Postcolonial Images of Spiritual Care

Postcolonial Images
of Spiritual Care

Challenges of Care in a Neoliberal Age

EDITED BY

Emmanuel Y. Lartey

AND

Hellena Moon

FOREWORD BY

Abdullahi Ahmed An-Naʿim

EPILOGUE BY

Bonnie Miller-McLemore

PICKWICK *Publications* · Eugene, Oregon

POSTCOLONIAL IMAGES OF SPIRITUAL CARE
Challenges of Care in a Neoliberal Age

Pickwick Publications
An Imprint of Wipf and Stock Publishers
199 W. 8th Ave., Suite 3
Eugene, OR 97401

www.wipfandstock.com

PAPERBACK ISBN: 978-1-5326-8555-2
HARDCOVER ISBN: 978-1-5326-8556-9
EBOOK ISBN: 978-1-5326-8557-6

Cataloguing-in-Publication data:

Names: Lartey, Emmanuel Yartekwei, editor. | Moon, Hellena, editor. | An-Na'im, Abdullahi, foreword. | Miller-McLemore, Bonnie, epilogue.

Title: Postcolonial images of spiritual care : challenges of care in a neoliberal age / edited by Emmanuel Y. Lartey and Hellena Moon.

Description: Eugene, OR : Pickwick Publications, 2020 | Includes bibliographical references.

Identifiers: ISBN 978-1-5326-8555-2 (paperback) | ISBN 978-1-5326-8556-9 (hardcover) | ISBN 978-1-5326-8557-6 (ebook)

Subjects: LCSH: Pastoral care. | Postcolonialism.

Classification: BV4011.3 .P69 2020 (print) | BV4011.3 .P69 (ebook)

Permission received from Omid Safi to reprint the following article in its entirety as the prefatory reflection as well as portions of it for the epigraph: Safi, Omid. "How to Reach Out to Someone Who Is Struggling." *On Being* (blog), October 11, 2017. Online. https://onbeing.org/blog/omid-safi-how-to-reach-out-to-someone-who-is-struggling.

Manufactured in the U.S.A.   09/18/20

This volume is dedicated to all care providers faced with the tasks of caregiving in the midst of situations of social, political, and economic hardship resulting from colonialism and neoliberalism.

To Julyann, Stephen (1972–2003),
Elbert, Madeleine, and Benjamin

Free your loved ones of the energy they spend to hide their brokenness from you. Free them of the shame of coming to you as they are.

Let them spend that energy on surviving, on healing, on thriving. Let us love one another as we are, so that we may become all we are meant to be.

—OMID SAFI

Contents

Contributors

Abdullahi Ahmed An-Na'im is Charles Howard Candler Professor of Law at Emory Law School. He explains in his website that his presentation of his research and professional work is "in the first person because I am privileged to have areas of personal and professional concern so intertwined, and I write from a position of individual responsibility."

Bilal Ansari is Faculty Associate of Muslim Pastoral Theology and Co-Director of Islamic Chaplaincy at Hartford Seminary and Assistant Vice President for Campus Engagement at Williams College. He received his Doctor of Ministry from the Pacific School of Religion.

Natalie Bernstein has been an elementary school librarian at The Paideia School in Atlanta, Georgia since 1995. The focus of her work is teaching about the importance of reading, not just for academic success but also as an entry into the interior lives of characters, which helps build resilience and empathy. She is scheduled to retire in the Spring of 2020.

Alexander Brown is a University student in the South. He is currently working towards a degree in clinical psychology with the intent of helping others in positions similar to his own in the near future.

Gregory C. Ellison II, PhD, is the Associate Professor of Pastoral Care and Counseling at Emory University's Candler School of Theology. He is also the Founder and Senior Strategist of Fearless Dialogues, a non-profit organization that creates unique spaces for unlikely partners to engage in hard, heartfelt conversations.

Greg M. Epstein serves as the Humanist Chaplain at Harvard and MIT and as the Convener for Ethical Life at MIT's Office of Religious, Spiritual, and Ethical Life. Ordained as a secular humanist rabbi, he is the author of the New York Times bestselling book, Good Without God: What a Billion Nonreligious People Do Believe.

Cedric C. Johnson is the Assistant Director of Training for Redeemer City to City. He is a pastor, psychotherapist, and former Associate Professor of Pastoral Theology and Congregational Care at Wesley Theological Seminary. His research interests include pastoral care and neoliberal globalization, trauma theory, and African American pastoral care.

Sumi Loundon Kim, formerly the Buddhist chaplain at Duke University, now serves at Yale University. She is the founder of the Mindful Families of Durham (North Carolina) and author of *Blue Jean Buddha*; *The Buddha's Apprentices*; and *Sitting Together: A Family-Centered Curriculum on Mindfulness, Meditation, and Buddhist Teachings*.

Lori Klein is a Board-Certified Chaplain and Director of Spiritual Care Services for Stanford Health Care. She worked as an oncology chaplain at Stanford for seven years. She has taught health care providers, attorneys, and spiritual leaders, both in the United States and in Central Europe.

Emmanuel Y. Lartey is Charles Howard Candler Professor of Pastoral Theology and Spiritual Care at the Candler School of Theology and the Graduate Division of Religion at Emory University. He has taught at Trinity Theological Seminary, Legon, Ghana; The University of Birmingham, UK; and at Columbia Theological Seminary, Decatur, GA. He is the author of *In Living Color: An Intercultural Approach to Pastoral Care and Counseling*, which is read worldwide on courses in Pastoral Care and Counseling.

Amani D. Legagneur is the Manager of Spiritual Health and Education for the Northside Hospital system, an ACPE Certified Educator, and an internationally-recognized trainer of spiritual and organizational leaders. Amani holds an MDiv from Harvard Divinity School. She is an ordained minister in the United Church of Christ.

Jeremy Lewis is the Executive Director of Urban Recipe, a non-profit organization in Atlanta, GA, known for its innovative approach to creating food security alongside low-income families. He is married to Beth, who teaches special education, and they have three children—Isaiah (twelve), Naomi (seven), and Olivia (twenty-one months).

Melinda McGarrah Sharp is Associate Professor of Practical Theology and Pastoral Care at Columbia Theological Seminary in Decatur, GA. She is the author of *Misunderstanding Stories: Toward a Postcolonial Pastoral Theology* (Pickwick, 2012) and *Creating Resistances: Pastoral Care in a Postcolonial World* (Brill, 2019). Her work connects pastoral theology, ethics, and postcolonial theory.

Bonnie Miller-McLemore is E. Rhodes and Leona B. Carpenter Professor of Religion, Psychology, and Culture at the Divinity School and Graduate Department of Religion of Vanderbilt University; author of numerous publications; international leader in pastoral and practical theologies; and recognized for her work on families, women, and children.

Hellena Moon is part-time Assistant Professor at Kennesaw State University in the Interdisciplinary Studies Department. She is the author of *Mask of Clement Violence Amidst Pastoral Intimacies: A Feminist Liberation Critique of the Violence Against Wo/men Discourse* (Pickwick, forthcoming).

Bruce Rogers-Vaughn is Associate Professor of the Practice of Pastoral Theology and Counseling at Vanderbilt Divinity School in Nashville, TN. He has also maintained a continuous practice as a pastoral psychotherapist for over three decades. He is the author of *Caring for Souls in a Neoliberal Age* (Palgrave, 2016).

Omid Safi is Professor of Islamic Studies at Duke University. His most recent book is *Radical Love: Teachings from the Islamic Mystical Tradition*. He leads a spiritually-oriented adult tour to Turkey and Morocco called Illuminated Tours (illuminatedtours.com), which is open to people of all faith backgrounds.

Foreword

— ABDULLAHI AHMED AN-NA'IM —

EMORY UNIVERSITY SCHOOL OF LAW

IN THIS BRIEF FOREWORD, I argue that spiritual care includes the concept of mutuality: spiritual care as reciprocal self-liberation, whereby both sides are at once recipients and providers of care to each other and to wider society for reaffirming the value of spiritual care. I see this as mutual self-liberation because all sides are contributing to their own liberation by providing spiritual care for other persons in exchange for the care *they* receive. As this exchange model is accepted and practiced by more people, the source of care becomes as plentiful as the need for it. Another advantage of this exchange model is that it upholds the dignity and self-worth of all recipients of care because they give of the same resources from which they receive.

Drawing on the Muslim Sufi tradition that defines my worldview and spiritual perspective (or equivalent in other traditions),[1] I propose that the conception and practice of the provision of spiritual care is the means to *mutual* self-liberation, instead of being a hierarchical relationship of a presumably "compassionate" care provider to a passive care recipient. The relevance of the Sufi tradition in this context is that it transforms what may be a source of selfish pride, into that which contributes to the spiritual growth of the provider. Another advantage of citing the Sufi tradition is that it is likely to remind people of institutions of equivalent resources in their own traditions.

I should emphasize, however, that some aspects of the broad Muslim Sufi traditions (in the plural) which prevailed over vast regions that spread across several centuries, was also as diverse and contested as the Sunni and Shia theologies of the Muslim population at large. Yet, the Sufis of the various

---

1. An-Na'im, "Individual and Collective," 45–75.

Sunni traditions across the expanse of the Muslim world (from west Africa to southeast and central Asia) also had to negotiate, contest, and reaffirm aspects of their tradition. In modern terms, one can speak of "progressive" and "traditional" Sufis, although I believe that traditional Sufis were still more progressive than the progressive of the broader Sunni perspectives. To conclude this brief digression, progressive Sufi Muslims still had to struggle to enlighten and humanize their wider Sunni communities.

As a Sufi Muslim, I have struggled most of my life (since the 1960s) to uphold what I believe to be my progressive Muslim convictions. It is this reality which derives my determination to ensure the freedom to engage in civil and orderly contestation of religious and other views among Muslims and in their relationship with humanity at large. Such spiritual contestations and the need to preserve the social and political space for them are better known historically as struggles for human dignity and social justice. The challenge for advocates of modern human rights discourse is whether this framework can be identified as a human rights discourse or not.

The question of the universality of human rights is at the core of this challenge, especially in view of the geopolitical and economic relationship between former colonial powers and their former colonies. In my view, for instance, the long shadow of former colonial relations continues to influence postcolonial relations between the former colonized and former colonizer. The closer the focus is on immediate postcolonial relations, the more colonial those relations seem to be. Conversely, the further away the analysis moves from the colonial period, the more autonomous and independent will the former colony appear to be. Although it may seem that the continuity of postcolonial relations depends on the degree of economic, political, security, and other forms of dependency the former colony has with its former colonial power; I believe that the situation can change, depending on the ability of people to liberate themselves.

I am also proposing a shift in terminology to use the term "entitlement," instead of "right," and by-passing the state altogether by relying on people-centered strategies of protection instead of legal enforcement through the state.[2] Avoiding the liberal narrow definition of the term, "right" as a justiciable claim that is enforceable by the domestic courts of a country is closer to the global non-liberal terminology used as the clear majority of societies in Africa, Asia, and indigenous South American communities. This shift in terminology also invokes the principle of reciprocity, whereby the value of the Golden Rule is enhanced by the *exchange* of spiritual and material

2. An-Na'im, "Spirit of Laws," 255–74.

service to become a stronger motivation for both sides to engage in the process of promoting mutual benefits.

In this light, I believe that spiritual care is a universal entitlement of all human beings by virtue of their humanity. This proposal is more accurate in applying to a universal human right because it affirms the entitlement of every human being as such to the benefit or fulfillment of the promise of care, without any distinction on such grounds as race, color, gender, religion, or nationality. The term "nationality" is not commonly used in human rights discourse, but I use it here deliberately to emphasize the irrelevance of political national identity to entitlement to the human rights of all human beings by virtue of their humanity.

Since human rights are necessarily universal because they are the rights of all human beings by virtue of their humanity, none of the states of the entire world has risen to the level of conformity with human rights in the sense of true universality of protecting the rights of all human beings, equally and without discrimination. Even a state which has ratified all human rights treaties (without any reservation) and immediately implemented the rights provided for by each treaty, the outcome would be civil rights (i.e., rights of citizens and lawful residents) and not for every human being who may have crossed the border of the state illegally, or was "arrested" or tortured by agents of the state abroad.[3] In view of the realities of present human rights *practice*, it would be tragic to continue judging the human rights paradigm by the practice of states which claim self-appointed leadership in the field while violating the most fundamental principles of the rule of law in international relations.

The thrust of my argument here is that human rights norms are what peoples in their communities accept as the entitlement of all human beings, regardless of the policies and practice of states. Indeed, the Preamble of the Universal Declaration of Human Rights (UDHR) clearly stipulates the following:

> The General Assembly Proclaims this Universal Declaration of Human Rights as a common standard of achievement for all peoples and all nations, to the end that every individual and every organ of society, keeping this Declaration constantly in mind, shall strive by teaching and education to promote respect for these rights and freedoms and by progressive measures, national and international, to secure their universal and effective recognition and observance, both among the peoples of

---

3. Reference here is to the global response of the USA to the attacks of 9/11.

Member States themselves and among the peoples of territories under their jurisdiction.[4]

It is therefore ironic that states have succeeded in highjacking the high moral mantle of universal human rights in order to advance their narrow, relativist purposes. By the same token, however, supporters of human rights must strive to recover the initiative to uphold the principle of the universality of these rights. Unfortunately, these competing perspectives are not mediated on the merit of each perspective.

Although the UDHR does not entrust states with the right or obligation to implement the UDHR as such, Member States of the UN have in fact hijacked the Declaration and assumed the authority to operationalize and implement it. Moreover, instead of adopting appropriate strategies for the implementation of this unique document, throughout which, it addresses individual persons as the exclusive rights-holder; states assumed that they have the obligation to implement the Declaration through the application of traditional international law. Since states are the exclusive subjects of traditional international law, they are the only entities that can have rights and obligations under international law. States are the only entities which have the standing to sue and be sued under international law. The paradox of the international protection of human rights is that individual persons are the exclusive holder of human rights against the state; yet, states hold the exclusive power to enforce or implement those rights.

In the final analysis, the meaning and implication of human rights norms is the product of negotiations among states, whereby rights are binding only on states and can only be enforced or implemented by states. It was inconceivable from that perspective for human rights norms to be defined, interpreted, or applied independently from the same states that hold the exclusive ability to violate as well as the obligation to protect those rights. To conclude this foreword, postcolonial relations are often what they inspire human beings to do or be, like what the Mahatma Gandhi is reported to have said: "be the change you want to see in the world."[5] I see this volume and the contributors' chapters as an important step in challenging ongoing paradigms of what constitutes the *human* in human rights, as well as demonstrating that spiritual care is a human rights practice. As stated (implicitly or explicitly) in almost all of the following chapters, recognizing the dignity and self-worth of humans is spiritual care. It is a *human* right to be treated with dignity.

4. United Nations General Assembly, *Universal Declaration of Human Rights*.

5. There are many competing claims of authorship of this powerful thought, but the point for me is what this phrase inspires people to do, regardless of who said it first.

Prefatory Reflection

"To Love One Another as We Are,
to Become All We Are Meant to Be"[1]

———————— OMID SAFI ————————

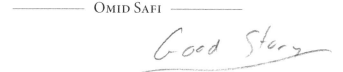

THERE IS A STORY told and retold in the Middle East about how to help someone who's drowning. The story goes that a man had fallen into a river. He was not much of a swimmer and was in real danger of drowning. A crowd of concerned people wanted to rescue him. They were standing at the edge of the water, each of them urgently shouting out to him:

Give me your hand, give me your hand!

The man was battling the waves and ignored their urgent plea. He kept going under and was clearly struggling to take another breath. A saintly man walked up to the scene. He too cared about the drowning man. But his approach was different. Calmly he walked up to the water, waded in up to his knees, glanced lovingly at the drowning man, and said:

Take my hand.

Much to everyone's surprise, the drowning man reached out and grabbed the saint's hand. The two came out of the dangerous water. The drowning man sat up at the edge of the water, breathing heavily, looking relieved, exhausted, and grateful. The crowd turned towards the saint and asked in complete puzzlement: "How were you able to reach him when he didn't heed our plea?" The saint calmly said:

---

1. This article first appeared as Safi, "How to Reach Out." The title has been changed with permission from the author.

You all asked him for something, his hand. I offered him something,
my hand. A drowning man is in no position to give you anything.

Let us remember not to ask anything of someone who is drowning.

I saw a friend of mine over the weekend. It was the first time I had seen him since turbulent events in my own life, and he lovingly asked about that. I know him to be a loving father, a caring husband, one whose face glows when he speaks about his children. So I inquired about his family. He shared with me the difficult news that his own daughter had gone through some of the same challenges I had. We spent the rest of the time discussing how we can best be there for the people we love.

He shared, with a pained voice, how hard it was to see someone he loves so much hurting. It almost sounded like it would be less painful for him if he could be the one carrying the burden. We talked about the energy our loved ones spend to shield us, to protect us from their pain at the times when they are most in need of having someone take them by the hand and lead them to the shore.

We talked about this issue of how to be there for, and with, someone who was hurting, drowning. In other words, how to lend a hand, rather than asking them to give us their hand.

One thing we talked about stayed with me: When a person is breaking, broken, they are so exhausted, so drained. Asking them to come to us and share their brokenness is asking them to do more when all they can do to stay alive is to tread water.

And then there is shame. So many of us have felt a great shame when our lives, our marriages, our careers fall apart. To come to the people who can help us with our shame is . . . well, shameful. Ironically, we end up spending more energy trying to shelter our family and loved ones from our brokenness. This is energy that we don't have, energy that we should be using to tread water.

So if you are that saintly soul, if you want to reach out to someone who is struggling to stay above water, go to them.

But don't ask them to give you their hand. Instead, offer them your hand. Don't ask for their heart, offer them your heart. Offer them your ear, your love, your shoulder. Release your friends, your family, from the shame of their brokenness. Let them know that you love them through the brokenness, because of the brokenness, and God-willing, after the brokenness.

Free your loved ones of the energy they spend to hide their brokenness from you. Free them of the shame of coming to you as they are. Let them spend that energy on surviving, on healing, on thriving. Let us love one another as we are, so that we may become all we are meant to be.

Acknowledgments

WE, THE EDITORS, WISH to sincerely thank the many people who have been involved in the production of this book. We would like to thank the editors at Pickwick for all the email correspondence they have had with us in the preparation of the text. Hellena would especially like to thank Matthew Wimer and Daniel Lanning for their supportiveness and patience throughout the editorial process. We also wish to thank Omid Safi for allowing us to reprint his blog reflection for our prefatory reflection, as well as a portion of it for our Epigraph.

This book project was inspired by Madeleine and Benjamin's (Hellena's children) discursive practices of "epistemic disobedience." Several years ago, in the middle of reading a book, my (then-seven-year-old) son wanted to locate something on the globe. He sees the African continent and thoughtfully asks, "Mama, if the first people were African, and we were made to look like God, how come God looks white? Shouldn't God be Black?" Benjamin was referring to Michelangelo's Sistine Chapel ceiling painting of Adam and God. Immediately, my daughter (who was nine-years old at the time) said, "I think I know! The rich people in power get to hire who they know to paint the fancy paintings we see in museums, and they were famous white men, so they painted God to *look like them.*" A few recent follow-up conversations on religion are also worth mentioning: my daughter alluded to the importance of challenging European historicism in religions and respecting religious pluralism by stating (in, of course, less adult-centric language) that "God didn't create us. We created God. God was created by humans, Mama, so God keeps changing in different times and places depending on what people are thinking. And some people didn't have Gods, they have each other." My own chapter on the "immured spirit" was inspired by Madeleine's comment,

"God is stuck in our heads, and who knows what humans will create in the future." I am so proud of their deep thinking on power and the social construction of race, gender, and religion. We have had such amazing spiritually critical discussions on so many topics that I really think James Fowler's *Stages of Faith* are radically challenged in light of how my children seem to bypass what he alleged, were universal stages. On that note, I, Hellena, would like to thank their elementary school teachers at The Paideia School for the classroom atmosphere they create in cultivating such critical thinking skills. I especially want to acknowledge Natalie Bernstein, a contributor to this volume, as she retires from her position as librarian at the school. Natalie has been instrumental in fostering a love of reading in my children. My kids love the library—and more so, the librarian—at the Paideia School. Our family wishes Natalie the best in her retirement.

Hellena would also like to offer deep gratitude to Robert Dykstra who was incredibly generous with his time in discussing the vision for the project and giving her suggestions on how to proceed with the initial stages of the book. Finding a co-editor, he suggested, should be the next step. Hellena is deeply grateful to Emmanuel Y. Lartey, co-editor, for his work to make this project a reality. All the book's contributors were phenomenal in working and writing to meet deadlines and in answering the numerous questions we had for them. We express our hearty thanks to you for making this book project a reality.

We would like to express profound appreciation to Bonnie Miller-McLemore, who was more than just the person writing the Epilogue. Hellena has been in correspondence with her on this and other writing projects, on which she gave great support. She has been a mentor to me, despite not having taken any of her classes. I have read her works over the years and am honored she takes the time to support my projects.

Hellena would like to honor and acknowledge her sincerest gratitude to Emmanuel Y. Lartey for the support he gave her throughout the years of her studies for her PhD. He was her advisor and mentor for her academic work in the Graduate Division of Religion at Emory. Several times along the PhD journey, she questioned whether her ideas were even fit for the GDR. Had it not been for Dr. Lartey's support, I would not have finished the PhD, nor would I have had the opportunity to make this book project vision a reality. He helped me to attain both. His work paved the way for many of us interested in the project of Third World liberation via a postcolonial path in 'spiritual care.' His classes (seminars and individual readings and research) helped shape my own scholarship. Beyond the academics, I appreciate his kindness, patience, and deep spirituality. He cares deeply about the issues on which he writes and researches. Through his work, he has brought meaning to the spiritual lives of many.

I, Hellena, would also like to thank my partner in life, Elbert Chun, who has been the steady support I needed, offering positive and much needed encouragement. I have learned much in our seventeen years of togetherness and caretaking. Despite our busy parenting schedules, I am grateful we took the time for each other in our play together. Finally, no one knows the realities, pains, beauty, and hardships of caretaking like my sister, Julyann Moon. She has been by my father's side in Suji, Korea, engaging in the deep, genuine spiritual practice of loving another being steadfastly. She has been present for the struggles of our dad, suffering in his illness like I have never known another human being to experience. She has given him her unwavering love like I have never seen anyone give. People say that only a parent knows that kind of love for their child—but my sister has that kind of love for all of us in her circle. I dedicate this book to my family: my sister, Julyann, our beloved brother, Stephen J. Moon (1972–2003); my partner, Elbert Chun and our two children, Madeleine and Benjamin. You all have been my greatest teachers on the life-long project of unwavering love.

Together, as editors, we would like to say how grateful and thankful we are to each and every one of you who has made it possible for this anthology to reach an audience of caregivers. Our hope and prayer are that this work will be beneficial in furthering our caregiving in the face of an increasingly xenophobic, oppressive, nationalistic, and uncaring world situation.

Hellena Moon

Emmanuel Y. Lartey

December 2019

Introduction

THIS ANTHOLOGY ENTERS THE revolutionary history of the struggle of victims of colonialism in its many forms to overcome the deleterious effects of imperialism and colonialism, at one of its crucial points—that of the care of persons. In recognition of the many different forms of oppression, injustice, and violence in the world today that are traceable to the legacy and continuing effects of colonialism; various authors have contributed to the volume from diverse backgrounds in terms of ethnic identities, religious and cultural traditions, gender and sexual orientations, as well as communal and personal realities. The volume commences with the juxtaposition of Abdullahi An-Na'im's legal, analytical discourse of spiritual care as human rights practice, with Omid Safi's poetic and eloquent story of care. Both An-Na'im's and Safi's contributions are variations of radical love—to love one another radically and meaningfully means allowing people to be who they are through the practice of mutual reciprocity and deep listening. An-Na'im's vision of radical love challenges the legal framework to allow self-love and self-determination to flourish. An-Na'im underscores the centrality of mutuality in spiritual care in that he sees "spiritual care as self-liberation, whereby both sides are at once recipients and providers of care to each other."[1] An-Na'im's human rights paradigm also shows that only through deep listening to the needs of others can we arrive at an overlapping consensus as to what is important to, and valued in, a community.

Safi's reflection also highlights mutuality and deep listening. His story demonstrates the power of language and genuine empathy. One is struck how a drowning man was expected to hold out his hand; this demand could not be comprehended in the face of impending danger. When the

---

1. See An-Na'im's "Foreword" in this volume.

language was re-framed for the drowning man to take the helper's hand, it was more readily accomplished. Herein lies the beauty of offering unaffected care and sincere listening when it is not forced on us. Offering care versus demanding someone to do something becomes key to building trust and relationality. All of us have been both the saint and the one struggling in the water. To know that we can be in the position of needing care can help us better provide the care when we are in such a situation. In this volume, we offer such perspectives and practices of care. We offer diverse perspectives and stories, narratives and voices of difference, and we offer images for radically re-imagining spiritual care.

The title of Safi's reflection, "To Love One Another As We Are, To Become All We Are Meant to Be," eloquently encapsulates the work of all the contributors and also becomes the principal aim for this volume. While Omid Safi identifies as a Muslim, his voice is a *human* voice—his story evokes quotidian spiritual practices that are contextually translatable into various cultures and communities. In this regard, the contributors in this volume similarly demonstrate that the sacred practice of allowing others to flourish in their becoming—and to support such becoming—*is* the rich work of spiritual care. Decolonized spiritual care embraces the *human* in human rights discourse; it becomes human rights practice.

Why Spiritual over Pastoral Care

Decolonized spiritual care entails practices of mutuality, reciprocity, and deep listening. In that regard, the editors give preference to the terminology of spiritual care, over that of "pastoral care."[2] While pastoral theologian Robert Dykstra does defend the shepherding model of care; the term, "pastoral," historically has been associated with a hierarchical, top-down model of care.[3] We are not arguing, however, that the term is exclusively a Judeo-Christian concept as some do. As early as the eighteenth century (1681–1762), a shepherding model of "pastoral care" was used in Korea by Neo-Confucian scholars of practical learning in the work of Yi Ik. The Practical Learning scholars focused on political matters and care of the people. Chong Yagyong's most well-known work focused on the understanding that in order to have good society, one needed good governance/ good rule. Good government began with care for the people—this was

2. While we do not object to the use of "pastoral" (several contributors to the volume use the word), we prefer to use the term "spiritual care" as more inclusive to all cultures, communities, and spiritual practices.

3. Dykstra, *Finding Ourselves Lost*, 14–24.

written in his *Core Teachings for Shepherding the People*.[4] Pastoral care and governance were imbricated and not separate ideologies in Korea prior to the people's exposure to Christianity via Catholicism.[5] Yet, this pastoral care/shepherding model was very much a top-down, hierarchical, patriarchal, and paternalistic model of care.

While the concept of pastoral care, therefore, is not exclusive to Judeo-Christian or monotheistic care models, we problematize its usage for several reasons. In historicizing "pastoral," the term was used primarily to convey a metaphorical model of shepherding care that showed authority and power of one species (i.e., the human) who was considered superior to the sheep (i.e., unthinking animal who needed guidance). This communicates an uneven message of leader being superior and human, while the image of flock somehow is beneath that of the leader and less than fully human (read: colonialism). We, the editors, therefore associate "pastoral care" with the Linnaean classification and hierarchical system that became the prime tool for colonial and imperial conquests, as well as environmental devastation, leading to the subjection and subjugation of Africans, Asians, and native peoples in the Americas. We in the field of pastoral theology are challenged by the legacies of colonialism and the ways in which "care" is—and has been—a colonizing practice, especially when Third World spiritual practices were not recognized as legitimate or as on par with that of Christian practices.

This volume seeks to challenge the association of the concept of pastoral care with such historicist understandings of the term. In that regard, we acknowledge the need to have a thoroughly historicized critique of the term, especially in the ways the image of shepherding has been used to reinforce Christian-centered norms in the practices and theories of spiritual care. We need to rehabilitate the term, "pastoral," just as "queer" has been rehabilitated from the pejorative ways it has been used in the past. At the same time, some contributors have chosen to use the term "pastoral" in their chapters. In using such language, they disturb its conventional meaning, thereby upending the assertion that it is unique to Judeo-Christian care.

As a postcolonial critique of spiritual care, this anthology highlights the plurality of spiritual voices and concerns that have been overlooked or obscured because of the politics of race, religion, sexuality, nationalism, and other structures of power that have shaped what discursive spiritual care entails today. US society tends to "normalize" and not *problematize* what the West has dictated as constituting religion or spiritual practices (what is sacred and what is deemed "barbaric" and profane). We have

---

4. Hwang, *History of Korea*, 92.

5. Baker, *Catholics and Anti-Catholicism*.

blindly obliged to the oppressive categories constructed for "us" by Renaissance and Western European Enlightenment (seventeenth and eighteenth centuries) thinking.[6] Prior to and after these periods of European thought, the boundaries of what was considered to be religion and what was secular/ sacred and profane were redrawn and gerrymandered multiple times to favor European Christian thought as normative. The creation of a discipline of Religious Studies was to support what practices and beliefs Europeans saw as most compatible (or comparable) with Christianity, or what might most follow the trajectory of Enlightenment "rational" thinking. Some "religious" practices were "othered" and categorized as extremely different from Western Christian sensibilities. The alleged superior mind of the West was rationale for engaging in a civilizing "pastoral" mission to shepherd and guide the allegedly less enlightened (sub-human) peoples. The image of shepherding that is associated with pastoral care, then, is extremely problematic, racist, and colonizing.

This logic of European racist thought is explicit in the philosophy of G. W. F. Hegel, who saw persons from the Asian or African continent as not fully developed humans and as inferior to those races with white skin.[7] The Hegelian view of Asia and Africa as "static, despotic, and irrelevant to world history" has shaped Western thinking about its people and cultures.[8] Hegel's account of race is embedded in his conception of personhood, where he believed in biological distinctions between persons. He saw the soul as embodying racial distinctions. According to Hegel, Europeans/White subjects were seen as the very paradigm/model of freedom and rationality because of their biology. He states, "It is in the Caucasian race that spirit first reaches absolute unity with itself," while the people of the Orient and Africa were considered to be ignorant and superstitious.[9] Third world peoples have apparently improved through our contact with European civilization and Christianity.[10] Hegel saw Africans and Asians as inferior—with regard to Mongolians and Chinese (et al.), he critiqued their religious practices as unworthy of free persons because they did not embody a "faith" tradition.

6. The European Enlightenment was an intellectual movement that dramatically changed the intellectual environment of Europe in the areas of nature, reason, God, and science. The goals of such Enlightenment thinking were freedom, knowledge, and happiness. The Renaissance period (fourteenth to seventeenth century) had its clearest manifestation in the arts, through which artists highlighted the dignity of "man"— referring to the white, Christian man.

7. Moellendorf, "Racism and Rationality," 246.

8. Said, *Culture and Imperialism*, 168.

9. Hegel, *Philosophy of Subjective Spirit*, 393.

10. Said, *Culture and Imperialism*, 168.

This Hegelian mindset—of the European person as the model of full human subject-hood and that "religions" have to be a separate corporate "belief"—is still operative in politico-economic arenas, human rights discourses, and US society today. This volume postcolonializes[11] the nineteenth-century ideology that foregrounded such racist, dehumanizing Eurocentric philosophy and thought that colonized what constituted "spirit" and defined spiritual or pastoral care. A goal of this anthology, therefore, is to decolonize spiritual care as defined by a Hegelian understanding of spirit and history, as well as Western understandings of what constitutes "religion" or "spiritual." Religion has been a tool, a methodological weapon for colonizing the two-thirds world by creating and constructing categories of what were considered secular, sacred, and profane—obliterating practices that were considered unrecognizable and illegible to the civilized Western knowing subject; as well as dehumanizing the practices of local communities in the Americas, Africa, and Asia. We need to reinvigorate the meaning of spiritual care in light of how Hegel's meaning of spirit has dictated what is spiritual and what is not.

Most of the non-white world did not believe in a monotheistic G*d or Savior (until the period of colonizing conquests in the 1500s). This by no means denotes they were not spiritual or as human as their white Christian subjects. Today, atheists and humanists have to constantly defend their right to spiritual care (to convince others they have spiritual needs and to argue that they can be providers of spiritual care as well). We *do not* think for a practice to be pastoral and/or spiritual, it must also be corporate or linked to and rooted in a faith community and its traditions. We understand that "religious traditions" are socially constructed or invented European categories, which are constantly changing.

"Spiritual" or "pastoral" care should not be circumscribed to "faith" traditions. Such a mindset limits what is considered spiritual or even religious. If by "faith" or belief system, one refers to a broadly understood faith meaning as it was understood in medieval times, then "faith" refers to a concept of trust in someone, not belief in an epistemological sense of higher beings.[12] If we apply such a definition of a faith community, then atheists who state, "I believe there is not a God as understood in Christianity," would be considered part of a faith community. A postcolonial critique of "spiritual" includes scrutinizing how certain humans were excluded and seen as subhuman because their personhood did not fit the Hegelian definition of "spirit." Knowledge of "what was considered to be human" changed and

---

11. Using the language and method of Lartey, *Postcolonializing God.*

12. Asad, "Thinking About Religion, Secularism, and Politics."

shifted throughout the centuries. When we limit what is "spiritual" to "faith" traditions, it reinforces Christian hubris: a combination of white Christian superiority as normative, with racism intertwined in those standards of the norm. Toni Morrison poignantly stated how racism

> keeps you from doing your work. It keeps you explaining, over and over again, your reason for being. Somebody says you have no language, and you spend twenty years proving that you do. Somebody says your head isn't shaped properly, so you have scientists working on the fact that it is. Somebody says that you have no art, so you dredge that up. Somebody says that you have no kingdoms, and you dredge that up. None of that is necessary. There will always be one more thing.[13]

Intersecting with Morrison's statement on racism, it becomes daunting and overwhelming for non-Christians or non-white Christians to have to prove to others that they are as *spiritual* or as *human* as their white Christian colleagues or neighbors—whether in the workplace, schools, clinical pastoral education settings, seminaries. It is de-humanizing to constantly have to prove one's humanity by explaining they are "spiritual"—but not religious, or spiritual but atheist!

Metaphor or Image of the Work

This project was partly inspired by the book, *Images of Pastoral Care: Classic Readings*, edited by Robert Dykstra.[14] Published in 2005, none of the contributors were of any other religious background, apart from Christianity. All of the contributors were white Protestants, except for one scholar/minister. We have brought together diverse voices, beliefs, and work backgrounds for a book that more adequately reflects the spiritual practices of United Stateseans (Janet Halley's neologism).[15] The editors of this volume are well aware of tokenism or narratives depicting the single voice as authoritative or as speaking on behalf of all in a particular community. We want to emphasize that these following chapters are but a few voices within a kaleidoscopic lens of spiritual care. Spiritual care is as rich and varied as the billions of people, plants, and fauna on this earth.

This anthology hopes to contribute to the voices of practical and pastoral theologians, academics, spiritual care providers, religious leaders, students,

13. Morrison, "Twelve of Toni Morrison's Most Memorable Quotes."

14. Dykstra, *Images of Pastoral Care.*

15. Halley, *Split Decisions.*

and activists working to provide greater intercultural spiritual care and aware-ness in the areas of healthcare, community work, and education. The proj-ect highlights the expertise of spiritual care from those who may not have institutional power. The volume is not a "how to provide pastoral care"—as many volumes purport to do. Rather, the contributors share the knowledge of spiritual care garnered from their deep-listening work with patients, families, students, and community members. As these chapters attest, those in power are not the only ones who get to decide what constitutes spiritual care. It is our hope that this book provides a much-needed impetus for listening to many more voices, stories, and histories of spiritual care.

As co-editors, we believe in the necessity for greater spiritual care lit-eracy in the training of spiritual care providers who work in public spaces. Having deliberated on how to bring the diverse chapters together and or-ganize the text, we have identified a few, overlapping central themes in the chapters. Each of the author's images contribute, in some form, to disman-tling colonialist and white supremacist ideological frameworks in spiritual care. Through the work in this volume, we hope to expand and widen the discourse of spiritual care and participate in the ongoing paradigm shifts in the field of pastoral and practical theology.

Chapters

We have ordered the chapters in relation to the breadth of subject, com-mencing from the micro-focused (personhood) through sociality (society, community) and into globality (culture, international politics). Themes of neoliberalism, economics, resistance, and care in the face of injustice reverberate through each of the chapters since these all affect persons in the current global nexus. In addition, each chapter contributes to the theoretical framework of spiritual care as decolonizing and challenging the dominant *inhuman* human rights paradigm. An-Na'im rightly states that human rights laws and frameworks are colonized.[16] Institutionally, norms were agreed upon by States and by people who were not representative of their own communities. He argues that state-centric legality was a crucial element of European colonization, spreading ideas of norms to non-Euro-pean countries. States allegedly were—but have not been—in the business of protecting human rights.

Spiritual care recognizes the importance of the de-institutionalized religious practices that emerge from the daily lives of people that give them the tools to find their agency and flourishing. Spiritual care is concerned

16. An-Na'im, "It's Time to Decolonize Human Rights."

about caring for self, for those in our community, and for improving the daily lives of people by recognizing and underscoring agency in their lives. A central goal of spiritual care is to liberate and empower the wholeness of human beings, families, and communities. In that regard, these chapters uphold the *human* in human rights discourse and work towards the de-colonization of human rights norms. We contest the neo-liberal, capitalist, de-humanizing values that have shaped and structured human rights norms and what is considered to be spiritual care.

Another theme or thread of commonality in the chapters is the revelation of a "third space" that occurs via postcolonial spiritual care. In the words of postcolonial theorist Homi Bhabha,

> Legitimating narratives of cultural domination can be displaced to reveal a "third space." Most creative forms of cultural identity are produced on the boundaries in-between forms of difference, in the intersections and overlaps across the sphere of class, gender, race, nation, generation, location.[17]

Spiritual identities are produced in concert with cultural identities of the third space. Not only are our spiritual identities fluid and constantly changing; we argue that the field of pastoral theology itself needs to be open to the many apertures and closures, fissures and fractures when it comes to diversity and inclusion within an academic discipline. These "third spaces" are the interstitial spaces that are overlapping and laden with new theories. By being present with—and listening to—the stories of youth, students, the elderly, the poor, et al., the contributors conjure a discursive "third space" and reinvigorate the sacrality of humanity and community that is constantly being challenged in a neoliberal world. For too long, the discursive space of pastoral care has been exceedingly narrow and provincial. It has elided the diversity of spiritual practices and voices, because we have focused on what is considered to be the dominant "norm" of society. This volume seeks to overturn normative structures of spiritual care by engaging and energizing the margins of the 'third space', the holy in-between space where we can authentically explore stories and practices about our *becoming*.

Part One: Spiritual Care of the Person

Professor Emmanuel Lartey's chapter explores the concept of relational holism in African life and thought. He references the work of practitioners of African spirituality in its rich and varied forms by examining its

17. Bhabha, *Location of Culture*.

significance in the care of persons across the entire world. At the heart and center of personality within African notions of personhood lies, not a soul, but rather 'spirit.' Spirituality in African life and thought is a matter of relationality, and spirituality comprises five inter-related and inter-connected dimensions. These are: (a) relation with the divine, (b) relation with self, (c) relation with (an)other, (d) relations among groups of people—community, and (e) relation with nature/earth/space. African spiritual practices aim at relational holism resulting from harmonious relations along all five of these dimensions.

As the Director of Spiritual Care at Stanford Hospital, Lori Klein articulates an image of "cultural humility and reverent curiosity" for the work of intercultural spiritual care in a hospital setting. Patients, their loved ones, and staff come to hospitals embodying complex identities. They draw upon intersecting cultures and norms to meet expectations of their gender, communit(ies), and religious tradition(s). They come with histories of access, privilege, vulnerability, and/or discrimination. Medical centers in the United States also function based on often unacknowledged cultural norms. Klein beautifully demonstrates how to navigate this people-and institution-scape to provide spiritual care, while adhering to cultural humility and being with people in reverent curiosity. The chaplain's goal is to help all people experience the hospital as a place of compassion and healing. Accompanying people through decisions made in grief's shadow, transitions, loss, and uncertainty can lead to meaningful transformation not only for patients and their loved ones, but also for chaplains. It is transformative mutuality.

Buddhist chaplain Sumi Kim explores the interconnectedness of humans and nature. She observes the current paradigm shift in which our interconnectedness with local economies is entwined with globalization, and how racial and social injustices are understood through systemic oppressions. Our survival is now clearly dependent on Earth's ecological web. She concludes her chapter by reflecting on how we find personal agency while feeling trapped in large-scale political, economic, and social systems. The image of the flower of interbeing, as taught by the Vietnamese Zen master Thích Nhất Hạnh, serves as her metaphor.

In *Images of Pastoral Care*, Robert Dykstra contended that pastoral theologians have long used metaphorical images as guiding frameworks for theoretical analysis and therapeutic practice.[18] To frame Greg Ellison's teaching and practice as a pastoral theologian and new faculty member at Candler School of Theology in 2010, he published a journal article to cast his own image of pastoral care, entitled, "From My Center to the Center of All

18. Dykstra, *Images of Pastoral Care*.

Things: Hourglass Care (Take 1)." A decade later, he contributes his "second take" on that original article. He makes some revisions, which highlight the importance of pilgrimage, fearless dialogue, and a full-sensory pedagogy, to aid students in caring for self and other.

Amani Legagneur, manager of Spiritual Health at Northside hospital, asks the following questions: "Is your healing welcome to you? Is my healing welcome to me?" These questions serve as touchstones and guides for spiritual care responders who may identify themselves as *healing welcomers*. A *healing welcomer* is a spiritual care responder who intends to offer a respectful, hospitable presence to those served while endeavoring to facilitate the amelioration and/or alleviation of their pain and suffering. Legagneur demonstrates how *healing welcomers* seek to promote restoration, positive connections, comfort, hope, self-compassion, and grace as they encourage greater spiritual wellbeing in those for whom they care.

In experiencing the welcoming healing of self-love, we introduce the beautiful work of Alexander Brown, an undergraduate student at a university in the South. He contributes a most poignant, thoughtful piece of his ongoing spiritual journey, as he reflects on his gender, religious, and sexual identity. Weaving his own personal Muslim-Christian spiritual narrative with the theories of feminist and womanist scholars and activists, he constructs a spiritual care prescriptive for transgendered individuals.

Part Two: Spiritual Care of Communities

Bilal Ansari, Muslim chaplain, contributes a brief synopsis of his work-in-progress on the image of the Black Sheep and how shepherding and care of one's flock is a repeated theme in the Qur'an, *hadith* (prophetic narratives), the prophetic biography, Islamic jurisprudence, theology and spirituality. There is a clear pastoral theology and concept of care in Islam. Muslim pastoral care can be imagined and best understood as the marginalized Black Shepherds and sheep. This brief chapter comes from his dissertation work, which will be published in the near future. By introducing his work in this volume, he hopes to diversify the notion and image of pastoral care to include the deep roots inherent in Islam, expand the identity of Muslim caregivers beyond the relegated Christian realm, and contribute meaningfully to the professional literature in the field of pastoral theology and spiritual care.

Pastoral theologian Mindy McGarrah-Sharp's chapter begins with the imagery of basketry as a metaphor for what is necessary for pastoral care in a "flammable" world. Baskets bear intergenerational, intercultural wisdom while also carrying future stories. Baskets are also flammable in a world shaped by colonial impulses. The second part of the chapter describes an image of collective phoenix poetry that arises amidst such dehumanizing risks. The chapter argues that intercultural, postcolonializing pastoral care practices cultivate the conditions for and contribute to phoenix poetry in a flammable world where persistent joy and prophetic grief co-reside.

Greg Epstein, humanist chaplain at Harvard and MIT, offers the image of midwifery for spiritual care. With a dramatic rise in the number of atheists, agnostics, humanists, and nonreligious people in the United States today—in particular among young, highly educated people (self-professed atheists and agnostics now outnumber all Christians combined at Harvard and MIT, according to detailed recent surveys of campus demographics)—there is a strong need and called-for demand for professionally trained helping professionals who can work with members of this population to address spiritual questions on topics such as meaning and purpose, death and despair, and ethical well-being. Epstein describes the rich ways he has connected to students in this anthology by sharing some of his own ethical struggles and challenges in his spiritual journey.

Elementary school librarian Natalie Bernstein's chapter explores the variety of ways that an elementary school library offers support to students, parents, and teachers. The space itself is welcoming and comforting, offering a quiet place to be calm, read, or ask for help. The relationship between the librarian and individual library users can be surprisingly intimate, with individual consultations about choosing a book sometimes developing into personal confessions about fears or hopes. At the heart of the library program, however, are books—especially stories—that create connections to personal experience, deepen our understanding of the interior lives of others, help solve problems, build resilience, and, ultimately, nurture compassion. Bernstein embraces a Paolo Freirean method in the library to allow for liberative critical thinking and reflection. She focuses on teaching, modeling, and cultivating the joy of reading—whether individually or communally—and through that reading, has taught children how to appreciate themselves and connect empathically with others. Bernstein invites us into her elementary library sanctuary, where we are privy to her awe-inspiring work and spiritual practice of reading and engaging in community-building with children, parents, and teachers.

The next chapter looks at the compassionate care and community organizing work of Baptist pastor Jeremy Lewis and the members of a food co-op in Atlanta called Urban Recipe. Urban Recipe is not a typical food bank or food distribution center for low-income families. The rituals of gathering, distributing, and organizing the food is not done in a paternalistic or hierarchical manner. The co-op endeavors to create community and food security for its clients in a way that respects and honors the dignity of each individual of the community. Food is not simply handed out; the members participate together and deliberate, organize, distribute the food, etc. The members do the bulk of the co-op tasks themselves, as well as help solve whatever problems may arise. The co-op members have dignity in their shared responsibility with one another, and through that agency, they help each other to build community based on radical love for one another. Rhythms and routines of life have formed and shaped the co-op members, as well as the care they give and receive from one another. In this chapter, Lewis explores the rhythm of one person's relationship with her co-op at Urban Recipe (and how the rhythm of each individual is integral in shaping the unique dynamics of the co-op). The expression of care articulated in this co-op model provides helpful insights into other life contexts and communities with regard to spiritual care. Resources (such as love and care), when provided, can contribute to building a thriving community.

Part Three: Spiritual Care and Global Well-Being

Pastor, academic, and activist Cedric Johnson investigates neoliberalism as a central framework through which to investigate the human suffering that has resulted from a growing economic divide that is now global in its scope. The image of the cultural broker metaphorically structures various realms of practice that inform soul care in the neoliberal age. Cultural brokering is defined as the act of bridging, linking, or mediating between groups or persons of different cultural backgrounds for the purpose of reducing conflict or producing change. Cultural brokers also function as mediators, negotiating complex processes *within* communities and cultures. The practitioner of prophetic soul care in the neoliberal age is called upon to build bridges of communication, manage the dynamics of cultural and socioeconomic difference, help groups mediate those differences, and advocate for transformation. The image of the cultural broker thus brings into view continuities among critical realms of practice that otherwise appear to be unrelated.

Theologian and scholar Bruce Rogers-Vaughn discusses the changing structures of colonialism and proposes a reimagining of spiritual care that includes an understanding of how the internet has become an effective tool of this global colonization. Rogers-Vaughn asks us to complicate and re-imagine Bonnie Miller McLemore's "living human web" metaphor. He suggests attending to the "dark web" as a way to visualize the decolonizing gaps, recesses, and interstices of the human web. After delineating the corrosive alterations of human subjects within today's dominant web, producing what he calls "dying human documents," he identifies four practices exist-ing within the dark web—hope, humility, love, and mourning—that might guide spiritual care in the current age.

Feminist theologian Hellena Moon metaphorically illustrates how the "immured spirit" is the spiritual erasure and oppression of communities due to the European categorization of religions deemed sacred (those beliefs seen to be similar to European belief systems) and profane (that which was categorized as unimportant). Not only does the "immured spirit" symbol-ize the marginalized or "caged" spiritual practices of previously colonized communities to prevent their/our true liberation; it also symbolizes the immured g*d—that is, the lack of imagination and creativity that could emerge if we engaged in the true work of decolonization. The possibility and vision for liberation is immured in the traps of "freedom" established by a neoliberal world. The *living human* web has been a Eurocentric web—with a desperate need for the infra-human. The freedom and liberation of white Euro-Americans have been dependent on various forms of violence (colonial, imperial, neo-liberal, capitalist) wrought on human and nonhu-man communities. While the structural and physical forms of violence have been theorized and critiqued, the clement and curative forms of violence have been less discussed. The metonym of an immured spirit is a heuristic for us to contemplate the less noticeable, yet equally toxic, forms of violence (clement and curative) that are perpetrated against—and endured by—in-frahumans, thereby circumscribing our genuine liberation. In contemplat-ing our freedom, Moon also considers how our liberation has been tethered to other forms of violence, such as our dependence on fossil fuels. In that regard, how free are any of us when we are so utterly immured by the forces of nature? While we are responsible for environmental damages, *we* are the ones who are suffering the consequences. The Earth can continue without us, but we cannot continue without Earth. Paradoxically, we are destroying the very force that gives us life.

Conclusion

We see the potential of metaphors to help contribute to—and expand—the language, vision, and practice of spiritual care. It is our hope that new meta-phors can stimulate our imaginations to create new language and creative ways of theorizing and envisioning what constitutes spiritual care. Spiritual care is the care of the everyday that is part of our circadian rhythm. It is a vision, an image, of the ordinary work of people in their everyday healing (healing of self and being present with others). Postcolonial spiritual care creates the situations that allow our dignity, as well as that of others, to be granted so that we *can become* who we were meant to be. We hope readers can journey with us into the quotidian practices of care. We want to emphasize the importance of the de-institutionalized religious practices that emerge from the daily lives of people whereby their agency and dignity are able to flourish. Mutuality of listening and support, as An-Na'im and Safi have described, creates a space for the emergence of dignity and for becoming who we were meant to be, and *this* is a synecdoche for spiritual care.

Emmanuel Y. Lartey

Hellena Moon

Part One

Spiritual Care of the Person

1

Be-ing in Relation

The Goal of African Spiritual Practice

—— Emmanuel Y. Lartey ——

In engaging a study of spiritual care through postcolonial lenses we necessarily privilege and give pride of place to unacknowledged, despised, marginalized, subjugated, and down-played voices. We allow and raise these voices precisely because the hegemonic forces of colonialism have suppressed them, denigrated them and rendered their contribution to any subject of study unappreciated and irrelevant. It is true that there are many notions and expressions of spirituality, and as such what spiritual care might be is not easy to define, pinpoint or specify. As a contribution to the exploration of spiritual care the focus in this chapter is on African notions drawn from African life and experience. African ways of framing spirituality, I wish to suggest, offer important insights into practices of spiritual care in the world today.

All of Life Is Sacred

One of the central features of African life and thought is a widely and generally held affirmation of the sacrality of all of life. Magesa argues correctly that, in contrast to a Durkheimian separation of "sacred" and "profane" domains of life and therefore spirituality, African experience offers a quite different way of understanding spirituality and religion. "In Africa," Magesa points out, "there is an essentially 'transcendental' perception of all life because all reality is situated in the sacred realm, which is a spiritual sphere. A people's life is their religion, so that "religion," or "spirituality" for that matter is not identifiable as a separate institution but permeates the whole society. The spiritual is not opposed to the physical or material, but both are intricately merged."[1] In fact, as Magesa goes on to say, "the idea that there is a "spiritual life" distinct from any other kind of existence is foreign to the African mind and spirit. All reality is spiritual and has ethical implications."[2] Not only is there no effective separation between a so-called "sacred" and a so-called "profane" in African life but rather spirit and spirituality constitute the essential core of human being.

Magesa is emphatic about the centrality of spirituality in African thought and practice. He puts it this way: "African thought and action, both of which structure culture, are rooted in spirituality. This is the culture by and through which Africans as agents identify themselves."[3] Spirituality then, is the root and center of African life. It is also the identifying and self-defining core of human existence.

Spirit and Spirituality Are Central

At the base of African anthropologies and healing traditions lies a central organizing aspect of the human personality. The Akan peoples of West Africa refer to this central core of personality as *okra* or *kra*. To the Gã people of Ghana, it is called *kla*. For the Ancient Egyptians it was *ka*. The Yoruba peoples of Nigeria and Benin refer to it as *ori*. The reference in all these examples is to a God-given essence that is received or uniquely chosen in the divine realm prior to one's entry onto the earth. This essence serves as the core or key driving force of a human being's life, purpose, and personhood. It is this component of one's personality that links one with the divine and is also the core of one's psychology.

Decades ago, in the 1950s, Anglican Bishop John V. Taylor explored African religion in the face of the increasing presence of Western Christianity in sub-Saharan Africa. Taylor, unlike other European thinkers, correctly articulated the essence of African understanding and practice of spirituality. Quoting French Roman Catholic priest and anthropologist Placide Tempels, with approval, Taylor argued that the Bantu peoples of Southern Africa do not conceptualize "man [*sic*] as an individual existing by himself, unrelated to the animate and inanimate forces surrounding him." Taylor continued his quote of Tempels in critique of the oft-thought 'sociality of African peoples,' asserting that "it is not sufficient to say that he [African man] is a social being; he feels himself a vital force in actual intimate and

1. Magesa, *What is Not Sacred?*, 24
2. Magesa, *What is Not Sacred?*, 26
3. Magesa, *What is Not Sacred?*, 25.

permanent *rapport* with other forces—a vital force both influenced by and influencing them."[4] In other words, Africans are not merely social beings but rather see themselves as spiritual beings in active quest of *rapport* and relationship with other forces. Taylor is right to assert that to the African, "A man's [*sic*] well-being consists in keeping in harmony with the cosmic totality."[5] In this African view then, "man's [*sic*] position vis-à-vis the world is not one of exploitation but of relationship."[6] The sense of humanity as a vital spiritual force among other forces continues to be widely felt and expressed in Africa and across the African diaspora. This belief has fueled and continues to be expressed in the many African Heritage Religions such as Cuban *Santería*, Brazilian *Candomblé* and Haitian *Vodou*, that increasingly thrive in the Caribbean and the Americas.

The fact of African spirituality as central to African personhood is not in doubt. But the intriguing question concerns the nature of African spirituality. What then are some of the characteristic features of African spirituality?

African Spirituality Is Relational and Action-Oriented

In African life and thought, as Magesa makes clear,

> [Spirituality] is based on interactive relationships among human beings and between humans and the entire order of existence. It understands this relationship to be the essence of religion, the sacred. . . . It is an approach that is absolutely relational and completely unitary. It perceives all reality, whether seen or unseen, as composed of sacral mystery and destiny.[7]

African spirituality is indeed a matter of interaction and relationality. It is also practice-oriented based very squarely in action and activity. Magesa highlights the pragmatic and active nature of African spirituality by declaring that in the African worldview,

> Spirituality is more of an activity than a passive quality. Rather than a "state of being," it is a way of behaving or, rather, relating. It involves dynamic relationships between visible and invisible

4. Taylor, *Primal Vision*, 74.

5. Taylor, *Primal Vision*, 74.

6. Taylor, *Primal Vision*, 75.

7. Magesa, *What Is Not Sacred?*, 24

power. Better yet, it entails the mutual exchanges of energies among all beings.[8]

Spirituality Is Dynamic and Can Be Developed

The Akans of Ghana and La Côte D'Ivoire, term a crucial dimension of human existence *sunsum*. The Gã of Ghana refer to this anthropological dimension as *susuma*. *Sunsum* is conceived of as a spiritual aspect or element in a person's personality accounting for their character, disposition, intelligence, ability to inspire or motivate self and others. One's *sunsum* is said to be subject to change for it can be developed, educated, or trained from a state of being "light" to one of being "heavy," strong, or hard. A lightweight personality can—through ritual and/or training—become a heavyweight social presence. A person with a strong *sunsum* can repel evil spiritual agents, whether human or non-human. A highly developed or educated *sunsum* is manifest in a person's appearance, social demeanor, self-confidence, ability to motivate or influence others, leadership qualities and strong personality. It is also the case that not only individuals possess *sunsum*. Whole families forming a clan are also spoken of as having *sunsum*. Fathers are believed to transmit their *sunsum* to their children.[9] A whole community of peoples can be strong or healthy in spirit. This is a most desirable value to which spiritual care is directed.

In addition to *okra* and *sunsum*, Akans speak of *mogya* (which literally translated is *blood*) as an element of personality that is received from one's mother and constitutes a relational bond with her while also placing one within a matrilineage; which the Akans, being matrilineal in their kinship and inheritance systems, argue defines one's place in society. Furthermore, the physical body in which we reside the Akan's term *nipadua* (literally "person-tree"; *nipa* = *person*, *dua* = *tree*) emphasizes humans' connection with nature or earth (tree).

Relational Holism

What is observable therefore, in the conceptualizing of the Akan and other African people groups, is just how relationally constituted humans are. One's *kra* relates one to God in a personal and unique way giving divine

8. Magesa, *What Is Not Sacred?*, 26

9. For a fuller consideration of Akan notions of personhood, see Lartey, *Pastoral Counseling*, 50–57.

relational ground for one's being. One's *sunsum* which is educable, links one relationally with one's father and father's extended family. One's *mogya* relates one with one's mother and locates one in a matrilineage, ensuring place and inheritance within a specific community in society. These components of personhood are inter-related, with each being capable of affecting the other. Illness results from disharmony or imbalance between these interpenetrating facets of a person's life as they interact in one's *nipadua* (body), the visible aspect of one's life which itself relates one with the earth and nature. In sum persons are relational beings in every respect—each component of their beings is relational. An African view of personhood can therefore be characterized as relational holism. Every constitutive element of a human's being is relational. Each element is related to other forces in a cosmos that is relationally defined and constituted. The whole cosmos is thus a network of relationships that need to be in harmony and balance for health and wellbeing to exist.

Spirit Is Essentially the Capacity to Relate

Clinician Joann Wolski Conn studied both religious and non-religious usages of the concept of spirituality, arguing that, "general or universal religious spirituality refers to the actualization of human self-transcendence (i.e., capacity for relating, knowing, committing ourselves) by whatever is acknowledged as the ultimate or the Holy."[10] On the basis of her thoughtful study she concludes, underscoring the African perspective on the true essence of spirituality: "In summary then, both classical and contemporary sources demonstrate a common theme-with-variations. *Relationship is the goal of spirituality and the pathways to it are a means of developing and sustaining relationship*"[11]

Spirit, in African thinking, lies at the core of human's capacity to relate. Here the essential meaning of "spirit" is the energy or driving force of relationship. In African thought, this capacity or energy is the defining feature and essential characteristic of humanity. What is spiritual about us is our ability to relate, and to speak of spirituality therefore is to refer to characteristic ways in which we relate across various dimensions of our being and with different forces in existence. I have elsewhere spoken of this capacity as a "vector" rather than a "scalar" quantity because it possesses both magnitude and direction.[12] One's spirituality can be directed and harnessed

10. Wolski Conn, "Spirituality and Personal Maturity," 38

11. Wolski Conn, "Spirituality and Personal Maturity," 41 (emphasis added).

12. Lartey, *In Living Color*, 142.

towards beneficial or else harmful ends. It can also be strengthened through various activities and rituals or weakened, impoverished or diminished by other kinds of activities or powers.

An African view of spirituality is encapsulated in a definition I offered in 2003, which has been the energizing and operative force within my intercultural pastoral care and counseling: "*Spirituality* refers to the human capacity for relationship with self, others, world, God and that which transcends sensory experience, which is often expressed in the particularities of given historical, spatial and social contexts, and which often leads to specific forms of action in the world."[13]

Spirituality from an African perspective is about our characteristic styles of relating and the pathways and means by which we develop and strengthen healthy relational patterns particularly along the five dimensions of our living specified. Further, it is necessary to bear in mind that these dimensions, far from being isolated or singular, are inter-related and inter-connected, inextricably intertwined with each other. Let us now examine each of the five dimensions.

Relationship with the Divine

Typically, in African experience spirituality affirms the universal human capacity to experience everyday life in relation to dimensions of power and meaning which are transcendent to our lives. No matter how that transcendence is spoken of, understood, or defined; it is the case that Africans tend to experience human life as in many ways related to an unseen world in which the Creator or Originator of all life, deities, natural spirits, ancestors, and unseen forces reside. Religious language is not the only means available to articulate this experience of life. The Orisha traditions, for example, understand orishas as "forces of nature" which need not be interpreted in religious terms. Often music, and the rhythmic movement of bodies in dance is the means by which this dimension of life is expressed. One does not have to be theist to recognize transcendence. There are African atheists and agnostics who affirm humanity's capacity for self-transcendence. The affirmation that there is a dimension of our human experience that lies beyond our total grasp leads us in a direction of awe and wonder at our own and all of creation.

Relationship with transcendence is the bedrock upon which our whole lives may fruitfully be based. Relationship with God is deeply personal as well as absolutely cosmic in its ramifications. Practices such as prayer,

13. Lartey, *In Living Color*, 140–41.

meditation, contemplation, and worship have the potential to deepen, strengthen, and nourish an abiding relationship with that which lies beyond our capacity to encompass or subsume under physical, mental, or social categories. Spiritual care practices need, among other things, to be directed at nurturing and enhancing our deepest sense of the divine or of transcendence in our human experience.

While this aspect of spirituality is crucial and often lies at the base of the whole of human's spiritual experience, it is also true that it cannot and must not be considered as exclusively what spirituality entails. When it becomes one's sole definition of spirituality, it manifests itself in an otherworldliness that may put one out of touch with the other aspects of what should be a holistic human experience. Spiritual care practices may help us develop a healthy balance between all aspects of our spiritual lives including—but not exclusively focusing—on the divine dimension. Reductionism is the bane of spiritual pursuits for it can result not in health, but rather in narrowness and harm.

African spirituality tends to understand the whole of creation to be God-infused. As we have seen, there is no sharp distinction made between a "sacred" and a "profane" or "secular" aspect of life. In Exodus 3:1–6 Moses encounters God in the midst of a bush that was burning but not consumed by the fire. To the African, every bush is burning. God literally and figuratively reveals Godself through every created thing, animate or inanimate. Everything has a sacred character and potential. As such, nurturing spirituality entails those ways in which we are helped with a sense of reverence for the entire created world and cosmos since all life is sacred. Reverence of this kind can inspire us to explore and examine the nature of the earth and all of creation as a feature of our worship of the Creator. It can also keep us from wanton destruction of the earth for personal profit and other selfish ends.

Relationship with Self

Another dimension of spirituality that must not be neglected nor seen as inferior to a superior "relation with the divine," is that of relationship with self. Self-awareness is as crucial to spirituality as God-awareness. In fact, our awareness of the divine is often mediated through a deep sense of self. We are likely to develop greater divine awareness through activities in which we go deep within ourselves.

Spiritual Director Wilkie Au, and Jungian analyst Noreen Cannon, offer a helpfully integrated approach to spirituality in their book, *Urgings of the*

Heart.[14] They argue that spiritual and psychological growth go hand in hand. In a necessary corrective to reductionist and exclusivist notions, they assert: "Neither a spirituality that ignores the dynamics of psychological growth nor a psychology that denies the spiritual nature of the human person can serve as an adequate guide today for people who seek to live with greater harmony and integration."[15] Exploring spiritual transformation, Au and Cannon offer the sense that spiritual transformation entails two movements namely what they term "self-appropriation" and "self-transcendence." Because in my view spirituality is deeply a matter of relationship with self, I find their explanation of self-appropriation helpful: "Self-appropriation involves self-knowledge and self-understanding. Practically, it means knowing what is going on inside ourselves: knowing who we are, knowing why we choose what we choose, why we do what we do and what our feelings and desires are."[16] This requires a practice of self-reflection which can truly be a means of coming to terms with our deepest spirituality.

In many situations of ill-health, one's way of viewing oneself is found as the culprit. When we think too lowly of ourselves or else denigrate and downplay our very selves, we enter into the deep abyss which has been described as "low self-esteem." There is no end to the damage that is done to one's personhood when one is perennially subject to low self-esteem. Those who would offer spiritual care must take time to explore with those they are seeking to help the nature of their "relationship with self." This relationship can be indicative of deep challenges to well-being. On the other hand, a true love of self can result in a healthy self-giving. Love of self is a prerequisite for love of neighbor.

Relationship with (An)other

The ability to cultivate an *I–Thou* relationship, as arguably best presented by Martin Buber,[17] with another person in which mutuality, respect, accountability and friendship are sustained, is truly a spiritual endeavor. The yearning for intimacy, closeness and union with the beloved, which is the center of sexual attraction, has furnished the vocabulary for the articulation of the longing of mystics of different religious traditions for union with God. Thomas Merton speaks of the heart as the center of human personhood: "The inner sanctuary where self-awareness goes beyond analytical

14. Au and Cannon, *Urgings of the Heart.*

15. Au and Cannon, *Urgings of the Heart,* 2.

16. Au and Cannon, *Urgings of the Heart,* 3

17. Buber, *I and Thou.*

reflections and opens out into metaphysical and theological confrontation with the Abyss of the unknown yet present one who is more intimate to us than we are to ourselves."[18]

What is spiritual about us has to do with the quality of relationships we have with others. The powerful connection between an honored teacher (guru) and a novice or newly initiated person (chela) is the vehicle of much spiritual growth within Eastern Religious traditions. In the teaching of Jesus "love of neighbor" is ranked a close and related second to "love of God." In the letter of John anyone who claims to love God whilst hating his or her brother is nothing but a liar (1 John 4:20). Spiritual care then has to be accounting for, reviewing, and exploring the dyadic relational dynamics that are typical for anyone seeking help. Spiritual care providers need to assist people examine ways in which these one-on-one relationships can promote or hinder health and wholeness.

Relationships among People

Community is commonly assumed to be a focus and is often a locus for the development of spirituality. Spiritual disciplines shaped and framed by particular luminaries in community is often the basis upon which persons develop their personal sense of the spiritual. We speak of the spirituality of Franciscans, Carmelites, Dominicans, Augustinians, Methodists, Anglicans, Jews, Muslims or Hindus as distinct forms or traditions within which persons may find spiritual fulfillment. As such it is possible to speak of the spirituality of a group of people. This would be manifest in the nature and intensity of relations between members of the group, as well as through the disciplines and practices by which relationship with God is strengthened or developed within the group.

The late great African philosopher and theologian John Mbiti commented significantly on the communal nature of African spirituality in the following words:

> To be human is to belong to the whole community, and to do so involves participating in the beliefs, ceremonies, rituals, and festivals of that community. A person cannot detach himself from the religion of his group, for to do so is to be severed from his roots, his foundation, his context of security, his kinships and the entire group of those who make him aware of his own

18. Merton, *Contemplative Prayer*, 33.

> existence. To be without one of these corporate elements of life
> is to be out of the whole picture.[19]

It is the solidarity of belonging that is expressed through participation that is lauded and encouraged within African society.

One can also speak of the spirituality of an institution and, as we have been doing all the way through this chapter, of a people or a culture. As such a hospital, an agency, or an organization can be spoken of as having a spirituality. Simply put, an important way to gauge that spirituality is to examine the patterns of relationship that exist within the institution. This calls for a systemic and structural approach to spiritual care. Institutions, organizations, and in fact whole cultures can promote and maintain healthy communities. Nations, political groupings, organizations as well as neighborhoods can facilitate health for persons. Cultures, in which social forces, signs, symbols, and ideologies are disrespectful of persons, or else denigrate minorities and marginalize groups, cannot foster health. Corporate forms of spiritual care are called for to address this corporate dimension of spirituality. These corporate forms often take shape in social activism and in movements for social justice across the world.

Relationships with Place, Space, and Things.

Spirituality in African view is deeply linked with material culture, space, nature and place. As with Native American thinking, in which all existence is spiritual, African spirituality is deeply connected with the land and geographical features like rivers, mountains, trees, and material objects like wood carvings, sculptures, and works of creative arts, and crafts. The Akans of Ghana and La Cote D'Ivoire have a saying that captures this sense powerfully: "If you wish to say something to God speak it to the wind." There is this sense that earth, wind, fire, and every other element symbolizes, represents, and may mediate the divine presence. What is perhaps most significant in African thought about the spirituality of the material is that the link between the physical world and the divine realm is strong. All of the created order is infused with the breath of God. As a result, African understanding is that one may approach the divine through nature. African mystic, Ishmael Tetteh repeatedly declares that "nature is his teacher," and that much of his spiritual instruction is derived from nature. Far from fearing or else lacking an understanding of God as the source and origin of all that exists, Africans, and especially those who espouse a mystical pathway, affirm the crucial example

---

19. Mbiti, *African Religions and Philosophy*, 2.

of nature for true spirituality. Such present us with ways of developing and nurturing relationship with nature as spiritual care.

So many people have their most sublime experiences of transcendence, the presence of God, and intimacy with the divine, as they commune with nature on a walk, climb a mountain, or else engage some other physical activity. Spirituality very clearly has to do with the way in which we encounter the created world. It also has to do with our manner of engagement with the 'built environment' and all the features and structures of the social environment that humans have created and within which we live our lives. The economic systems, employment systems, the educational systems, health care systems, criminal justice and legal systems, all of which impact the wellbeing of persons and groups of people, need to come into the purview of spiritual care provision. Spirituality in this sense has ecological and environmental dimensions that must be engaged for health in individuals and communities to exist.

Conclusion: Orchestral Music Needed

Spiritual care giving has to do with caring for what is spiritual about us as human beings. As we have seen, our spirituality encompasses a wide range of relationships which are inter-connected into networks of well-being or disease. All human beings, whether they participate in religious groupings or not, regardless of whether they assent to particular credal or doctrinal statements or not, live in and through sets and systems of relationships. What is spiritual about us is our capacity to relate. Spiritual care then is concerned with facilitating healthy relationships—with God, with self, with others, and with the environment.

Nurturing and fostering healthy ways of being in relation with the divine is a necessary part of spiritual care. Examining one's attitudes and responses to one's self is another. This is neither a purely psychological nor an exclusively 'theological' matter. It is the result of realizing the interconnectedness of all our life issues. Relationships with a loved one, a child, friend, spouse or parent are important and needed arenas for spiritual care analysis and activity. Exploring relationships with and among groups, organizations, institutions and whole cultures is another necessary aspect of spiritual care. Ecological and environmental relationships constitute another important area of concern and activity for spiritual care givers.

No singular spiritual care provider can undertake on their own to provide care for—and in—all of these dimensions. There is clearly a need for specialization and focus. However, what is crucial is that the vision of what spiritual care is about needs to be kept broad and comprehensive. As persons focus on the task at hand, it is important that they see themselves as part of an orchestra. Each individual instrument is needed for the full sound to be heard. No singular instrument or player can produce the full sound on their own, but each by focusing on their particular part can make possible what is a wholesome experience of music. Each spiritual care provider may see themselves as partly responsible for the whole instead of wholly responsible for a part. Our individual efforts in particular aspects need to be seen as contributing to a whole which is itself greater than the sum of the parts. Spiritual care in postcolonial vein needs to be no less.

2

Cultural Humility and Reverent Curiosity

Spiritual Care with and beyond Norms

LORI KLEIN

Introduction

THE CHAPLAIN'S GOAL SHOULD be to enable all people to experience the hospital as a place devoted to compassion, healing, and equity. Achieving this goal requires training and self-awareness guided by cultural humility and reverent curiosity. By earning the trust of patients, their loved ones, and hospital staff; the chaplain can serve as a cultural broker, helping all parties to navigate a landscape of intersecting and interacting cultures. This chapter will describe the vantage points that led me to adopt cultural humility and reverent curiosity as professional guideposts, demonstrate how hospital medicine in the United States is its own culture, and provide examples of chaplains acting as cultural brokers. Accompanying people through decisions made in grief's shadow, transitions, loss, and uncertainty can lead to meaningful transformation not only for patients and their loved ones, but also for chaplains.

Vantage Points

My intersecting identities and cultures inform how I navigate an academic medical center. My identities are marked both by privilege and the lack of privilege that accrues to non-dominant or oppressed people. Shifting assemblages of privilege/lack of privilege flavor my interactions. As a "white"[1] woman in a room of people of color, I may be quiet, especially if we discuss the individual or structural effects of racism. As a lesbian in a room with people identifying as heterosexual, I will be more outspoken, especially if the topic of homophobia arises. Even though I have been middle-class, my great uncles' stories of being sent to an orphanage by their recently widowed, immigrant mother, and my grandparents' stories of hunger during the Depression help me identify more personally with people living close to the financial edge. As a Jewish person, I understand what it means to live on the margins of a predominantly Christian society.

Living with one foot in and one foot out of dominant paradigm(s) gifts me with the perspective of an insider and outsider, allowing me to cast a compassionate yet critical eye in all directions. For example, sometimes when I am asked by a staff person to attend to family members who they perceive as disruptive, I will find a family that is Ashenazi Jewish, or African-American, or from another ethnic background in which it is culturally normative for people to stand a little closer, talk a little louder, become more emotionally expressive at times of stress. I recognize the staff person may view the family's behavior as disruptive out of an unconscious cultural discomfort, especially if that staff member comes from culture(s) that emphasize emotional restraint or distance. The staff person also acts within a medical system that values quiet, asking that family members subdue their reactions to terrible news or a loved one's death, so that physicians and staff can focus on their work and other patients can rest. As a chaplain, I know the resilience that comes from allowing a person to express their emotions, even if that expression creates discomfort for me or anyone else. As a hospital employee, I also am obligated to observe rules that emphasize quiet to promote healing. So my interventions may include gathering a family into a fervent prayer circle in a waiting area, or escorting wailing family members into the room of their deceased loved one, then bearing witness until their first rush of expressed grief eases. Navigating these situations demands that I facilitate the coexistence of conflicting behavioral norms. My multiple vantage points of privilege and lack teach me to approach these situations consciously and strategically.

---

1. I believe whiteness and race are social constructs, yet I understand my "whiteness" grants me privilege.

Coming to Terms

How did I adopt "cultural humility" and "reverent curiosity" as my watchwords? I grew up and live in a story-based culture and religion: Judaism. While reading may add intellectual grounding, life stories remain a fertile source of my formation. Also, terms such as "cultural competency" or "cultural humility" do not make sense to me without context. This section tells stories to trace how these concepts came to live in me vividly enough to guide my spiritual care work. In 1968, Anne Moody wrote *Coming of Age in Mississippi*, a memoir of living through the transition from the Jim Crow south through the early Civil Rights era. My mother gave it to me, her third-grade daughter. I read slowly, horrified by the racist cruelty she endured. Anne Moody's life differed from mine, yet I aspired to emulate her courage and persistent determination for equal treatment. That early exposure helped inoculate me against seeing people of color or any other group outside the dominant paradigm as "less than," and stoked my hunger to understand how and why prejudice flourished, hoping my understanding could contribute to change. I read voraciously.

In the 1990s, I served on the Santa Cruz AIDS Project board of directors. In an unlearning racism workshop, we learned we should include bicultural staff, attract bicultural volunteers, and become more bicultural or multicultural ourselves. I told a fellow board member I did not think I could call myself "bicultural"; I needed to own my "whiteness" and do my best to understand other cultures from that starting point. Jay, an African-American man, said he had to learn to be bicultural to function in a white-dominated society. Jay highlighted that my privilege allowed me to avoid that learning, to dip in and out of painful awareness of discrimination and inequity. This conversation changed me. The stakes became more personal to me not only when I felt disempowered, but also when I benefited from structural power.

My first immersion in the concept of cultural competence came as I advocated for a young mother. Before my rabbinic ordination in 2006, I worked as an attorney. In one case, I represented G. T., a mother raised in the Philippines, recently immigrated to the United States, whose son was placed into foster care based on evidence she physically abused him. At a review hearing, the trial court rejected the mother's psychological expert evidence that she should have received culturally competent, individualized parenting instruction. On appeal, I wanted to argue the trial court should have found reasonable reunification services had not been provided. At that time, no published California appellate opinion required trial courts to order culturally competent reunification services. Numerous social work and child welfare journal articles detailed the institutionalized bias faced by families of color in the child dependency system, as well as the need for culturally competent case evaluation and reunification services. However, the appellate court would not permit me to rely on these sources. This case exemplified encountering structural bias that allows a system to claim it is treating individual participants equitably, while maintaining norms and rules that privilege white, acculturated "Americans" who are fluent in English. I was unwilling to let this case go. I published a law review article about the issue so that other attorneys would not encounter the same obstacles that prevented me from arguing that reasonable reunification services must be culturally competent.[2]

This case stung me as an example of power and unconscious bias used to delay or prevent inclusion with the significant result that G. T. would not raise her child. In more recent times, this experience nurtured my awareness that the potential for discrimination lurked underneath seemingly neutral hospital norms: that the "patient" is only the person in the hospital bed, that unconscious patients may have only one surrogate decision maker at a time, that informing the patient of all relevant medical information is always the preferred alternative.

The concept of cultural competence first appeared in social work, nursing, and medical education literature between the early 1980s and early 2000s.[3] Chaplains, too, have fostered cultural competence to better understand patients' and families' emotional, existential, and spiritual needs, distress, resources, and requests. Stanford's patients and staff come from a wide variety of cultural, ethnic, and religious backgrounds. I agree with the laudable goal of learning to recognize cultural cues and allowing that knowledge to inform our care. However, some of the resources used by chaplains left me wary, as they reinforce incorrect cultural assumptions formed by members of dominant culture(s). A handbook on the Health-Care Chaplaincy Network website treats Judaism as a religion,[4] even though many Jewish people also regard themselves as part of a distinctively Jewish culture, such as Ashkenazi, Sephardic, or Mizrachi, and these cultures differ based on the patient's or family's lineage and nation of origin, including how directly affected they were by the Holocaust, nineteenth-century pogroms (anti-Jewish terror) or by living in anti-Semitic Communist societies. These cultural lineages can affect whether patients are open about their Jewish

---

2. Klein, "Doing What's Right," 20–44.

3. Gallegos et al., "Need for Advancement," 51–62.

4. Wintz and Handzo, *Patient's Spiritual and Cultural Values*, 19–21.

identity, whether they regard Judaism as a spiritual resource, whether they can trust a largely non-Jewish health care team.

Even when discussing Judaism as a religion, this handbook contains basic errors that would make a chaplain less able to understand or address a patient's or family's spiritual care needs. For example, the handbook states that Jewish, Christian, and Muslim traditions share a belief in heaven and hell after death, and that the primary difference between Judaism and Christianity is that Jews do not believe that Jesus was the "Christ," the savior of humanity.[5] While there are a variety of Jewish views about what happens in the afterlife, ranging from "nothing happens" to various formulations of a "World to Come," to reincarnation, there is no mainstream Jewish belief in heaven or hell as conceived by most Christian denominations. Also, it is a Christian-centric view that "the" primary difference between Judaism and Christianity is that Jews do not believe Jesus is the Savior. A Jewish person might say another primary difference is that Jews do not believe in original sin, or that humanity is fundamentally damned and therefore in need of saving in order to avoid hell after death. Even more fundamentally, the handbook's statement that "all Jews believe" is itself a paradigm coming from a Christian faith tradition. Judaism is not a "faith" tradition but a religious tradition. It does not rely on every Jew believing the same thing. Judaism is a deliberately constructed culture of questioning, valuing minority opinions and dissent. At best this handbook is a starting place. For example, the death and dying practices described can help formulate questions to identify a patient's or family's end of life needs.[6]

If this well-meaning but prescriptive and formulaic handbook is inaccurate about my religious tradition and culture, how can I trust its ability to teach me about cultures with which I am too unfamiliar to critically interpret the handbook's summary statements? The limitations of this and similar resources led to my dis-enchantment with the concept of cultural competence. For me, "competence" implies arrival at a set knowledge base, and I do not think I have arrived or could ever arrive. Striving toward cultural competence encourages us to focus on the more visible aspects of an individual's cultural identity, rather than the less or in-visible influences that affect responses and decision-making.[7] Monolithic understandings of cultural competence do not fully take into account individual or collective agency, intersectionality, acculturation to the dominant culture, or hybridity.   *Decísm*

---

5. Wintz and Handzo, *Patient's Spiritual and Cultural Values*, 7.

6. Wintz and Handzo, *Patient's Spiritual and Cultural Values*, 20.

7. Spencer-Oatey, "What Is Culture?," 3–6.

In more recent years, our CPE Educators teach our chaplain students to approach every spiritual care interaction with cultural humility.[8] Cultural humility is the "ability to maintain an interpersonal stance that is other-oriented (or open to the other) in relation to aspects of cultural identity that are most important to the [person]."[9] The term cultural humility arose as a counterpoint to cultural competence.[10] Advantages of a culturally humble approach include devotion to life-long learning, listening, reflection, and self-critique, the imperative to approach each patient with respectful openness to their unique matrix of intersecting identities and abilities, and a correction to the power imbalance between health care workers and patients or families.[11]

The aspect of cultural humility which warns against making assumptions based on prescriptive book learning resonates for me. The essence of good spiritual (or emotional or medical) care is learning when and how to respectfully ask questions. At times, I am saying "educate" me to patients and families; save me from ignorance, but it is not so that I can learn, for example, why the history of medical treatment and experimentation without informed consent or systemic under-dosing of pain medication might leave communities of color wary of hospital staff.[12] Learning about those disparities is part of my commitment not to burden people of color with educating me about racism. Rather, I ask questions to serve patients and families with better attention to their particular needs.

For example, the handbook produced by the HealthCare Chaplaincy Network tells me that, for Buddhists, "traditionally, there is a 3–5 day period when the body is not disturbed following death."[13] While this may be a broadly true statement, it does not help me in the hospital, where it would be impossible to leave the body of a deceased patient undisturbed for several days. Further, after-death religious care varies among Buddhists. At Stanford, family members of a dying Vietnamese Buddhist patient gave me instructions written by their priest requesting both that the body not be touched for at least eight hours after death, and that all lines be removed and the patient placed in a fresh hospital gown before after–death chanting begins. We can often accommodate a request that a deceased patient remain undisturbed for

---

8. Thank you to Chaplain and CPE Educator Candidate Jennifer Dillinger.

9. Hook et al., "Cultural Humility," 2.

10. Tervalon and Murray-García, "Cultural Humility," 117–25.

11. Ortega and Coulborn Faller, "Training Child Welfare Workers," 27–49; Tervalon and Murray-García, "Cultural Humility," 117–25.

12. Skloot, *Immortal Life*, 48, 165, 169; Maina et al., "Decade of Studying Implicit Racial/Ethnic Bias," 219–29.

13. Wintz and Handzo, *Patient's Spiritual and Cultural Values*, 22.

eight hours to allow for religious ritual. However, since many lines cannot be removed until after the patient dies, the combination of these two requests seemed incompatible. Believing that the Vietnamese Buddhist priest must have considered these contradictions, I asked when he considers a patient to have died for purposes of the proscription against touching. The priest replied they do not consider the patient to have died for ritual purposes until the physician pronounces the patient dead. By seeking wisdom from the family member's priest, we had our answer: once the nurse determined the patient had died, we did not ask the physician to pronounce until the patient was free of lines and clothed in a fresh gown.

And yet, perhaps because I spent years wedded to the goal of cultural competency, adopting a stance of pure cultural humility, even with its emphasis on learning and openness, feels too passive to me. And so, I balance my own cultural humility with a goal of reverent curiosity. When I ask a patient or family member to tell me their lived experience, needs, hopes, and goals based on their cultural location, I frame my question so they understand I only want to respect and serve them better, not to feed conventional curiosity. I want my seeking answers to be grounded in reverence so that my curiosity serves the person before me and the moment, not a self-absorbed desire to know. Calling my curiosity reverent reminds me that everyone's story is sacred. At the same time, I do not want to always rely on patients, their loved ones, and staff to educate me. Without any illusion that I will achieve competence, I read first-hand accounts of life lived and fiction written by people from a multitude of cultures. I expose myself to a variety of religious and spiritual practices, music, dance, and visual arts as a window into the emotional and spiritual lives of those I serve and work beside.

When my identities and commitments meet the multiplicity of identities and commitments of patients, loved ones, staff, students, and volunteers, the encounter brings us to a liminal space of *nepantla*. Chicana feminist philosopher Gloria Anzaldúa calls *nepantla* "the threshold of transformation":

> Nepantla is that uncertain terrain one crosses when moving from one place to another; when changing from one class, race, or sexual position to another; when traveling from the present identity to a new identity.

The hospital is "uncertain terrain" for all of us. In that liminal space, we can open ourselves to transformative encounters:

> En este lugar entre medio, nepantla, two or more forces clash and are held teetering on the verge of chaos, a state of entreguerras. There tensions between extremes create cracks or tears in

the membrane surrounding, protecting, and containing the
different cultures and their perspectives. Nepantla is the place
where at once we are detached (separated) and attached (connected) to each of our several cultures. . . . Nepantla is . . . a place
where we can accept contradiction and paradox.[14]

Within *nepantla*, I have helped transform and been transformed by Jewish
family members singing doo wop songs in a patient's final hours; enabled
a Muslim patient to honor his religious obligations while also receiving a
life-saving bowel diversion; witnessed the flexible theology of an evangelical
Christian patient remaining grateful and full of testimony even when the
miracle did not arrive.

The Setting for Our Work

The Stanford Spiritual Care Service team includes interfaith chaplains and
CPE students, a spiritually generous administrative assistant, and more than
150 volunteers. The team is diverse by race, ethnicity, national origin, immigration status, language ability, gender, sexual orientation, religion, and
spirituality. We serve a correspondingly diverse population. We serve in
nepantla together. Inclusion begins with hiring and recruitment. Our staff
chaplains must be passionate about providing spiritual care to people from
their own tradition. They also must whole-heartedly offer to meet the needs
of any patient or family member while holding appropriate theological, cultural, and religious practice boundaries. Chaplain students must be open to
providing non-judgmental and interfaith spiritual and existential care and
willing to learn and challenge their comfort zone. Spiritual Care volunteers
generally visit patients who share their religious tradition, but they must
have enough interfaith focus to care for the patient's loved ones who may not
share that tradition. Volunteers must also refrain from proselytizing, even
by urging more rigorous observation of the patient's religious tradition. We
hire skillful staff chaplains with an eye toward cultural contribution rather
than cultural fit, because looking for "fit" tends to decrease inclusion and
reproduce the current staff composition.[15]

In our work, we mix universalism and particularism. We open weekly
team meetings with a reading, prayer, or exercise from a particular or no
religious tradition that contains sentiments to which any of us could subscribe. We celebrate holidays in the Atrium and include speakers who can
speak about a particular religion without denigrating the belief or non-belief

14. Anzaldúa, *Light in the Dark*, 56.

15. Rivera, "Hiring as Cultural Matching," 999–1022; Rodriguez, "Hiring," para.
3–5.

of someone attending or passing by. We openly discuss how people from many cultures cope with illness, prepare for dying, wrestle with theodicy, describe the sacred. We teach each other about how to meet different needs without transgressing our own boundaries. For example, Jewish people end most prayers with a simple "amen." However, when I ended prayers with Christian patients that way, their body language sometimes communicated they felt I had slammed down the telephone. To compensate, they might add, "in Jesus name we pray, amen." I could not pray in Jesus' name, but did not want to undermine the comfort of prayer either. One day during my CPE residency, I observed a Lutheran staff chaplain leading a family in prayer, ending with, "we pray this in Your name, amen." I could say that! Each of us could infer what "Your" meant and pray collectively as individuals. I asked her about her liturgical choice. She said she did not know the range of beliefs in that circle and wanted to be inclusive.[16] I have used that ending in many situations since, and no longer elicit distress. Recently, more non-theistic students have joined our team. At team meetings, this has led several of us to question when to use prayer language such as "amen." Instead we might read spiritual poetry. Adding new team members can be a delightful or uncomfortable challenge to our internal biases; all of it is spiritual practice that we bring to our hospital work.

Medicine Practiced in a Hospital Setting Is a Culture

The definition of culture is contested and determined by each definer's culture(s). However, several definitions contain the same elements: ideas, values, norms, rituals, and stories held in common and socially transmitted over time by individuals and as part of systems.[17] By these criteria, medicine as practiced in a hospital setting is a culture. Practitioners of that culture, whether they are healthcare providers or teachers, need to incorporate awareness of that culture and humility when encountering people from other, sometimes conflicting cultures.

While a medical workplace may be racially and culturally diverse, the norms and values of hospital culture in the United States align with white, Euro-American conceptions of family, how power and decision-making occurs within families, individualism, privacy, and whether distressing medical information should be conveyed to a patient. For example, the pre-printed text of many advance directives assumes the adult patient will make medical decisions as long as the patient is mentally competent to do so. If the patient becomes unable to make medical decisions, that power transfers to

16. Thank you to Chaplain Susan Scott.

17. See Spencer-Oatey, "What Is Culture?," 3–5.

the health care agent. With patient consent, the medical team may discuss treatment options with additional loved ones, but they will look to the health care agent as the patient's voice, even if other family members disagree. However, some cultures value consensus decision-making above that of any individual; others follow prescribed norms, such as decisions being made by the eldest male person, or the parents of a "legally" adult child, as long as that child is unmarried and under the age of thirty.[18] Thus, the decision-making paradigms of the medical team and family can conflict.

Similarly, a cornerstone of medical ethics is supporting patient autonomy.[19] To make treatment choices, a patient must have adequate information about their diagnosis, prognosis, and the effects of possible treatments.[20] However, because discussion of terminal illnesses or end-of-life is taboo in some cultures, family members of a terminally ill patient may ask medical team members not to reveal a diagnosis or prognosis to the patient, making the patient's informed consent unattainable.[21]

Patients and families are not the only humans who suffer when a cure is impossible or values clash. Nurses, social workers, chaplains, and physicians may experience emotional, spiritual, and moral distress when sustaining life for a patient who is clearly dying and suffering physically.[22] Physicians may suffer when they see a patient dying despite their best efforts to find a cure, a repair, a path toward increased quality of life.[23] I once observed one of our staff chaplains leading ICU physicians to affirm each other after a week in which two young patients died in tragic circumstances. All but one of the physicians cried.[24]

What happens when the academic medical culture regards its own norms as the best way to make a decision, and then sees alternate methods as less valid? I have witnessed health care teams struggling to incorporate cultural or family values that conflict with medical norms, leading some staff to see those patients or families as more troublesome, stressful, or unduly time-consuming. We cannot take all of the emotional or spiritual pain out of decision-making at death's borderland. Even so, it is a better starting point to regard these encounters as a meeting of legitimate cultures. To be

---

18. Decision-making style related to me when caring for a young adult from India. See Su et al., "Family Matters," 175–82; Sharma et al., "Traditional Expectations," 311–17; Matsumura et al., "Acculturation of Attitudes," 531–39; Kwak and Haley, "Current Research Findings," 634–41.

19. Gillon, "Ethics Needs Principles," 307–12.

20. Stirrat and Gill, "Autonomy in Medical Ethics," 127–30.

21. Kwak and Haley, "Current Research Findings," 634–41.

22. Pauly et al., "Framing the Issues," 1–11.

23. See chapter 4 in Ofri, *What Doctors Feel*.

24. Thank you to Chaplain Samuel Nkansah.

culturally humble means also acknowledging our own values and the norms we uphold to achieve them. Only then can we see beyond our assumptions to respect competing values and norms.

Use of Cultural Humility and Reverent Curiosity in the Hospital

Acting from cultural humility and reverent curiosity enables us to deliver high quality person-centered care.[25] Providing person-centered care includes asking the patient what they would want you to know about them and their goals.[26] "Reading" patients and their loved ones as "living human documents" is a key skill in providing person-centered care.[27] Listening well to someone with whom we differ culturally (everyone) entails awareness of verbal and nonverbal cues, respect, listening for the emotion underneath the words, and following the speaker's lead.

When loved ones gather around a dying patient, they increasingly represent members of different religious or spiritual traditions. They may include humanists or atheists, or the family may be primarily comprised of atheists with a few religious members. Some of them may desire culturally familiar end-of-life ceremonies even if they no longer believe the accompanying religious precepts. Yet they intra-act as phenomena in the nepantla/uncertain terrain of the life-death transition.[28] Our role as chaplains is to co-create a ritual that allows for everyone to remain in the room to express their thoughts and feelings.

Cultural humility and reverent curiosity also enable chaplains to serve as cultural brokers. Navigating culturally and sometimes ethically fraught situations equips us for this role. Cultural brokering has been defined as "bridging, linking, or mediating between groups or persons for the purpose of reducing conflict or producing change."[29] Brokers mediate among patients, their loved ones, and hospital staff. Successful cultural brokers earn everyone's trust. Assuming everyone is doing their best under the circumstances helps build that trust. We try to maintain compassion toward health care workers whose fear of death may lead them to delay addressing a patient's desire to enter hospice. We help patients surface underlying suspicions about hospital care that may lead them to reject treatment options.

25. Saha et al., "Patient Centeredness," 1275–85.
26. Entwistle and Watt, "Treating Patients as Persons," 29–39.
27. Boisen, *Exploration of the Inner World*, 185.
28. Anzaldúa, *Light in the Dark*, 56; Barad, *Meeting the Universe Halfway*, 197.
29. Jezewski, "Evolution of a Grounded Theory," 14.

I offer a few examples of how cultural humility and reverent curiosity help us act as cultural brokers and provide person-centered care: (1) Providing empathetic care by offering to pray with the family who has asked "for a miracle," while not undermining the medical team's message that aggressive life-support is contributing to the patient's suffering. (2) Overriding an Interpreter's assumption that the patient will not complete an Advance Directive if organ donation is mentioned, then learning the patient finds organ donation a meaningful option. At the same time, understanding that many communities of color distrust Advance Directives, because they can point to historical and current experiences in which medical staff have provided them with sub-standard care. (3) Helping different staff members cope with an inpatient's traumatic death by leading a debriefing, then a guided meditation, then blessing the room with consecrated oil. (4) At a goals-of-care meeting, recognizing that a family's resistance to transitioning the patient to comfort care may reflect their desire to allow family members to arrive from far away, a request they are too shy to make unless prompted. (5) Understanding that a patient or family member who staff believe is in "denial" may be titrating knowledge that will cause emotional suffering. In fact, so-called denial may melt away once the chaplain and patient pray together and the patient asks for a peaceful death.

Coda

The bottom line is encountering each person as an individual, even as I use my ever-growing knowledge of cultures to better understand how they may have arrived at their response to their circumstances. We can allow others to be experts of their needs. Also, permitting ourselves to be culturally humble is a vulnerable state that helps equalize the power imbalance between ourselves as chaplains and the patient or their loved one who find themselves in the unexpected and unwelcome situations that arise when grappling with illness, injury, or dying. We accept that we are perpetually learning and that self-acceptance increases our compassion for all the learning beings around us. In turn, this enables others to trust us as cultural brokers, because we do not attempt a facade of unearned expertise.

Maintaining cultural humility and reverent curiosity is a practice, not a destination. It is one of my spiritual practices. The goal is to remain culturally response-able.[30] Within the nepantla of the hospital, this spiritual practice means I do not just affect change; I am changed as well.

30. Barad, *Meeting the Universe Halfway*, 392.

3

The Flower of Interbeing

—— SUMI LOUNDON KIM ——

Introduction

FROM THE VAST CANON of Buddhist teachings, one is emerging as a useful concept for our time: interconnectedness. As it is, we are already undergoing a paradigm shift reflecting an unfolding understanding of interconnectedness, with local economies seen as entwined with globalization, racial and social injustice understood through systemic oppression, and our survival now clearly dependent on the Earth's ecological web, to name a few. This chapter sets forth that this Buddhist-yet-universal teaching provides religious professionals with a framework to help others understand their identity; to strengthen the learning relationship between a chaplain and students; and to rethink how we teach. To support us in experiencing the ground of our interbeing, we examine the symbiotic practices of solitude and community. We further consider the impact of our use of internet-connected devices on spiritual development. The chapter concludes with reflecting on how we find personal agency while feeling trapped in large-scale political, economic, and social systems. The image of the flower of interbeing, as taught by the Zen master Thích Nhất Hạnh, serves as the core visual.

Concept

The renowned Vietnamese Buddhist monk Thích Nhất Hạnh (b. 1926) uses a flower to illustrate the nature of something's existence. How does a flower come to be? A flower grows through the relationship of a seed, soil, rain, sun, and air. Each of these elements are not themselves a flower, but when brought together, a flower comes into being. Nhất Hạnh calls the flower's existence "interbeing," because the being of the flower arises through these interrelationships.

The Flower of Interbeing

This flower exists through the interrelationship of a seed, soil, air, rain, and sun.

Sun

Rain

Air

Seed

Soil

© 2019 Sumi Loundon Kim

Artwork by Kimberley Cordray, based on the author's sketch

Interbeing is Thích Nhất Hạnh's own particular word for what Buddhists commonly call interdependence or interconnectedness. All three terms are themselves rendering of the Sanskrit word śū *nyatā*, which is most often translated into English as "emptiness,"[1] a word that continues to be used widely. Nhất Hạnh explains his innovative rendering from a classical Buddhist perspective:

1. "Because all phenomena are dependently arisen, they lack, or are empty of, an intrinsic nature characterized by independence and autonomy" (Buswell and Lopez Jr., *Princeton Dictionary of Buddhism*, 872).

Emptiness [*shunyata*] always means empty of something. A cup is empty of water. . . . We are empty of a separate, independent self. . . . Emptiness is the Middle Way between existent and non-existent. The beautiful flower does not *become* empty when it fades and dies. It is already empty, in its essence. Looking deeply, we see that the flower is made of non-flower elements—light, space, clouds, earth, and consciousness. It is empty of a separate, independent self.[2]

By anchoring śū *nyatā*on the word "being," Nhất Hạnh assists us in making the connection to something we fail to understand accurately, that is, the nature of *human* beings. From the Buddhist point of view, it is our mistaken belief in our separateness—that each of us is autonomous and self-determining—that is a major contributor to our suffering. As such, to begin healing this false sense of isolation and division, we start by revising our understanding of who we think we are. Nhất Hạnh clarifies,

> You cannot be, you can only inter-be. The word inter-be can reveal more of the reality than the word "to be." You cannot be by yourself alone, you have to inter-be with everything else.[3]

Changing our view of self from independent to interdependent changes how we view everything else, from the personal and interpersonal to the social and environmental.

In the last few years, I find that in my own spiritual development, inseparably entwined with my service as a Buddhist chaplain and minister, I keep returning to this teaching on interbeing. Although I practice meditation regularly and work to live from the basis of recognizing the interdependence of all things, I have long wanted to think as deeply as I could about how this teaching speaks to some of my own core issues. This includes working with personal identity, the practice of teaching others, the paradox of loving both solitude and being in community, the connection to my heavy use of devices and, most challengingly, how to dismantle and heal racism both personally and socially. I suspect you, along with many others, think about the same things.

Understanding Identity through Interbeing

One of the most striking developments in our time is the increasing complexity around personal identity. Globalization, immigration, and

2. Nhất Hạnh, *Heart of the Buddha's Teaching*, 146–47.

3. Nhất Hạnh, "Island of the Self."

intermarriage have given birth to greater numbers of multicultural and multiracial individuals. Moreover, how we conceptualize aspects of identity has also become more diverse. For example, while a decade ago we mostly referenced gender in binary, male/female terms, we now think of gender as a spectrum. As such, chaplains can no longer assume much about those we work with based on their appearances or biographical sketches. Rather, we may do best to think about students (and indeed ourselves) as the interbeing of no less than gender, race, nationality, ethnicity, home faith tradition, new faith exploration, languages, family of origin, culture, sexual orientation, educational opportunity, and economic access. Doing so helps us work more fluidly and dynamically with each student.

Interbeing also helps us address one of the most pressing lines of inquiry for young adults: their personal identity. Young adulthood is a time of defining and shaping who one is and who one wants to become. Each year of university chaplaincy, I hear the same set of questions, "How can I understand who I am? Am I being inauthentic or not true to myself when I find myself being a different person in different situations?" The questions themselves belie the search for some kind of single, fixed core of certainty. Interbeing provides a framework of interpretation that allows young adults to hold multiple and shifting identities that can be dependent on context. It allows them to imagine that who they are might change as they have new experiences, learning, and relationships. To assist young adults in rethinking the nature of a self, one could contemplate the many factors that led to the formation of oneself at this moment in time.

Identity continues to be a question for older adults as well, particularly when a life rupture promulgates a new identity: for example, onset of a disability or diagnosis, a major change in family life, or more basically, the inevitable aging of the body. Here again, the image of ourselves as the interbeing of histories and identities allows us to include prior incarnations while incorporating these changes. We tend to have a linear sense of self—"I was a college student but now I'm a professional"—or a fixed sense of self—"I'll always be judgmental and awkward." A sense of self that is more pliable, open, and shifting ameliorates the problem of typecasting our own self. This pairs nicely with a growth mindset and recent research that the brain is able to recode itself in very powerful ways. As it happens, mid- and later-life is often characterized, writes Sharon Daloz Parks, by a person becoming aware "of the depth and pervasiveness of the interrelatedness of all of life."[4] Such recognition of interdependence leads to maturation in multiple ways, including relationships, finding the balance of action with equanimity in

---

4. Parks, *Big Questions, Worthy Dreams*, 86.

response to inequity, community, and responsibility. In providing pastoral counseling for maturing adults, affirming this growing understanding of interbeing can be deeply clarifying and supportive.

Pastoral Care from a Place of Interbeing

Relationship between Chaplain and Student

As we address questions of identity through the lens of interbeing, we can bear in mind that the very relationship between ourselves and the student becomes a part of their being, too. In my early twenties, I worked as an admissions officer at the Harvard Divinity School; yet, I was shy and slightly awkward. I was in awe of my boss Anne who exuberantly welcomed everyone who came through the door with a broad smile, warm handshake, and often, a big hug. I decided to simply imitate her to see if I could get better at greeting visitors. It was difficult at first, but I got the hang of it. I began to enjoy meeting new people and, as my kids will tell you, these days I will strike up a conversation with just about anybody. Sociable Sumi was created through interbeing with Affable Anne. It might be humbling to consider that we, as pastors, are co-creating others, but that responsibility can inspire us to be our best possible selves, too.

Likewise, we can take joy in the ways our students inter-be with and shape us. My students have nudged me to places of compassion and open-mindedness that could only have happened through relationships (and not in therapy, for example). I used to jump to conclusions about who a person must be based on their appearance, to the point that I could discount someone entirely without knowing a thing about them. In one of my first classes on meditation for a university research project, there was an older student who resembled Imelda Marcos. She wore all white, tinted glasses, heaps of jewelry and makeup, and appeared to be fabulously wealthy. She said she was taking the meditation class to help science. She did not show up for several classes nor do her homework. One class, we were sharing what we had learned in the last week. She raised her hand. My eyes rolled at the thought that she'd have anything substantial to say. She said,

> I don't know if this counts as meditation, but my dog had a seizure this past week. It was really bad. I took him to the vet and as we were waiting, he was breathing rapidly and shaking all over. I was also very upset. I could see that my fear was making him worse. I thought, "Oh no, you can't die on me. My husband died this past year, my son died the year before—you're the last one left to me."

So I gathered him in my arms and I began breathing slowly and deeply. His panting began to subside. Eventually, we were breathing together, slowly and deeply. And we both calmed down.

"Imelda" was just one of dozens of students who knocked prejudgment right out of me. Seeing the mutual shaping between student and teacher opens the teacher to being a student, too, such that learning is not top down but co-created in a mutually beneficial way.

A sense of interconnectedness with our students or parishioners also mitigates interpersonal frustration and, at the extreme, burnout. One cause and also sign of burnout is the hardening of boundaries between oneself and others. Interbeing allows for breathability between ourself and another. One year, I had a doctoral student with razor sharp intellectual capacities who publicly corrected me on Buddhist terminology several times and sought to engage in long conversations about orthodoxy. For a few months, I found myself mentally spinning through debates and counterpoints with him, at times tempted to write long explanatory emails. I wondered how fast he would graduate. At some point, I asked myself, why does this person bother me so much? Very quickly, I saw that his questioning touched a tender spot of insecurity, as I always doubted whether I was sufficiently qualified for my position. And I saw that his own obsessiveness and strained social interactions with peers was a source of suffering for him, too. We spent the rest of the year working on noticing and softening fixations, and I spent some time resolving my insecurities. If I had clung to a fixed identity that I am the knowledgeable teacher and the student needs correction, this rigidity would have perpetuated an embattled mentality of separation that would further drain us both. Instead, seeing our dynamic from a place of interconnectedness allowed me to breathe and thereby to learn and grow.

Learning Spaces

The viewpoint of interbeing can also help us reimagine how we teach in the classroom and in sacred spaces of spiritual development. Educator Parker Palmer lays out a useful model in his classic *The Courage to Teach*. Traditionally, teachers posit that there is some kind of objective reality or truth that exists on its own. The teachers have access to that truth and then transmit knowledge of it to students. This linear, top-down model has significant problems, particularly with regard to authority, power, and claims to the truth. But foremost among those problems is that academia itself no longer thinks of fields as defined by an autonomous, objective truth. Rather, scholars understand their own fields in increasingly interdisciplinary, complex, and interconnected ways. Parker cites a leading thinker of modern science, Ian Barbour: "Nature is understood to be relational, ecological, and interdependent. Reality is constituted by events and relationships rather than separate substances or separate particles. . . . [We should see nature as a] historical community of interdependent beings."[5]

Given that academic fields themselves are understood through interconnected causes and conditions perhaps, hints Palmer, we should rethink how those fields are *taught*. He suggests that a different process for generating knowledge would be to place the *subject* (as opposed to working from an *object* we call "objective truth") in the center of a circle of thinkers who consider the topic from various angles. Here, students enter into relationship with each other, the teacher, and the subject. Each person draws on what they know and engage with others in learning. Palmer writes, "As we try to understand the subject in the community of truth, we enter into complex patterns of communication—sharing observations and interpretations, correcting and complementing each other."[6] Through the interbeing of ideas and relationships, the subject comes into view. In this model, the teacher, too, becomes an active participant and therefore student, even as she holds and facilitates the space. Palmer, citing Ian Barbour's *Religion in the Age of Science*, writes, "Reality is a web of communal relationships, and we can know reality only by being in community with it."[7]

What are the implications of this model–of knowing in community–for spiritual development? In my own lineage, Theravada Buddhism, teachers traditionally give "dharma talks" on the teachings of the Buddha. These can run from forty-five minutes to several hours, and, even more traditionally, there's no question and answer period. When I began as a university chaplain, I replicated this model. Not only did the already-exhausted students get drowsy—no matter how many jokes or references to pop culture I made—but I highly suspect a year on, no one remembered a thing. However, I noticed that during the brief question period at the end, the energy in the room came up and then rose exponentially when the students dared to engage each other directly, bypassing the teacher.

I found myself, in time, increasingly using two other teaching formats: storytelling, followed by discussion, and what I might call the workshop format. Both formats generated a charged space that engaged students and facilitated personal insights. Significantly, students enjoyed meeting each other and deepening relationships through their conversations. This

5. Palmer, *Courage to Teach*, 99.

6. Palmer, *Courage to Teach*, 106.

7. Palmer, *Courage to Teach*, 97.

community-building kept students returning right through to the end of the semester: they were coming back for each other as much as for their own needs.

The workshop format is comprised of a series of exercises, reflections, and discussions in which 80 percent of the airtime and effort is given to the students in the room. The remaining 20 percent is for me as the facilitator/guide to briefly introduce the topic, set the agenda, step the group through it, and provide reflection, summary, and shepherding. During discussions, I sit to one side at a short distance in order to let students feel they have full permission to talk with each other. I listen, nonetheless, and if a conversation veers too far off, goes dead, or something totally wrong comes out, I step in for a brief facilitation. The workshop format provides a practical process for fostering relationships among students, the teacher, and subject, thereby implementing learning through interconnectedness.

The Practices of Solitude and Community

Interbeing can be realized through two practices that are seemingly in opposition: solitude and community. Solitude is removing oneself from the ordinary busyness of daily life and withdrawing the senses from the usual stimulations of the world. One turns inward, releasing vexations about the past and anxieties about the future. In a safe, quiet, hedonic-reduced environment, the body, heart, and mind release and relax. Real solitude is not a vacation, which revolves around consuming sense delights. Rather, real solitude take discipline, because as soon as we settle, the temptation to get busy and distracted again is high. Then, as the discursive mind quiets, one begins to notice the sounds previously drowned out by the noise of thinking. Crickets, children in the distance, one's own breath. Slowly, the senses connect to what is occurring in and around oneself. Solitude allows us to drop into subtle attunement with the events of the present moment. As the heart and mind relax, they expand, until a feeling of connection spreads outward and unbounded, shifting from the tight swirl of self-concern to an intimate care with life. One feels interbeing somatically.

The second practice is that of community. We tend not to think of community as a practice—we think of it as a thing. But creating and sustaining a spiritually fulfilling community takes intentionality and effort. Yes, we can gather with others and chatter about the news or latest gossip. This has its own value, but we won't necessarily feel nourished by it. So what kind of practices do we undertake to develop spiritual community? The Buddha himself provided guidance more than twenty-five centuries ago:

> Students, there are these two kinds of communities: [shallow and deep]. . . . A shallow community is one in which the members are restless, puffed up, vain, talkative . . . with muddled mindfulness . . . with wandering minds, with loose sense faculties. A deep community is one in which members are not restless, puffed up, vain, talkative . . . but have established mindfulness . . . are concentrated . . . with restrained sense faculties.[8]

Hence, deep community is built on an agreement that we are comfortable with silence and speak when it's meaningful, that we are aware of ourselves and others (mindful), and that we are content and at ease with a minimum of sense delights (restrained sense faculties). Many churches, temples, synagogues, monasteries, and retreat centers are set up to facilitate deep community.

In the context of a quiet mind and mouth, we are much more attentive to the words of others when they share with us. Here, this listening and caring, while also sharing of ourselves with thoughtfulness, leads to deepening friendships. It is through these meaningful relationships that we begin to glimpse how who we are is comprised of threads of reciprocal care. In the relative safety and belonging of community we begin to relax the primitive reflex of hoarding and defending I-me-mine to find contentment, gratitude, and generosity. In community, we again feel our interbeing: we are formed by others and we in turn shape those around us.

Solitude and community are not mutually exclusive: indeed, the great traditions structure intensive spiritual formation so that these are practiced simultaneously. The documentary *Into Great Silence* beautifully illustrates a community of Carthusian monastics together in silence, practicing interiority and communion with the divine, but together. The replication of this model throughout the religious world speaks to how a certain form of solitude and community work companionably. A well-known passage in the Buddhist texts attests to this combination, as well. The Buddha's cousin and attendant Ananda comes to him one day and asserts that good friendship comprises *half* of the spiritual life. The Buddha corrects him, saying,

> Not so, Ananda! Not so, Ananda! This is the *entire* spiritual life, Ananda, that is, good friendship. . . . When a dharma student has a good friend . . . it is to be expected that they will develop and cultivate the noble eightfold path [which is] based upon *seclusion*.[9]

---

8. Bodhi, *Buddha's Teachings,* 111.

9. Bodhi, *Buddha's Teachings,* 89 (emphasis added).

Another passage from the Buddhist texts draws a connection between the twin practices of seclusion and community with the insight of interconnectedness. The Buddha notices that one of his foremost disciples, Shariputra, is especially radiant. Shariputra says that he's been meditating on emptiness, which prompts the Buddha to further teach that one can realize emptiness while going for alms (Buddhist monks traditionally beg for food):

> When a [monk] puts on his robe, takes his bowl and walks with a group of monks down into town to beg for almsfood, that monk should guard his six senses,[10] should hold himself in such a way that confused thinking does not arise, so that he is able to completely dwell in peace, freedom and happiness with each step. Going for almsrounds in that way he already realizes the concentration on emptiness [interbeing].[11]

This model need not feel far away and long ago, nor feel we need to lock up our office and run for the Abbey of Gethsemani in the hills of Kentucky. Rather, access to a felt sense of interbeing can occur through everyday moments, just as a monk could realize interbeing while begging for food. For example, if we talk just a bit less while abiding with kind-hearted awareness, we'll find others open up to share. Or, if we take a few minutes to step outside by ourself and intentionally reconnect our senses with the sounds, experiences, smells, and sights of our environment, we'll move out of our head and touch the pulse of the world as it is now.

Devices and the Internet

An everyday person will find the spiritual image of interbeing highly accessible because the internet is a firmly established paradigm. Since the 1990s, many have gradually adopted interconnectedness-like mental maps of relationships, communications, commerce, and more through both the use and model of the aptly named world-wide web (www) service. In terms of spiritual cultivation, it would appear that personal device technology and internet access provide three essentials: the concept of interconnectedness, solitude, and community. Community is found through social media, video conferencing, forums, etc. while solitude is enabled by the home-delivery of goods and services. We would expect, therefore, that

10. In Buddhist psychology, the mind is considered as one of the senses because, like the nose, ears, eyes, etc., it, too, can receive sense impressions.

11. Nhất Hạnh, *Soulmate of the Buddha*, 7–8. Nhất Hạnh's rendering of a classical Buddhist sutra titled "The Purification of Almsfood" (MN 151).

these conditions would favor an upwelling of very happy, spiritually nourished, and perhaps even enlightened people. And yet, the opposite appears to be the case. Studies consistently find rising rates of depression, anxiety, loneliness, and suicidality, with higher rates having a striking correlation to the duration of screen time.[12]

What's going on? To understand the dynamic, we need to look more carefully. The impact of internet-connected devices is of special concern for those of us in pastoral capacities, because we need to understand the degree to which tech and social media are potential contributors to suffering and factors in claiming a life of sanity. It could even be that these, when out of balance, are antithetical to spiritual development.

We might begin this inquiry with an observation: humans have bodies. Somehow, perhaps through evolution, we need physical touch with others in order to develop properly. Infants who do not receive normal levels of touch are at significant risk for behavioral problems and functioning.[13] The need for touch doesn't abate with adulthood: the "cuddle hormone" oxytocin is primarily released through touching in hugging, nursing, and sex. What, then, happens to us when we receive difficult news or experience emotional distress through online activity when we are alone?

I experienced this starkly the day of the Sandy Hook Elementary School shooting in December 2012. That morning, as I read the extraordinarily painful news, my six-year-old daughter was in class at her elementary school. Between event updates, I kept returning to Facebook to connect with friends to try to make sense of it all. Everyone was upset. By mid-day, I noticed that I was not feeling comforted and had actually become increasingly distraught. My friends postings were whipping up emotions. I closed my laptop and headed out to simply make contact with real humans. I received hugs and talked face to face with colleagues. Those interactions, even with people I knew less well than my online friends who lived far away, provided the soothing we all needed in that moment. Later, I learned that research shows that soothing hormones such as oxytocin only kick in when we are with someone with all five senses and that it cannot be produced through online interactions or reading.[14] For example, a study of 11,000 adults ages fifty-plus showed that face-to-face contact reduced depression and, conversely, lack of in-person contact—even if the person stayed in touch through phone, letters, or email—increased the risk for depression.[15]

12. For example, see Twenge et al., "Increases in Depressive Symptoms."

13. Gunnar, "Salivary Cortisol Levels," 611–28.

14. See interviews with Gloria Steinem, such as Stuermer, "Meet the Muse."

15. Teo et al., "Mode of Contact."

Circling back to the practice of solitude, it could be for good reason that most faith traditions have us practice solitude with others, in community. That setup might not merely be for providing food and shelter. It may be that, *even when we are at our most interior,* as humans with bodies, we need to be in the company of others relatively often. Thus, while the new internet and tech setup offers the possibility for us to be solitary, in an extended form through weeks and months it could be that it is the wrong kind: this type of aloneness, without access to in-person friendship, leads to loneliness, isolation, and disconnection.

If indeed we need to be physically around others, then can we feel spiritually nourished if we're together with others but absorbed individually on our own device: for example, a crowded bus, bodies close together, but heads down, eyes locked on a personal screen? Scholar Sherry Turkle, in the prescient 2012 TED talk "Connected, But Alone?" maintains that longform conversation both creates meaningful relationships with another while paving pathways for inner dialogue with ourselves: social media shortchanges both. She continues,

> How do you get from connection to isolation? You end up isolated if you don't cultivate the capacity for solitude, the ability to be separate, to gather yourself. Solitude is where you find yourself so that you can reach out to other people and form real attachments. When we don't have the capacity for solitude, we turn to other people in order to feel less anxious or in order to feel alive. . . . We slip into thinking that always being connected is going to make us feel less alone. But we're at risk, because actually it's the opposite that's true. If we're not able to be alone, we're going to be more lonely.[16]

In other words, sitting on a bus with others but connected to far away friends on a device robs us of both time to be close with ourselves and to be in contact with those around us.

Moreover, we could extend the Buddha's discernment of shallow and deep communities to our online experience: mostly we participate in shallow communities in which we are *restless* (clicking among twenty tabs and apps), *vain* (my vacay posts on Insta), *talkative* (hello personal blog, endless comments section), with *loose sense faculties* (binge-watch Netflix between an Amazon purchase). So, even though in a certain way we are in community online, most of the time it is not the variety that fosters spiritual depth.

Not only does excessive screen time disconnect us from people physically near us, but it could be that using devices is so absorbing that we lose

16. Turkle, "Connected, But Alone?"

touch with our very own body. I remember being in a state of oneness with my laptop in the dining hall at Duke University. After several hours, my bladder reminded me that all that coffee wished to "interbe" elsewhere. As my attention broke from the screen, I observed how each sense reconnected one by one in slow motion. First, the clanging of dishes and chatter of people—my hearing. How was I *not* hearing these things while tasking? It was a wonder to me. Then, my eyesight: I looked up and around to experience depth, color, and atmosphere. This was followed by discovering I had a body, and that my legs and shoulders were none too pleased to be cramped in one position for so long. Next, the aromas of lunch being prepared and whiffs of the nearby bathroom as the doors swished. Ah, then my lungs took a big inbreath: I had been computing with a high, shallow, barely discernible breath. Finally, oh, other human beings, moving in space, talking, and with whom I could converse!

The difference between the moment before and after was so distinct that I extrapolated: perhaps the awakening the Buddha taught is like waking up from the attenuated, two-dimensional device world to the expansive, three-dimensional human reality. Could enlightenment therefore be like going from this three-dimensional experience to a kind of "fourth-dimension" reality beyond what our limited minds can imagine? And if the aim of the Buddhist path is to awaken from this dream we take to be "reality," then isn't getting sucked into this online world, which is itself but a representation of reality, actually taking me one step *back* from spiritual waking up?

Of course, the internet has provided countless people—particularly in finding affinity groups beyond one's physical location—with new sources of meaningful friendships and vital support, unthinkable in past eras. And, it is becoming an important venue for spiritual caregivers to reach out to, help, and teach students, integral to our work. At another level, however, excessive internet and device use, particularly to the exclusion of in-person socializing and undistracted alone time, may be contributing to feelings of isolation, hyper-busyness, fragmentation, anxiety, longing, and disconnection from our bodies. In terms of spiritual fulfillment, heavy internet and device use may be usurping more intimate forms of community and authentic solitude because of the way these mimic—but do not entirely fulfill—both. As spiritual caregivers, we may need to guide people toward balancing their online friendships with face-to-face socializing and human touch. We may need to teach students how to be unafraid of sitting alone quietly, in an undistracted way, with their thoughts, feelings, and present moment. Internet and device use are no longer a minor part of our lives, impacting physical, mental, and spiritual health as much as diet, exercise, and sleep. As such, we spiritual caregivers must take this factor into consideration for both our students and ourselves.

Personal Agency within Systems

At the end of the two-day workshop on the roots of racism in the United States, we sat in a large circle. I felt deep grief and pain, both for those who have been and continue to be oppressed, as well as for myself and other white people who have been inculturated with racism and supremacy. Many of us in that circle felt raw, numb, stunned. I also felt curiously liberated, set free by seeing that my racism and supremacy was not personal to me but built from historical, ideological, and cultural structures. At the same time, I felt deep disgust that I had unwittingly been born into, participated in, and unconsciously perpetuated a racist system that harmed so many.

Since then, I have become increasingly aware of how most of the world around me, and indeed my own personhood, is a refraction of vast systems that have risen through the interactions of millions of people, nations, and institutions. For example, I see how climate change and environmental degradation are both due to large-scale consumer systems. This awakening puts me, as it does many others, into a crisis. Where is the efficacy of one person in systems of millions? How can I not participate in oppression, and more importantly, how can I change anything? While seeing the world as imbricated systems made things less personal, it also led to feelings of disempowerment and therefore despair. Resolving this dilemma is essential for any of us providing pastoral care, for both us personally and for those with whom we work.

On an individual level, undoing my racism has been entirely actionable, though requiring consistent effort to recode my thoughts. There's a wonderful teaching in the Buddhist world that says, "*You are not your anger, but you are responsible for it.*" Likewise, I can understand that I am not my racism, but I am responsible for it. But most of us are not satisfied with just changing ourselves: we want to dismantle these systems of harm.

Here again our understanding of interbeing addresses the challenge. This is beautifully imagined in a remarkable, slender Buddhist book titled *What in the World is Going On?* by Penny Gill. We are asked to picture an awakening person as a tiny stream running down a mountainside, believing that it is alone in its efforts. The trickle of water gradually meets up with other small streams, each discovering they're not alone and finding belonging in a small pool together. Now a larger stream of water, they continue together down the mountain, surprised to find other strong streams who again collect in a pond.

One can picture this journey and expansion over many iterations, "each race downward to a new plateau shifts the dominant self-understanding, eroding the sense of particularity and specialness, and making it increasingly clear it is participating in something large and powerful."[17]

In practical terms, an individual should act to transform the world knowing that one is not alone and will, in time, join other streams. Together, these efforts become a river that have the power to reshape the land. This came home to me several years ago when I needed to include notes about deforestation in an article. I had to do several google searches and go somewhat deep into the pile to find what I needed. What leapt out were countless grade school students, university students, activists, scientists, moms, businesses, and more all leading efforts to prevent deforestation—some locally, some nationally, some globally. While each may have felt isolated in their efforts, stepping back one could see little streams interbeing to form the river of change.

Conclusion: Contemplation

In keeping with a vision of learning through interconnected engagement with a subject, we will close with instructions for a practice in which you, the reader, can generate insights of your own. Head outdoors and find a flower or, if seasonally necessary, a tree. Read this teaching by Thích Nhất Hạnh out loud, practicing the notes in brackets.

> [Breathe deeply three times, with the inbreath starting deep in the belly. Observe how you are breathing in the air produced by plants around you.]
>
> *Looking into a flower, you can see that the flower is made of many elements that we can call non-flower elements.* [Look carefully at the flower and name some elements.]
>
> *When you touch the flower, you touch the cloud.* [Touch the flower gently.]
>
> *Cloud is a non-flower element. And the sunshine . . . you can touch the sunshine here. And sunshine is another non-flower element.* [Touch the flower again, sensing the sunshine in it.]
>
> *And earth, and gardener . . . if you continue, you will see a multitude of non-flower elements in the flower.* [As you touch the flower, contemplate all the non-flower elements of the flower before you.]

17. Gill, *What in the World Is Going On?*, 95.

In fact, a flower is made only with non-flower elements. It does not have a separate self. A flower has to "inter-be" with everything else that is called non-flower. That is what we call inter-being.[18]

[Breathe deeply three times. Notice how your outbreath provides air for the flower. Sit quietly with your eyes closed, holding space for any reflections to come to you.]

---

18. Nhất Hạnh, "Island of the Self."

4

From My Center to the Center of All Things

Hourglass Care (Take Two)

—— Gregory C. Ellison II ——

Introduction

"Everything this week is a circle with a triangle in it." These were Dr. Walter Earl Fluker's introductory words to nearly one-hundred African American male students gathered on the first night of the 2009 Coca-Cola Pre-College Leadership Program at Morehouse College. "A circle with a triangle in it?" I wondered. I was not alone in my wonderment. On the confused brows of these pre-college students, I recounted my bewildering days of high school geometry. I had no clue how much Fluker's theorem would shape my perspective and pedagogy of pastoral care and counseling.

Moments following, I zeroed in on the master teacher as he invited all in attendance to envision the dynamism of these two interacting shapes.[1] Fluker exclaimed, "This is a liberated circle. It spirals outward for infinity and inward simultaneously. This is a liberated circle and together we are a part of this cosmic dance. Spiraling in. Spiraling out." Then referencing two of the program's central themes—the need to form beloved community and live with integrity—he concluded by stating, "We can't create a beloved community outside, unless we do so inside." Many remained clueless to these geometric philosophical abstractions, but clarity was closer than imagined.

---

1. In the summer of 2009, I led a team of two doctoral students, Marc Cordon and Jermaine McDonald, to conduct a mixed-method study and internal review of the Coca-Cola Pre-College Leadership Program at Morehouse College.

With pedagogical swiftness, Fluker moved from abstract theory to embodied practice. He invited all in attendance to join in a ritual that symbolized
the interrelatedness of our centers with the center of all things. He instructed
the dozens of students and staff to form a large circle that stretched to the
edges of the meeting room. In baritone pitch, Fluker taught us a song meant
to channel energy between self and community. Minutes later a meditative
chant filled the room as we sang in unison: "Spiraling into the center, the center of the wheel. Spiraling into the center, the center of the wheel. I am the
weaver. I am the woven one. I am the dreamer. I am the dream."

Led by Fluker, who held a hand-carved ("talking") stick in the air, all
except two hands were joined, and we created a circle with one opening.
Together we began spiraling into the center of the room, singing the song
we just learned. While coiling to the center, Fluker instructed us to "look
in the face of your brother." Once in a tight coil in the room's center, we
spiraled outward and unraveled into a larger circle. Following this experiential exercise, students were individually invited to the center of the
circle. Surrounded by the larger community of their peers and staff, these
fearless young leaders were given space to reverently hold the "talking
stick" and speak their truth "from their center to the center all of things."
The center of the liberated circle provided these young men a space to
share their innermost truths, to empathically see and hear each other, and
to occasionally glimpse the divine.

Weeks later, in preparation for my first year of teaching Introduction
to Pastoral Care and Counseling at Candler School of Theology, I imagi-
natively revisited the image of the liberated circle and the corresponding
"spiraling" ritual. I put more thought into the themes of wholeness and the
dynamic interplay between self and community. In the midst of this contemplation, I heard three words from my *own* center: "Self. Care, Hope."
Shortly thereafter, I envisioned these words moving fluidly like grains of
sand through an hourglass.

An hourglass is an invertible device with two connected glass bulbs
containing sand. It takes one hour for the sand to stream from the top bulb
through a narrow center to the bottom bulb. After further reflection on the
shape of an hourglass, I realized that when viewed two-dimensionally from
a top-down perspective an hourglass is, in fact, a "circle with a triangle in it."
Upon this realization, the hourglass model of care began to take shape. The
circular top and bottom bulbs of the hourglass would represent what Philip
Culbertson calls the "wholeness wheel," with one bulb representing self and
the other representing community. The three sides of the hourglass' funnel-
like triangles would represent the themes of self, care, and hope. Lastly, a narrow pass holds the two bulbs of an hourglass together. This center is the point

of convergence between self and community, and it is said to be the site of divine wisdom. The hourglass, complete with two circles and two triangles spiraling into an identifiable center, would emerge as a practical metaphor for pastoral caregiving, underscored by themes of wholeness, self-awareness, context-sensitive care, and the generation and sustenance of hope.

For ten years I have utilized the spiraling ritual, the wholeness wheel, and the image of the hourglass, to introduce hundreds of first-year Master of Divinity students to the theory and practice of pastoral care and counseling. On day one of these classes, I clarify that for decades scholars in Pastoral Theology have employed metaphorical images as guiding frameworks for theoretical analysis and therapeutic practice. In *Images of Pastoral Care: Classic Readings*, Robert Dykstra highlights nineteen different images that have shaped pastoral theological theory and practice (e.g., Seward Hiltner's solicitous shepherd, Bonnie Miller-McLemore's living human web, Henri Nouwen's wounded healer).[2] These image-focused frameworks are provocative tools to articulate how pastoral theologians conceptualize their work. For one, they offer caregivers memorable metaphors that often translate into ministerial action. They also provide a myriad of options to assist practitioners in choosing a framework that best suits a specific context (i.e., the wounded healer image may be more beneficial with a grieving parent than the metaphorical image of the wise fool). In this long history of crafting images of care, my hope is that the metaphor of the hourglass, which was borne out of personal reflections on my center in relation to the center of all things, will enliven possibilities of self-discovery and creative approaches to care in community.

In 2010, "From My Center to the Center of All Things: Hourglass Care (Take 1), was published in *Pastoral Psychology*.[3] One decade after first introducing the hourglass image of care in my classes, I now revisit the image and refine my thoughts. In "Take 2," I deconstruct and analyze the component parts of the hourglass: the circle as a creative revision of Philip Culbertson's "wholeness wheel"; the three sides of the triangle (S.E.L.F., C.A.R.E., and H.O.P.E.); and the center as the site of divine wisdom. Finally, this article closes with reflections on the dynamism of the hourglass model.

2. Dykstra, *Images of Pastoral Care.*

3. Ellison, "From My Center."

Component Parts of the Hourglass:
Circles, Triangles, and the Center

After presenting the metaphor of the hourglass as a "circle with a triangle in it" to my class, a student drew my attention to a marble sculpture displayed in Candler School of Theology's building that I had never noticed. Interestingly, it was a circle with a triangle in it. Research discovered that this sculpture was of historic significance. Since the Middle Ages the triangle has occupied great significance in Christian iconography. According to art historians Didron and Millington, "An unbroken area, terminated by three angles, expressed, with wonderful exactitude, the unity of one God in three persons."[4] Furthermore, a circle around the triangle represented the Trinity's eternal nature. Additional research also uncovered that a circle with a triangle in it has contemporary relevance, as this symbol was officially and unofficially employed as the logo for Alcoholic Anonymous. The organization's website explained that, though still employed unofficially by members today, the logo was used officially from 1955 to 1994: "The three legs of the triangle represented the three legacies of recovery, unity, and service, and the circle symbolized the world of AA."[5] Recognizing the historic and contemporary significance of a triangle embedded in a circle, it is necessary to clarify the meanings of these two shapes and the identifiable center, as component parts of the hourglass model of care.

A Liberated Circle: Creative Revisions
of Circles and Wheels

The circle has significance in pastoral care. In *Here and Now: Living in the Spirit*, Henri Nouwen referenced the importance of the circle in pastoral care by metaphorically speaking of the circle as wagon wheel. In a reflection entitled "The Hub of Life," Nouwen explains, "Wheels help me to understand the importance of a life lived from the center. When I move along the rim, I can reach one spoke after the other, but when I stay at the hub, I am in touch with all the spokes at once."[6] Though Nouwen's reflections speak explicitly of the hub as the center of the circular wheel, connoted are the many facets of one's identity represented by the individual wheel spokes. For the hourglass model, the liberated circle is a composite of seven unique, yet

---

4. Didron, *Christian Iconography*, 58.

5. Alcoholics Anonymous, "Frequently Asked Questions."

6. Nouwen, *Here and Now*, 23.

complementary, identity traits. When considered collectively these seven traits represent wholeness.

Philip Culbertson furthered Nouwen's notion of the spoked circle by presenting what he calls the "Wholeness Wheel" in the opening pages of *Caring for God's People: Counseling and Christian Wholeness*. In this text, he differentiates wholeness from oneness, sameness, and even perfection, because few individuals or communities can ever attest to being fully healthy or completely whole. For Culbertson, wholeness refers to interconnectedness, as "no single element of the whole is thought of as functioning independently of the other components."[7]

Similar to Fluker's declaration when introducing the liberated circle that "we can't create a beloved community outside, unless we do so inside," Culbertson stresses the importance of self-awareness as a prerequisite step for caregivers to connect meaningfully with others. Culbertson uses the visual image of a "Wholeness Wheel" to stress that all parts of one's identity "are related to each other and that health [and wholeness] must be understood as inclusive and comprehensive."[8] Recognizing the limits of a two-dimensional drawing to show the dynamic interplay between the parts of one's identity, Culbertson uses the diagram to contradict the tendency of "[splitting] off parts of our self and [treating] them as though they are not . . . integrated."[9] In this regard, instead of viewing the diagram as compartmentalized portions of identity, asserts the wheel's pieces are interactive. Therefore, one could intuit that it is difficult to be socially unhealthy, but spiritually healthy because any unhealthy aspects of the self affects all the healthy aspects and vice-versa.

Culbertson's wholeness wheel identifies six segments or component parts of identity. They are the following: mental, emotional, social, physical, spiritual, and volitional. For the purposes of the hourglass model, I added a seventh part, the cultural/historical. Each segment, according to Culbertson, is shaped by issues such as gender, culture, and life experience. Thus, physical health may be defined differently for those who are physically disabled, social health may be interpreted differently for heterosexual persons and LGBTQII persons, and volitional health may have a different meaning for a teenager, adult, or senior citizen. The seven segments are considered briefly below.

7. Culbertson, *Caring for God's People*, 5.

8. Culbertson, *Caring for God's People*, 5.

9. Culbertson, *Caring for God's People*, 5.

1. *Mental health*: As the source of creativity, active memory, and vision, the healthy mind, for Culbertson, is typified by malleability and openness to change.[10]

2. *Spiritual health*: Spirituality extends beyond the ritualized, systematic faith of institutionalized religion, and "requires repeated awakening and deliberate nurturing of the spirit."[11]

3. *Social health*: While this element of wholeness may vary between cultures, social health is the creative balance between self and community and is demonstrated in respecting and empathizing with others.

4. *Physical health*: Physical health recognizes the body as sacred and worthy of care. To this end, physical wholeness involves a healthy and appropriate equilibrium of activity, intimacy, and rest.

5. *Emotional health*: Emotionally healthy caregivers have the ability to find, name, and address emotions appropriately. The emotionally mature seek assistance from others (i.e., counselors, support networks, clergy groups) and are sensitive to the cultural norms and practices of others.

6. *Volitional health*: Volitional health requires caregivers to balance their own freedom with that of others, therefore, "our choices are not imposed upon us by the group, nor do we impose our choices on others."[12]

7. *Cultural/historical health*: Though humans may share common physiological and psychological capabilities, all persons emerge from unique cultural and historical backgrounds that shape their worldviews. Cultural and historical wholeness attends to these matters of origin with care.

Culbertson finalizes his treatment of the wholeness wheel by exclaiming that "no part is beyond the reach of healing . . . [or] the love of God."[13] Though Culbertson explains that one can never be perfectly whole, he does imply that through intentional nurture and the love of God, the healing of broken segments of one's wheel is attainable. This bespeaks of the theological concept of sanctification, and the state of becoming more holy—or even more whole—through God's grace.

Sanctification, as a gift from God and goal for human striving, also has communal implications when reflecting on Culbertson's wholeness wheel.

10. Culbertson, *Caring for God's People*, 6.
11. Culbertson, *Caring for God's People*, 6.
12. Culbertson, *Caring for God's People*, 7.
13. Culbertson, *Caring for God's People*, 7.

In this regard communities, like individual caregivers, are challenged to ac-knowledge and attend to the seven segments of the wholeness wheel. Like in-dividual persons, communities have interconnected parts that are susceptible to atrophy. Communities, too, through intentional nurture and the grace of God can be sanctified and move ever closer to wholeness.

Sanctification is a significant point for the hourglass model of care. The hourglass has two bulbs and, in turn, two liberated circles—one representing the self and the other community. These circles are liberated (and liberating) because they are comprised of seven interconnected parts that have the po-tential for wholeness. In this model the caregiver who is critical of *self*, has the power through *caring* to model awareness of and attention to the seven component parts of the wholeness wheel. This caregiver, who is formed by community while simultaneously informing the community, serves as an agent of *hope* and catalyst for communal introspection. Such introspection is a precursor of wholeness and sanctification. The following section explores the three sides of the funnel-like triangle: self, care, and hope.

Siding with Self and Other:
S.E.L.F., C.A.R.E., and H.O.P.E. as Tools for Caregiving

S.E.L.F.

Wholeness begins with the desire to know and care for one's self. Within the hourglass model, S.E.L.F. is an acronym that highlights "seeing, encounter-ing, listening, and feeling" as sensory foci necessary to attend care+fully to the dynamism within one's essential being. Self-awareness as a starting point for caregiving is not foreign to pastoral care. In *The Wounded Healer*, Henri Nouwen speaks of the caregiver's necessity to bind her own wounds one at a time in order to be able to respond quickly to the needs of others. Nouwen's accentuation of binding one's own wounds before tending the needs of others is instructive. As previously stated, lack of attention to parts of one's wholeness wheel contributes to an overall state of imbalance and ill health. Additionally, as noted by Pamela Cooper White in *Shared Wisdom*, the caregiver's unprocessed countertransference phenomena serve as po-tential threats to boundary violations and the livelihood of those receiving care. Outside of precautionary measures to be aware of one's personal and professional boundaries, awareness of self concretizes purpose.

In the twenty years that I have been associated with theological educa-tion—as a student and now a professor—it is becoming increasingly clear, that scores of students, both young and old, flock to theology schools in search of purpose. Through attentiveness to self in the hourglass model, one is conditioned to contend with issues of vocation. "Vocation," is derived from the Latin word *vocare* meaning "to call." However, the minds of countless seminarians are filled with competing voices that impair the ability to hear God's instruction for their lives. In a reflection titled "How Good to Center Down" mystical theologian Howard Thurman likens these competing voices to "endless traffic" whose clashings and noisy silences distract us from purpose.[14] I have learned that both students and seasoned caregivers alike must consciously attend to the endless traffic that impairs them from hearing the divine voice of God calling and instructing them from their center. An inability or unwillingness to hear this "strong pure purpose" positions caregivers to exceed the boundaries of their gifts and become reckless caregivers. In addition, established boundaries and vocational discernment, sensory awareness is vital to the self-aware caregiver.

In my first book, *Cut Dead But Still Alive: Caring for African American Men,* I question, "In the hurried traffic of our daily routine, how many people do we snub completely and deliberately ignore?" To this query I respond, "The primary role of the caregiver is to see that which is overlooked and to hear that which is not spoken."[15] Over the past decade, I have accentuated that attentive seeing and listening requires not being consumed by the endless traffic occupying our daily calendars and becoming hyper-attentive to persons and communities hidden in plain view.

Caregivers must have "ears that hear and eyes that see—the Lord has made them both" (Prov 20:12 NIV). But, do we see the people who maintain the grounds of our campus, empty the trash at our office building, and operate the cash register at the local fast food chain? Do we hear the concerns of abused children, battered wives, youth in the church balcony, or the gifted international student reluctant to speak in class? Even more hidden are the concerns of the seemingly powerful. Do we see the wealthy businesswoman who commands respect in the office, but is little more than a pinion in the eyes of her family? Do we hear the silent tears of the ever smiling, positive-minded mega-church pastor, surrounded by beloved parishioners, none of whom he can trust? We need not only look to jails, senior citizen centers, or inner city park benches to find the muted and invisible, for the unacknowledged are all around us, but we must sharpen our vision and attune our hearing to care.

---

14. Thurman, *Center Down,* 29.

15. Ellison II, *Cut Dead But Still Alive,* xiii–xiv. I am grateful to Abingdon Press for granting me permission to use the following three paragraphs, which are copied directly from *Cut Dead But Still Alive.*

In all of my teaching, I offer strategies to help leaders and caregivers more clearly see and hear those who are muted and invisible. How we choose to see or not see and hear or not hear those around us speaks to our ability to identify the presence of God in others. Biblical wisdom tells us that the Good Samaritan has been labeled "good" throughout the annals of time because he suspended judgment and left the traffic of his daily routine to see and hear. Such a self-aware caregiver, who is willing to alter vision and shift pace, becomes uniquely equipped to care with others, particularly those who are unacknowledged and marginalized.

C.A.R.E.

As the wholeness wheel connotes, connection with others is contingent upon self-awareness of one's physical home, spiritual home, volitional home. However, Brita L. Gill-Austern wisely explains, "We never fully know home until we have left it, until we have made a pilgrimage to somewhere else. . . . [Pilgrimage] dislodges us from the known and familiar and . . . becomes transformative when it displaces the self from the center of reality."[16] On pilgrimage, caregivers move from the familiarity of home. Further, they encounter difference, feel discomfort, experience epiphany, and face the challenge of integrating theory and practice. In order to dislodge students from the familiar, I customarily frame one-third of every course I teach off campus. This way, through pilgrimage, students experience context-sensitive learning alongside community leaders. During the introductory course, these pilgrimages have included class sessions to learning sites such as: orphanages, domestic violence shelters, senior citizens residencies, funeral homes, and non-profit organizations that support immigrants.

Pilgrimage pedagogy frames the second third of the course around C.A.R.E., also an acronym in the hourglass model, that asserts "*contexts and relationships* [are] *essential.*" Contextualized care is grounded in the understanding that people do not come seeking care as "blank slates." Instead, every moment of care is specific and unique, and emerges from a particular space, time, and person. Attentive caregivers, who have invested time scrutinizing their own wholeness wheel, are better equipped to embrace the uniqueness and commonalities of others and use these similarities and differences to offer situation-specific, context-sensitive care.

In Emmanuel Lartey's *In Living Color: An Intercultural Approach to Pastoral Care and Counseling,* he asserts that context-sensitive caregiving should be guided by the maxim that "Every human person is in some

16. Gill-Austern, "Engaging Diversity," 40.

respects (a) like all others, (b) like some others, and (c) like no others."[17] According to Lartey, these three spheres, like the component parts of the wholeness wheel, are in constant and continual interaction as humans learn, grow, and change.

On pilgrimage, context-sensitive caregivers are challenged to see how every individual is "like all others," to affirm the humanity of others who are different and uplift the theological premise that all human beings are created in the image of God. Such reflection proves difficult for many students who are confronted with seeing their likeness in the eyes of a murder, rapist, or even someone on the other end of the political spectrum. Beyond the campus walls, sojourning students are encouraged to own their inherent power and social location, while also discerning how they are "like some others." From a vantage of open exploration, students must consider how factors like social class, cultural influences, gender dynamics, and faith perspectives, differentiate individuals.[18] Failure to do so places the caregiver at risk of paternalistic universalizing care. Finally, on pilgrimage, students come realize that individuals seeking care are "like no other." Every individual they encounter holds a unique life story and care must be specifically tailored. I recount the story of two African American mothers from the same neighborhood who have lost sons to gun violence at the same time and same place. Surely, these mothers are *like all* human beings who experience loss. They are *like some* African American parents who have buried their children much too early. Yet, these two mothers are completely *like no other* as they each shared unique relationships with their offspring. They grieve in disparate ways and lean on faith in ways no other could emulate. Context and relationships are essential for hourglass care, but so, too, must the attentive caregiver find hope where others only see despair.

H.O.P.E.

For years I defined hope as a "disrupting desire for existential change that is generated and sustained in a community of reliable others that names difficulties, envisions new possibilities, and inspires work toward transformation of self and other."[19] This definition underscores that hope is a communal act generated and sustained through the presence of reliable others. This community may be a multitude of well-intentioned, hopeful caregivers. However, it is not necessary for this community to be large or even

17. Lartey, *In Living Color,* 171.

18. Lartey, *In Living Color,* 172–73.

19. Ellison, *Cut Dead But Still Alive,* 82–83.

present in the earliest stages of development.[20] "Instead, this community may consist of just one well-intentioned, hopeful caregiver accompanied by the Reliable Other. In these cases, this singular reliable other at some point must entrust the well-being of the person in need to the care of others."[21] While a community of reliable others is central bolstering hope and assisting caregivers to stave off despair, apathy, and, shame, four years into my teaching career my understanding of hope expanded.

In addition to catalyzing existential change by serving as reliable others, caregivers also inspire hope by helping others practice excellence. In her timeless poem, "Celebration," my beloved teacher Mari Evans stresses, "I will bring you a whole person and you will bring me a whole person . . . and we will have us twice as much of love and everything."[22] Likewise, in *Out of Solitude*, Henri Nouwen asserts, "The friend who can be silent with us in a moment of despair and confusion . . . who can tolerate not-knowing, not curing, not healing and face with us the reality of powerlessness, this is the friend who cares." Evans and Nouwen both suggest that caregivers exudes hope when they show up as their most authentic self and model excellence. For Evans a whole self is not a perfect one, and for Nouwen excellence does not requires having all the answers. In fact, these sages have taught me that creating spaces for unlikely partners to engage in hard heartfelt conversation about taboo subjects is a form of care that invites authenticity and bolsters hope.

In 2013, days after the George Zimmerman verdict was announced, I put out a call on a local radio network for concerned citizens to gather at Emory for a hard conversation about protecting the lives of African American youth. Over three-hundred unlikely partners—from students, single mothers, and judges; to factory workers, faculty, and drug dealers—arrived for the dialogue. After that initial community conversation in July 2013, I founded "Fearless Dialogues." The movement has grown into an organization that has now worked with nearly 60,000 leaders worldwide. In addition to partnering with companies like Sun Trust Bank, the Atlanta Hawks, and Delta Airlines; "Fearless Dialogues" has worked with dozens of colleges and universities, and it has hosted leadership trainings for the United Methodist Council of Bishops and the Archbishop of Canterbury's staff at Lambeth Palace. I mention "Fearless Dialogues" in the context of hope, because I have found that the freedom and vulnerability I model in conversational

---

20. For more on the development of hope, see Ellison, *Cut Dead But Still Alive*, 83–90.

21. Ellison, "Late Stylin' in an Ill-Fitting Suit," 486.

22. Evans, *Dark and Splendid Mass*, 20–21.

spaces emboldens persons who have long felt invisible and muted to share their most authentic truth and showcase their most excellent self.[23]

The Center as Divine Wisdom

The center, also known as the core, nucleus, or nerve center, is defined by the *Oxford English Reference Dictionary* as "a point from which things, influences, etc. emanate, proceed, or originate."[24] This definition suggests that the center is much more than the middle point of a circle. Instead, the center is a site of both energy and origins. The hourglass model is centrifugal, meaning all its component parts, from the seven spokes of the wholeness wheel to the three parts of the triangle, are drawn to the center. This center is the seat of vocation, the source of creative genius, and the site of divine wisdom.

The Hourglass as a Dynamic Model of Care

As I move to place the component parts of the hourglass together, it is necessary to underscore that though the hourglass model is center-focused, it is most concerned with acknowledging and empowering the marginal. Along these lines, Connie Monson, a college English professor and a former student in my "Introduction to Pastoral Care class," stated in a correspondence that the sand in the hourglass model is analogous to the caregivers' intentions to see that from the margins which is characteristically overlooked. In her words:

> I think it's a perfectly apt model toward caring for "disappeared" populations. First, an hourglass has no corners. It does not admit of someone being swept off to the side and never seen or heard of again. Second, it seems doubly important to return through [the center] or I/eye that can see with perspective. The way I think this applies to marginalized populations is precisely in the circulating movement that you described. Yes, your model is center-focused. But it's impossible to stay in the middle of an hourglass, even if you knock it on its side![25]

23. For more information on the evolution, pedagogy, and theoretical influences of "Fearless Dialogues," see Ellison, *Fearless Dialogues*.

24. Pearsall and Trumble, *Oxford English Reference Dictionary*, s.v. "center."

25. The student-now-professor granted me permission to publish the above insights from her assignment for this paper.

To further Monson's profound insights, the hourglass' sand, like a sanctifying wholeness wheel consists of seven component parts that are inseparable in their swirl. In this circular spin, the attentive caregiver is drawn to see, experience, listen, and feel, to the self's callings toward vocation, warnings about appropriate boundaries, and yearning to stand alongside persons who feel invisible. The sand's journey toward center is a pilgrimage that alerts the caregiver to attend with C.A.R.E. to the commonality and diversity of individuals entrenched in unique communities. Finally, the path from one's *center to the center of all things* requires a hope that practices excellence, seeks the support of a community of reliable others, and draws upon the wisdom of the Reliable Other.

5

The Healing Welcomer

A Postcolonial Image of Spiritual Care Response

Amani D. Legagneur

"Everyone that Jesus healed died."

Time and time again, I am met with expressions of shock and dismay when I utter these words to groups of spiritual leaders. I am bemused by their surprise. Everyone that Jesus healed did die. Otherwise, I am pretty sure that they would be called "The Immortals," everyone would know precisely who they are, and believing in healing that proceeds from faith would be a whole lot easier.

If everyone that Jesus healed ultimately died anyway, what was the point of renewing their health or resurrecting their bodies in the first place? Was physical healing the full sum of his purpose in helping the blind to see, the deaf to hear, and the dead to rise again? Did Jesus weep when he reached the bedside of his deceased friend Lazarus because he was grieved by his demise or, perhaps, because he knew that even after the miracle he would perform to bring Lazarus back to embodied life, death would visit him again?[1] Questions pour forth to assuage the cognitive dissonance often experienced when people confront the idea that preserving physical life—life as we know it—may not have been Jesus' only or even primary aim in his healing ministry. A potential clue to his motivation may reside in a question that he often explicitly or implicitly asked in biblical encounters: "Is your healing welcome to you?" Jesus did not intrude, forcing people to answer according to his wishes. Instead, he invited them

---

1. See John 11:1–44.

to engage in a transformative process according to their own will, conscience, and faith. He was present to them—offering hospitality, grace, empowerment, and love. Jesus was a *healing welcomer.*

Defining the "Healing Welcomer"

This chapter offers the *healing welcomer* as a new image of postcolonial spiritual care predicated on the notion that healing is often relational and can be welcomed—invited, encouraged, and supported—through spiritual care relationships. A *healing welcomer* is a spiritual care responder (SCR) who intends to offer respectful, hospitable presence and accompaniment to those served while endeavoring to facilitate alleviation of their pain and suffering. "Healing" is variously and personally defined; and welcoming it often involves respectfully helping people to find their own path towards it. Healing refers to the process of recognizing, addressing, and seeking to resolve existential pain in any form that impedes holistic wellbeing. Implying more than the cessation of physical disease, healing in this paradigm includes the following: amelioration of spiritual distress through tending and relieving emotional, communal, or relational pain; connecting with the "ultimate" or "transcendent"; participating in meaningful rituals or customs; maintaining integrity in correlating behavior or decisions with religious, moral, ethical, spiritual, or other core identity-based beliefs; fulfillment of basic needs; and a plethora of other factors. As I discuss later, healing can also include relief of suffering through physical death.

Welcoming healing is a holistic enterprise. It includes all aspects of being—physical, mental, spiritual, communal, ecological, systemic, cosmic, and more. It does not simply operate in linear time through relationships of direct cause and effect dictated by planetary physics. Rather, for the *healing welcomer*, healing is deeply and fundamentally personal and relational, time-inclusive and timeless, and body-inclusive while ultimately soul-centered. It cannot be limited to the physical domain because of its spiritually relational source and nature.

Healing welcomers attempt to compassionately behold and be with those served through dignifying accompaniment and collaboration. If care seekers so desire, some *healing welcomers* encourage restoration, positive reconciliation, comfort, forbearance, hope, mercy, peace, empowerment, liberation, and grace. They also recognize the important role that acknowledging difficult emotions like anger, fear, doubt, impatience, sadness, and hopelessness can play in addressing existential pain. As appropriate, *healing welcomers* enable access to spiritual resources relevant to the belief systems of those served.

The*logical[2] and Vocational Positionality

The *healing welcomer* image is inspired by my work as a healthcare chaplain, leader of a multi-campus hospital system's spiritual health and education department, ACPE Certified Educator (aka CPE Supervisor), and ordained United Church of Christ minister. I work with patients, clinical pastoral education (CPE) students, and faith community members whose beliefs and commitments span a vast spectrum of religious and ide*logical[3] meaning-making frameworks. Some identify with faith-based language while others do not ascribe to any professed faith identity or affiliation. As Lartey observes, "Chaplaincies—for instance hospital chaplaincies, which have by law had to be multi-faith—have developed much expertise in recognizing, respecting and affirming the faiths of care-recipients, and collaborative work with caregivers from different faith perspectives."[4] Postcolonial spiritual care paradigms that recognize the tremendous variety of ways that people make meaning of their experiences have proven helpful in my multifaith, interfaith, and intercultural spiritual care and education contexts. The *healing welcomer* is intended to be such a paradigm.

Though I highlight Jesus as an exemplar of a *healing welcomer* from my own faith tradition, any SCR can display the orientation to care and traits of practice described in this paradigm. I am sensitive to the ways in which Christianity has been co-opted as a tool to overpower, oppress, and enslave people like my African ancestors who were abducted and brought to America. Therefore, I draw inspiration for the *healing welcomer* image from Christian the*logies of resistance like liberation, womanist, feminist, *mujerista*, LGBTIQ+, and others that lift up Jesus as a counter-cultural champion of equality and social justice—one who acknowledged the ubiquitous suffering of humankind and welcomed healing for people from diverse belief perspectives, cultures, and socioeconomic classes. This feature of Jesus' care posture is crucial in postcolonial spiritual care that celebrates diversity

---

2. Since theology means "speaking about God," I spell "the*logical" as an extension of spelling "G*d" with an "o" replaced by an asterisk. This challenges the use of androcentric language to describe divinity. The asterisk in "G*d" is analogous to the dash in orthodox Jewish spelling of "G-d," also referencing human limitations in fully expressing the unutterable name of the divine.

3. The asterisk in "ide*logical" replaces the masculine "o" for gender inclusivity.

4. Lartey, *Postcolonizing G*d*, 11.

and rejects oppression based on the supremacy of one's ide*logy over and against that of another. I am also inspired by other spiritual traditions that emphasize respect for humanity and the natural world and prioritize compassion as an elixir to suffering.

Is Your Healing Welcome to You?
Is My Healing Welcome to Me?

Becoming a *healing welcomer* hinges on keeping two questions at the forefront of one's spiritual care approach: (1) Is your healing welcome to you? and (2) Is my healing welcome to me? According to the gospel account, when Jesus invites a crippled man to pick up his mat and go home, he activates the man's agency to believe that he can be healed—to welcome his healing—even as his ambulatory ability is miraculously restored.[5] Jesus rubs a poultice on the eyes of a blind man seeking healing, and then activates his agency by inviting him to wash off the mud in the Siloam pool. The man welcomes his healing by accepting this invitation and regains his sight.[6] A woman with a hemorrhagic condition welcomes her healing as she pushes through a throng of people, believing that if she simply touches the hem of Jesus' garment she will be healed. Though her religion is unknown, Jesus tells the woman she has healed because of her faith. Through her own agency, she welcomes healing. The stories are plentiful, the message is the same: Jesus did not forcefully impose healing on these people, but instead welcomed them into collaborative relationship where they chose to employ their own resources of faith and action to achieve it.

Upon entering a patient's room, a healthcare chaplain may begin spiritual assessment by taking cues about whether or not the visit is desired. The patient may express hope to heal from a physical malady or to be relieved of related spiritual distress. Although chaplains are not tasked with providing medical care, they understand that relief of spiritual symptoms often correlates with a greater sense of wellbeing overall. Therefore, as a *healing welcomer*, a chaplain may form a companioning relationship with a patient to tend to spiritual distress by offering guiding, sustaining, reconciling, nurturing, liberating, empowering, comforting, inspiring, loving, helping presence and spiritual care interventions.[7] In order to accomplish this ethically, the

5. Mark 2:9–12.

6. John 9:6–7.

7. Pastoral the*logians are credited for these terms as follows: "healing, guiding, sustaining" (Hiltner, *Preface to Pastoral Theology*); "reconciling" (Clebsh and Jaekle, *Pastoral Care in Historical Perspective*); "nurturing" (Clinebell, *Basic Types of Pastoral*

chaplain must be attentive to how power is operative in the care encounter. Self-awareness helps SCRs to use their influence with greater precision.

It can be challenging to welcome healing for another person when one is unwilling to welcome it for oneself. Healing existentially defies terminal bifurcation between the self and the other, acknowledging that people cannot survive without some form of interdependence. Humans thrive in communities that support health, lovingkindness, and respect for self, others, and nature. Longevity, decreased illness, higher happiness, and greater connection with the transcendent are traits of people who live in blue zones—communities where equanimity, family, social engagement, clean diets, exercise, collaboration, care of the environment, and spiritual life are prioritized. Though positive connections are encouraged, *healing welcomers* recognize that spiritual healing requires maintaining deep respect for boundaries that protect people from intrusion, transgression, violence, or any other abuses of power.

Responsible maintenance of their own holistic health is crucial for *healing welcomers*. It is helpful to regularly ask, "Am I open to healing from anything that may present a barrier to spiritual care?" If, for example, a chaplain is aware of either attraction to or repulsion from a patient, discovering the underlying reason for that response may contribute to personal healing. *Healing welcomers* endeavor to take responsibility for their own reactions to care seekers rather than operating from unconscious projections; they bracket their own agenda(s) to convey authentically nonjudgmental presence in spiritual care. They maintain personal and role integrity by checking in with their own bodies, minds, and souls to address areas in need of support and care.

Cultural Humility

Cultural humility is a hallmark of the *healing welcomer*.[8] Culture encompasses the basic substance of who we are and how we are connected to others, including everything from genotypic and phenotypic identities to place of origin and from passing interests to cherished ideals. Awareness of cultural ecology helps us to consider elemental questions of being like: "Who am I?" "Who are you?" and "How can we relate to one another?" *Healing welcomers* with cultural humility realize that their personal cultures are not normative for all others, and that most people are multicultural. They remain open to

Counseling); "liberating" (Lester, *Hope in Pastoral Care and Counseling*); "liberating and empowering" (Lartey, *In Living Color*). The remaining modifiers are mine.

8. Tervalon and Murray-Garcia, "Cultural Humility."

healing any symptoms of self-deceit that would lead them to believe that they are fundamentally superior to another person.

Cultural humility is an antidote for supremacy. When *healing welcomers* become curious about points of disagreement with or misunderstanding about those they hope to assist, they may improve interpersonal communication and foster greater mutual acceptance. They can heighten the potential for rooting out aspects of their beliefs and behaviors that work as enemies internally while amplifying the potential for achieving peace externally. Displaying willingness to resolve internal prejudices and preconceptions that may serve as barriers to care, they cultivate awareness of how systems and social frameworks influence illness and dysfunction in myriad forms. As reflective practitioners, they understand that a desire for healing is not the same as access to it; they are, therefore, mindful of how those served are empowered or disempowered with respect to both practical and transcendent avenues of support.

Operationalizing Love

Jesus' concept of the faith necessary to welcome healing seems to paradoxically undergird and transcend religious identification. He acknowledges physically and socially desired values and outcomes in healing even while problematizing the notion that these are inherently correct or should be universally normative. In biblical accounts, Jesus most keenly focuses on "faith" as a spiritual precursor that facilitates processes of healing. For Jesus, faith connects humanity to love of G*d,[9] and for him, G*d is Love. He repeatedly acknowledges faith in people who do not share his religious affiliation. Lartey highlights Jesus' socio-religiously subversive affirmation of the faith of a Roman centurion as an example of this. When the centurion asks Jesus to assist his paralyzed, suffering servant, Jesus responds, "Truly I tell you, I have not found anyone in Israel with such great faith" (Matt 8:10 NIV). He then intimates that many people who do share his Jewish religion will be in heaven.

The "faith" that patients express to their healthcare chaplains often does not include G*d-language. For many, especially those who have had negative experiences with religion (or with people who describe themselves as religious), terms like "G*d" and "faith" can distance them from welcoming care. Questions like, "What gets you through the night?" or "What

9. My use of the asterisk in the word "G*d" is analogous to orthodox Jewish spelling of "G-d," similarly pointing to human limitations in essentializing the ineffable or expressing the unutterable name of the divine.

would you like to see happen?" regularly lend me more insight about patients' spiritual concerns than explicitly religious queries. The*logian Paul Tillich's famed definition of "faith" as one's "ultimate concern" and "G*d" as "the ground of all being" helps me to meet patients and students where they are according to their own spirituality.[10] Approaching people relationally rather than doctrinally is a common practice among chaplains and follows Jesus' pattern of response. As Lartey observes:

> Many who have actively engaged in interreligious dialogue confirm that in actual fact discussion of doctrine is the least useful starting point when persons of diverse faith traditions encounter one another. The example of Jesus in this is clear and salutary. Theological (doctrinal) discussion only usefully follows interpersonal empathic interaction that leads to the building of rapport and feelings of common humanity.[11]

For the postcolonial SCR, welcoming the healing of diverse array of others, not simply those perceived to be most like oneself, is a redemptive act of resistance against colonial hegemony and other paradigms of divisive, derisive, and violent dehumanization and oppression. As a woman and descendant of enslaved African people in America who were treated as subhuman and whose religious practices were disparaged as illegitimate, "heathen," or worse; this resistance is particularly vital to my understanding of the role of *healing welcomer*.

When Healing Is Unwelcome, Love Is Welcome Still

I believe that one of the most painful things that G*d and human beings experience results from offering healing that is not accepted. Nonetheless, in biblical narratives, Jesus allows those he encounters to make a real choice to heal or not to heal. When a rich young ruler approaches Jesus to ask what works he might do to achieve eternal life, he is met with an invitation to do so by keeping the commandments. The young ruler is dissatisfied, claiming that he has done so all of his life, and presses Jesus to tell him what he lacks. Jesus responds, "If you wish to be perfect, go, sell your possessions, and give the money to the poor, and you will have treasure in heaven; then come, follow me." The dismayed young man immediately realizes that the cost for this "healing" is too high for him to welcome. The pericope ends, "When the young man heard this word, he went away grieving, for he had

---

10. Tillich, *Dynamics of Faith*.
11. Lartey, *Postcolonizing G*d*, 11.

many possessions" (Matt 19:21–22 NRSV). Jesus does not anxiously follow behind him begging his return, strongarm, or shame him. Instead, he allows the healing that the young man desires—following a revealed path to eternal life—to be unwelcome to him at that time. Considerate acknowledgment of an individual's right to choose whether or not and how to heal is characteristic of a *healing welcomer*.

Prior to Jesus' acceptance of the young ruler's choice, there is a pivotal moment where he pauses. In the Markan account, this occurs right after the man vulnerably asks, "What do I lack?" Jesus' first intention and empathic response is recorded as follows, "Then Jesus beholding him loved him" (Mark 10:17–22 NIV). *Healing welcomers* may follow in kind with those they serve: to behold another with love is a radical act of hospitality which can catalyze transformative care even if a desired outcome is not agreed upon.

Many theologians chalk up the young ruler's decision to greed, power-hunger, and immaturity. Though we cannot know the full scope of his reasoning, we do know his choice is not unique. From an intersubjective perspective, similar factors that motivate his decision-making may motivate our own. Not welcoming healing, something that could be deemed spiritually irrational, is common because it is utterly, heartrendingly human. The young ruler could have "possessions" beyond material wealth. For example, he could be possessed by the following: his responsibility to function as a provider of financial stability to his community; loyalty to his family; desire not to leave or fail anyone to whom he felt obligated; reticence to heal unless everyone he loves is healed; or resistance to feeling guilt or other uncomfortable emotions if he leaves all he knows behind. What if he makes the "wrong" choice for what appear to be "right" reasons? It is a natural human propensity to identify with the stories of those who successfully welcome their healing than those who seem to fail, but, like the rich young ruler, anyone may make conscious and unconscious decisions not to heal. *Healing welcomers* recognize that spiritual distress often arises from a complexity of factors and does not signal that someone experiencing this distress is good or bad, right or wrong, faithful or faithless. Polarizing categorizations like these can lead both the distressed person and the SCR down a path towards further fragmentation and suffering.

Preventing Moral Injury

As persons of deep conviction responding to others in pain or crisis, *healing welcomers* may find themselves in positions where they feel that it could be unethical, immoral, or even sacrilegious to welcome healing as a care seeker desires. Moral injury can result from providing care that violates the core values of the care responder. In the best-case scenarios, when *healing welcomers* discover that they cannot respond with authenticity and integrity to their care seekers' beliefs, it is desirable to acknowledge this while remaining compassionate enough to refer them to other avenues for spiritual support, e.g., other SCRs, their inner resources, or means of connection to a community more in sync with their beliefs.

The*dicy, Spiritual Struggle, and the Healing Welcomer

I have often heard patients and their loved ones repeat the confounding mantra, "You can't question G*d. You can't question G*d. You can't question G*d ... " I will never forget my mother's advice when I asked her how to reply to that mantra respectfully when I believe differently: "Why not remind them that asking G*d questions is not the same as questioning G*d's existence?" I was grateful for her wisdom the following evening as I cared for the aunt of a child who had just survived a car accident where his mother and sister were killed. Overwhelmed with grief, she followed each expression of suffering with, "but you can't question G*d." After establishing trust with her, I ventured, "What if you can ask G*d questions?" She looked at me incredulously. I continued, referencing her Christian faith tradition, "People have cried out to the heavens throughout human history. Asking G*d questions isn't the same as questioning whether or not G*d is real (although I think G*d can take that too). Even Jesus asked, 'My G*d, My G*d, why have you forsaken me?' [Matt 27:46 NIV]." She paused and began to sob, wondering why her family members died this way and how to muster enough strength to tell the little boy on her own. Breaking through her religiously socialized façade of certitude enabled her to grieve and accept support. She implored me to help her tell her nephew about their deaths. I did.

Welcoming healing often entails engaging difficult questions that defy facile categorization or dogmatic assurance. SCRs can be tempted to invite those served to shift too quickly from processing pain in order to alleviate their vicarious discomfort. *Healing welcomers* offer safe space for questioning, seeking to be humble and resilient in the face of the unknown. This often requires mindfully integrating their own woundedness, vulnerability, morbidity, and mortality into conscious awareness in order to facilitate empathic, realistic spiritual care.

Healing welcomers refrain from quick fixes, platitudes, bromides, false assurances, or hyper-religious band-aids. They do not bypass the*dicy or spiritual struggle, instead offering caring presence in the midst of it. They also intentionally attune to each new care scenario, recognizing that inspirational words for one care seeker could sound abusive to another. For example, I have heard well-meaning SCRs tell parents experiencing perinatal loss, "Now you have an angel in heaven." This is comforting for some who believe similarly; for others it is traumatizing. People perceive healing differently. *Healing welcomers* understand that the person suffering is the subject matter expert about their own pain.

When Healing Includes Dying

"I want to go home! I want to go home! This is just like killing a person! I WANT TO GO HOME!" The only patient I have ever seen fully alert, oriented, and angry after a code motioned me over to her. As a CPE Resident in a room full of clinicians who had revived her just moments before, I was bewildered but obedient. "Will you tell them I want to go home?" the patient asked me, grasping my hand and shooting a look of exasperation at her doctor who stood at the foot of her bed. Stalling awkwardly because I did not know how to respond to her wish to die, I inquired, "Which home?" Squaring her gaze at me she replied, "You of all people should know. I want to go to my heavenly home, and they won't let me go. They just keep bringing me back." I had not yet introduced myself, but I felt like she recognized my soul. The doctor interjected with a small smile, "Ms. Jones,[12] it's my job not to let you go." Ignoring him, Ms. Jones began giving me messages for her adult children.

Desiring to respect and affirm her desire to die while tending to the reality that she was still alive, I prayed silently for guidance. "Ms. Jones?" I ventured, "I would be honored to deliver these messages. I am sorry that you are going through this. I know you want to go home." She visibly relaxed. After a significant pause and more conversation, I felt led to wonder aloud, "What if you deliver these messages yourself?" She said, "What do you mean?" I replied, "Well, since you're still here, what if you allow enough time to talk with your children yourself?" She looked into my face, studying it and reconsidering her position. After more conversation, prayer, song, and time together, she said, "Okay, I'm not going to die tonight. You should go to sleep." Since it was four in the morning, I was feeling exhausted. Recognizing that she needed rest too, I excused myself. Ms. Jones died three days later, to her doctor's surprise. In the interim, she ate well for the first time in a long while and spent meaningful time with her children.

12. "Ms. Jones" is a pseudonym.

For patients like Ms. Jones, the process of healing from existential pain involves dying. Wasted from metastatic cancer, Ms. Jones wanted to allow natural death to occur. She was frustrated by medical interventions that saved her physical life but did not allow her to decide what was most beneficial for her holistic wellbeing. The question of when dying becomes part of healing can be complicated. As a *healing welcomer*, displaying the willingness and resilience to engage that question with the people that we serve is a form of hospitality to their ways of making meaning about what matters most to them.

Healing in the form that one desires is sometimes unattainable. Healing welcomers contend with the reality that people are prone to illness, weakness, vulnerability, strife, inequality, violence, and death. Welcoming healing can mean railing against systems that do not view people as originally, essentially, and equally deserving of human rights such as the right to life, liberty, equality, and dignity. Welcoming healing challenges governments, powers, and principalities mired in injustice. It includes employing righteous anger as a resource to fight disease. The paradoxes of life and death are many—a body can be in pain and a spirit at peace, spiritual strength sometimes improves during physical weakness, and terrible misfortunes strike all of us in myriad ways. Standing in what Palmer calls the "tragic gap" between "the way things are and the way we know they might be" is the domain of the *healing welcomer*.[13]

Conclusion: Everyone Who Jesus Healed Died, but First They Lived Transformed

In spiritual care, chaplains and other SCRs often find themselves at bedsides or in crisis scenarios with people in the throes of existential struggle. Studies show that most people facing the end of life are not as afraid of death as they are of pain and isolation. In light of this, *healing welcomers* may help by showing up, welcoming an end to that pain, listening, extending love and compassion, bearing witness, performing appropriate rituals, prayers, blessings, songs, or simply allowing people who suffer to be validated exactly as they are. We continue to "live the questions now," following Rilke's alternative to insatiably seeking answers to life's mysteries.[14]

Though some wisdom traditions envision a future where pain and suffering no longer exist, spiritual care of itself is not purposed to bring the ultimate cessation of life's suffering. Spiritual care is meant to lend itself

13. Stamwitz, "If Only We Would Listen," 27.

14. Rilke, *Letters to a Young Poet*, 39.

to helping people to actively cope with suffering aided by a trusted, compassionate person and a transcendent source or meaningful ide*logy. Like welcoming love in any other form, welcoming healing can be counterintuitively challenging. It requires exercising agency to loosen the binds of personal and corporate spiritual suffering with the aspiration that something better can manifest. It requires a transformation of systems of injustice and oppression, inequality and resource deprivation, and ecological destruction that rob people of health on every level. My hope in advancing the *healing welcomer* image is that healing be available, be welcome, and come to pass for all who desire it.

Welcome?

Have I fallen in love with my own broken heart?
So familiar, at best, and near—
the pulse of not expecting more
feels almost like buffeting fear.

Have I fallen in love with my broken body,
too much to tend, protect, or feed?
Not wanting more is almost like
pretending I don't have the need.

Have I fallen in love with despair,
made a friend of misery,
or been seduced by the notion that holding it close
is better than setting it free?

Have I fallen in love with an illusion,
claimed self-sufficiency,
or simply resigned that there's nothing beyond
what I can do for me?

Do I love this broken heart enough
to gift it with uneasy truth—
what could bring healing beyond my grasp
is that for which Earth has no proof.

The Word offers grace and compassion
but the Whirlwind, a thorn in my side.
What can prevent me from suffering more
if this broken heart remains my pride?

"Faith is the substance of things hoped for . . . "
he says, " . . . the evidence of things unseen."
I fear a paltry excuse for faith
that permits a pain so mean.

The dark glass has left its razor shards
right here in my chest.
Though uninvited, I've made them at home,
and still there they've come to rest.

Is my healing welcome to me?
I struggle now to know.
Can I remember how real love feels
and take the risk to let it flow?

How can I welcome healing
when I distrust the Source,
disbelieving a good God could allow
such a breach in this vital life force.

It seems that I love my own broken heart
in terror that no one else will;
I can't be vulnerable to the next blow
if there's nothing left to kill . . .

Except, I can't help but wish sometimes,
even when it means agony.
I can't help but long for something real
to release the best of me.

My brokenness I have, cherished, adored,
because it seemed to be a friend;
and yet, what if, Love itself
is truer in the end?

Amani Legagneur

——— Part Two ———

Spiritual Care of Society & Community

6

The Transgendered G*d as Diversity and Inclusion

—— Alexander Brown ——

THE CONCEPT OF LIBERATION in Christian theologies has become a seemingly endless task for many people, especially for those living in the United States. While the United States was founded on the concept of pluralism, the multicultural and religiously plural society which we have become has been challenged by white nationalist ideology. The United States has formed its legacy on the premise of the incorporation of all people. With that idea in mind, individuals from many cultural backgrounds have chosen the United Sates to become their home. From personal experience, I am a first-generation Persian-American, living in the United States, raised by immigrant parents who came here with the intention of starting a better life. Not only would I be considered a minority in the mainly white dominated country on the basis of social structure, religion, and class; but I am also a member of the LGBTIQ+ community, which creates an even more substantial complication in the merging of my beliefs with those that are seen as the dominant majority in the United States. Both immigrant individuals and members of the LGBTIQ+ community are frowned upon and often not accepted within dominant US religious communities. In recent years, however, the ongoing struggle for LGBTIQ+ members' involvement in the church has become more prominent in liberation the*logies. As a society, we need to take a closer look into the lives of minorities and LGBTIQ+ members and learn to understand them in order to rewire our beliefs for the inclusion for all types of people in G*d's world.

Feminist the*logian Elisabeth Schüssler Fiorenza states that the ideas of a global neoliberal system of kyriarchy

> is best theorized as intersecting multiplicative social, economic, and religious structures of superordination and subordination, domination and exploration, and ruling and oppression. Kyriarchal relations of domination are built on elite male property rights and privileges as well as on wo/men's exploitation, dependency, inferiority, and obedience.[1]

Our country was built on the foundation of democracy and rights for all people. Yet, neoliberal society in the control of white privileged males impacts all aspects of our lives, including places of worship. Schüssler Fiorenza tells us that gender, power, and religions are social and political constructs, not religious mandates. The marginalizing and dismissal of individuals of the LGBTIQ+ community is not G*d given, but socially constructed via power structures. Schüssler Fiorenza insists that "religious texts and traditions must be reinterpreted so that wo/men and other 'nonpersons' can achieve full citizenship in religion and society, gain full access to decision-making powers, and learn how to live out radical equality in religious communities," because at this point, the idea of equality of all persons is merely a statement, not a reality.[2]

I have chosen personally to live a stealth lifestyle, in which I do not ordinarily share my LGBT identity publicly for the very reason that queer liberation exists today. When someone is a member of this community and identifies with it as LGBT, they are immediately labeled as "sinful" or "unjust." In many people's eyes, people like myself are just considered lost or confused and often sent to get "help" from specialists and doctors. I am a transgender, female-to-male individual, living my life with a completely male status. I choose every single day to live with my true identity as a male and hide the fact that I was given the female sex at birth. Due to the unfortunate white male-dominated society in which we live; in most cases, if a cisgender or assigned-male-at-birth individual were to find out my trans identity, he would no longer see me as their equal, but as his inferior. If I were to live with an open status about my gender identity, I would not be able to practice my religious beliefs at ease in many Muslim or Christian communities. In the eyes of a conservative Christian or Muslim heteronormative individual, individuals like myself are completely unaccepted and misunderstood.

A personal experience of mine that follows the major issues discussed in the context of liberation the*logy regards the issue of procreation in the queer community. Same-sex marriage, although legalized in many states

---

1. Schüssler Fiorenza, *Congress of Wo/men*, 53.

2. Schüssler Fiorenza, *Congress of Wo/men*, 53.

now, is still frowned upon by the general public. Since I was born female, anyone knowing this information can use it against me to try and validate the idea that if I were to marry a woman, it would be considered a same sex marriage, and that I am not actually a "man." They would argue that I am a lesbian taking the role "a little too far." In many cases, transgender individuals like myself have had some sort of sexual reassignment surgery, which allows them to change their (birth) gender marker to their desired one on legal documents such as their identification cards and birth certificates. In most cases, this is a very costly route, and it can be incredibly time-consuming and tedious. However, the gender marker matching our true identity still does not solve the problem of the inability to procreate with our desired partners. Although many cis-gendered individuals face obstacles with pregnancy, and while it is common for many individuals to just unfortunately be unable to procreate; we transgendered persons are seen in a different light because in a "normal" person's eyes, we are choosing to live this life.

My current partner—girlfriend of almost two years—told her mother and sister about my transgender identity before our relationship had become serious. She did not tell them to put me down or to cause attention to our relationship. She informed them about our relationship because she had just found out and needed someone to talk about this. After first being informed of this news, both her sister and mother ridiculed her and tried to convince her that she was no longer "straight." If she were to date me, she would then be considered a gay woman, even though I am male-identifying and years into my physical transition. Most people do not completely understand queer people in any light. I do not blame them, because it is difficult to understand things that one has not experienced first-hand; however, this is something that occurs quite often in our world. If they do not understand the situation, they can educate themselves and at least respect the persons involved.

Several months after my girlfriend had told her family about us, they eventually "accepted" her choice to be in a relationship with me and have never outwardly shown me any of their concerns. They still question her, however, and her mother brings up our intimate life and our plans for having children almost every time we see her. No matter how many times we try to explain to her that we would take the course of any "normal" or heterosexual cis-gendered couple trying for a child, she does not let the topic go. Her mother is extremely conservative and close-minded, which makes it difficult to talk to her in about these topics. Robert E. Shore-Goss writes a section on procreation, explicating clearly how I feel about the topic. He argues that justification for heterosexual marriage and the denial of same-sex marriage can no longer be sustained by the idea of procreation.[3] With today's technology and sources for assistance, anyone can have a child. The only deciding factor is how they choose to do it. This questioning and constant observation of hetero-cis individuals is a major factor behind why many members of the queer community live in silence and choose not to share their stories.

In a chapter of *Sister Outsider,* "Transformation Of Silence," Lorde preaches to her readers on speaking out on behalf of their insecurities and pain. I found that although she is writing from the perspective of a Black lesbian, I can relate to her work in many ways. Just as she endured racism due to her ethnicity, as well as homophobia due to her sexuality; I, too, was othered in the dominant community because of my race and religion, but also felt marginalized *within* my own culture as well. For years, I was hiding this pain that was growing inside of me because of the fear of being rejected by my own family. I was hiding my identity and feeling lost in my own skin. The idea of performing our gender is very ingrained in my Persian family. Both of my parents were raised in a Middle Eastern world where essentialism within their culture was very prominent. Men worked, while women stayed home to take care of the kids. Women were expected to be feminine, and men were expected to be masculine.

In the case of my family's background, essentialist markers have been put into place for the way men and women should interact in their daily lives. These markers create the gender roles we are expected to practice. This the*logy is not only visible in the culture of minorities, but it adheres to the very complexities of difference we are trying to avoid here in the United States. In the eyes of my ancestors, everyone was meant to live a heteronormative life, whether the individual liked it or not. If they chose to live a different lifestyle, they were often killed or abused through practices such as conversion therapies. Any person (or people) that did not abide by the "normal" or traditional standards of heteronormative life was seen as outliers or "others" in the community. This idea of "other" is explained by Zuleyka Zevallos, who writes, "the idea of 'otherness' is central to sociological analyses of how majority and minority identities are constructed."[4] If one group has a higher status or greater political power, they gain the right to become superior to their inferior, less powerful subordinates. Norms are created in such a way that involves such complexities of power.

Because of this knowledge I had with regard to what is expected and the consequences of stepping outside of the norm, I kept my silence. I

3. Shore-Goss, "Gay and Lesbian Theologies," 191.
4. Zevallos, "What Is Otherness?"

decided, however, to finally break the silence. Reading Lorde's *Transformation Of Silence* took me back to the very emotions I was feeling at the time of finally coming out to my family about my trans-identity. Lorde writes, "and I began to recognize a course of power within myself that comes from the knowledge that while it is most desirable not to be afraid, learning to put fear into perspective gave me great strength."[5] For many people, they choose to live in silence because of the fear of abandonment. In my initial coming out, I was rejected by my family and not accepted for my transgender identity. The idea of my true self was completely dissolved from discussion and was not brought up again. When it was brought up, my parents would try their best to persuade me that "it's just a phase," and that I needed to get this thought out of my mind. My mother would sit me down for hours and tell me that I needed to be a woman and marry a rich man, so I could bear his children and live a long "happy" life. My father would cry endlessly at the thought of losing his baby girl and being gifted a new son. Eventually, after several years of much trial and error, they learned to accept me for who I was and what G*d had created me to be.   *Not*

The ideation of G*d being our creator has played a strong role in the entirety of my life. My parents are practicing Muslims, and they raised my brother and me to be fairly religious. In that sense, growing up in the United States has given me the opportunity to live a somewhat Christian-influenced variation of Muslim tradition. I mainly identify as Muslim, mainly to avoid having long explanations. I do, however, attend Christian churches, work at a Presbyterian church, and participate in Christian spiritual practices. In addition to the Muslim holidays, my family has celebrated Christmas every year. In this regard, I practice and follow both spiritual traditions. Identifying as a Muslim, however, is just easier for people to understand because of my Persian background. *In Liberation Theologies*, Robert E. Shore-Goss speaks about transgendered the*logies, which I feel fits fairly closely to my own outlook on life. Shore-Goss writes a brief description about Justin Tanis, a female-to-male transgendered individual who has been a pioneer figure for transgender the*logies. After researching and interviewing several transgender individuals, Tanis was able to come to the conclusion that "through trans and intersexed bodies, G*d reveals G*dself to be a Creator who loves diversity and variation, a Creator who improvises and varies the melodies that call each person into being."[6] The purpose of Tanis's research was to open the minds of the people within a Christian the*logical

5. Lorde, *Sister Outsider*, 41.

6. Tanis, *Transgendered Theology, Ministry, and Communities of Faith*, 166, quoted in Shore-Goss, "Gay and Lesbian Theologies," 193.

framework to becoming more accepting and willing to understand trans-identifying individuals.

I can relate to Tanis's the*logy, due to personal experiences and acceptance of my own identity. It is difficult to live with an identity that the majority does not understand. Rather than accept the dominant conservative the*logical paradigm, however, I argue that religions actually cultivate and *allow* individuals like myself to have hope. If I did not truly believe that G*d put me on this Earth for the purpose of living out my life as a transgender individual, I would be completely lost in trying to figure out why I am the way I am. This is why I truly believe that transgender the*logy is a perfect fit for me. This also inspires me to continue to envision and construct a critical the*logy and spiritual practice that works for me.

In recent years, many LGBT Christians and the*logians have worked towards the incorporation of gays, lesbians, and other queer individuals into Biblical texts. Shore-Goss writes, "queer folks are made in the image of G*d and thus have the right to be included within the text."[7] Engaging in Biblical texts is a vital step forward in liberation for all queer individuals. A renewed critical queering interpretation of Biblical texts allows readers to read the text and incorporate their own understanding of it. I believe this is an imperative for the inclusion of queer folk into modern day Christianity. As a whole, I would expect for the Catholic and Protestant Churches to open their arms to queer individuals, as well as to oppressed people of any kind. Unfortunately, this has been proven to be immensely difficult, because there is a lack of true desire for acceptance towards individuals that are a part of the queer community. Shore-Goss shares this disappoint and laments that the dominant Christian community does not include the work of queer the*logians.[8]

Oppressed peoples would begin to see incremental change if, as a society, we were able to dismantle the dominant male-centered church, social structure, and hierarchy that continues to dominate our societies. Because of the ways in which our world, language, and traditions are structured; hetero-cis white male individuals are the standard of normative existence. If we are to create equality in a place to practice religion, or just to live in unity with one another, we must take a step in acknowledging our differences as well as admitting our faults in order to move past the oppression that marginalized groups of people have faced. A pertinent example of a much-needed shift in perspective is described in Lorde's chapter titled, "Scratching the Surface," where she speaks out on the common errors we

7. Shore-Goss, "Gay and Lesbian Theologies," 194.
8. Shore-Goss, "Gay and Lesbian Theologies," 199.

see between genders in our world. She writes, "it is based upon the false notion that there is only a limited and particular amount of freedom that must be divided up between us, with the largest and juiciest pieces of liberty going as spoils to the victor or the stronger."[9] Lorde expresses well, my own thoughts on the matter. It is not about who is better (i.e., male or female), it is about working together to reach a common goal. In this case, the common goal would be to attain equality for all people, without a huge downfall to any one group. We should move forward seeing men and woman as equals, as well as recognizing that there—will continue to be—major differences between cultures. Not only do our oppressors have to change, but the oppressed have to forgive. Both sides need to engage in deep listening to the other. If we were all truly created by the same G*d and living in the same world, we would just suffer in an endless cycle of the oppressed versus the oppressors until the end of time, if we do not learn to stop the vicious cycle of oppression and hatred now.

In conclusion, because of my personal identity as a transgendered Muslim Persian-American, I have experienced the intersecting oppressions of race, religion, and sexuality in a Western, white male-dominated society. White male privilege is a power construct that has been directly relevant to my own oppression. I do not know whether it can ever be dismantled, but we can continue to challenge it and show how it leads to the oppression of others, such as myself. Wielding white male privilege causes people with intersecting identities such as mine to feel inferior to everyone around them. As the oppressed and marginalized, I strongly believe it is our task to spread our stories, unlock the silence, and create a better understanding of our situation for those who may hold prejudices and hatred towards us. I also believe that in return, our oppressors should accept our differences and keep in mind that we are all G*d's creation, and that we all intend on living in harmony with one another. We need to put an end to the hypocrisy and repetition in the ladder of hierarchy. Separation between genders should no longer exist, as we are all people with the same end goal in mind. Queer liberation the*logies, as well as other liberation the*logies are the stepping-stones for the eradication of problematic essentialism, stereotyping, and premature judgement of a culture, race, or gender/sexual identity.

9. Lorde, *Sister Outsider*, 51.

7

Muslim Pastoral Theology

*A Brief Reflection of Black Shepherds
and Black Sheep*

BILAL ANSARI

A Black woman sentenced to life in prison in 1993 for a drug charge, immediately embraced Islam, but was denied by the prison her request to wear a headscarf *(hijab)* and long dress *(jilbab)* and to be photographed for her identification card in Islamic attire. She protested against pat searches by males, and she argued for Friday congregational worship led by a male imam and for access to Muslim pastoral care. She petitioned the court to recognize her religious identity, to accommodate the free exercise of her faith, and to provide greater equity for women staff and prisoners. The court granted all four of these requests. The legal decision would mean a need to hire not only female correction officers but a male imam willing to serve in a women's prison.

The Yale Law School contacted me when they learned of me through two newspaper articles describing my own gender equity and religious identity struggle as a Black American Muslim state prison chaplain.[1] They asked if I would be willing to serve Muslim women as Islamic Faith Leader in federal prison. I accepted. Now I would serve as Muslim pastoral caregiver to this Black female petitioner who had also endured years of harassment for her gender and religious identity. Even the Catholic

---

1. Islamophobic and racist acts against me by prison staff shortly after 9/11. Constant investigations and harassment, smashing my Islamic art, defacing my picture with white out, and writing "Nigger" on my portrait in my office were some of the challenges I endured. Nearly depleted from the fight, I was on the brink of leaving my calling in prison ministry that I had once loved.

and Protestant prison chaplains believed lay volunteers were all that was necessary for the Muslim prisoners because Islam allegedly has no theological tradition of pastoral care, especially for women. The professional decision to serve as a Muslim prison chaplain would mean a need to navigate as a Muslim religious leader the thorny intersections of gender, race, and theology in an American institution.

There was a common negative experience and perception of both of us—prisoner and chaplain—Black American Muslims. The institutional gaze had us framed as wayward, out of line, suspect, rogue, and perhaps evil. It was a time and space during which we both felt in our souls a sense of alienation, isolation, and persecution.

THE ABOVE CASE WAS among the most challenging professionally and equally debilitating for those in prison in need of my professional pastoral care. How do I minister as a Muslim Black Shepherd to those suffering similarly as the Black sheep? This brief essay is a response to that challenge and the limiting and denigrating ways that commonly accepted frames of pastoral care—and the unexamined assumptions within them—limit the understanding and acceptance of Muslim pastoral theology and care. Specifically, I want to address the overlooked postcolonial sojourn of the Muslim chaplain who effectively navigates hostile situations in the professional setting, emanating from exclusivist notions that pastoral care has roots only in the Judeo-Christian tradition. I was a graduate student in seminary during the time of this case. I struggled to find a generous enough image of pastoral care that I could appreciate without the effects of white supremacist underpinnings of Anglo Protestantism in chaplaincy. It was through this experience that the image of Black Shepherd was birthed. This essay is but a brief reflection and introduction of my dissertation work of that image.

A key question for Muslim chaplains, then, is how to shepherd a flock that faces a demonized identity. There is a noticeable absence of pastoral theological literature and reflection on theories and praxis of care when dealing in hostile circumstances within ministry. I found myself asking where to look when most literature on crisis care for congregations is framed through a Judeo-Christian lens for practitioners of Christian faith and meaning. Islam's tradition of such care has not been considered capable of being framed in a pastoral context. As a Muslim chaplain, I have endured persecution due to my racial and religious identity. I have had to navigate racial and gender religious discrimination, and I have not been supported professionally so that I can have the spiritual resources needed to support Muslim patients.

As a young minister, I faced several hostile situations in my own chaplaincy work in several rural prison institutions. I eventually came to notice within myself a fluctuating sense of alienation and diminished presence of belonging. The theological comfort zone I felt in my urban ministry context seemed to dissipate like evaporating fluid in these intensely heated environments. At times I struggled to grasp the aim and purpose of serving in a place that was hostile to my personhood and harmed me in the depths of my soul. I struggled with how to provide care to those people who were looking to me for transcendent relief from harm, because I myself was immersed in a spiritual struggle because of the marginalization and dehumanization I was experiencing due to my race and religion. I struggled to see what pastoral theological literature would be helpful for Muslim chaplains who face this on a daily basis as I did during the time of this pastoral case. My pastoral counseling and work have been to create and compile such resources for the Muslim community in light of my own life experiences. I felt I was forced off the beaten path, both as shepherd and sheep.

There were no written contemporary Muslim pastoral reflections, no inclusive Abrahamic people of faith literature to draw upon. The Society of Pastoral Theology had no seminary expertise to help a Muslim chaplain think through how to navigate such uncharted terrain as a caregiver. Where were the spiritual resources when such a marginalized shepherd was facing thorny patches and steep mountains while leading a marginalized flock? I found very few answers but the questions gave me the impetus to search deeper into the Islamic tradition, to chart my own way in the field. Pastoral theologian Robert Dykstra documents that the historical arc of pastoral theology as a profession is that it has no clear path or consensus of approach and that was actually the distinction of the field.[2] One common denominator was looking in scripture to find a hopeful sense that the months or years one spends with people who ostracized you would be among the most critical times of personal and professional opportunities of growth.[3] In the introduction it reads,

> Both the madness and the wisdom of pastoral theology and
> its resulting approaches to pastoral care and counseling derive
> from keen attention to life on the boundaries, making pastoral

---

2. Dykstra, *Images of Pastoral Care.*

3. This belief comes from a chapter in the Qur'an revealed during a troubling time for Prophet Muhammad. The chapter is called "ash-Sharh," or "The Soothing" in English. The idea that with every difficulty it is followed by ease and this is emphasized twice (Qur'an 94:5, 6).

theology's own questionable origins, as well as its frequent identity confusion, less its burden than its calling and destiny.[4]

Perhaps this rod providentially would become a staff for at least charting
the course for the development and integration of such crisis into a fabric
of meaning and purpose in the future. This image of pastoral care is written
to explain what it means to bear the cloak of ethical leadership as shepherd
and to thrive as a Black Muslim in American institutions as you overcome
your despised and devalued status.

Consequently, in my close reading of the foundational Islamic sources
for guidance in crisis in the absence of contemporary inclusive pastoral literature, I noticed that the theme of "the shepherd and the flock" kept reap-
pearing. I began to think that since the theme of shepherd and flock reappear
in Islamic texts, it might be well to apply it in my ministry context. It was
full of insights for those in prison facing present and past traumas. I thought
about shepherding as the role of the chaplain dealing with the effects of
the dynamics of perceptions of race, gender, and Islam. As a young Muslim
professional who worked as a prison chaplain throughout my undergraduate and graduate school years, I was viewed by many Christian colleagues
more as a "black sheep" leading other "black sheep." The identifier as black   _True_
and shepherd in the image of myself is meaningful when you understand
the psychological, sociological, and theological educational terrain I had to
personally and professionally traverse for my inclusion and equitable treatment. In psychology, the *black sheep effect* refers to the tendency of group
members to judge likeable ingroup members more positively and deviant
ingroup member more negatively than comparable outgroup members.[5]
This brief essay, then, is a reflection on my inward and outward navigational
tools under such conditions and to explore the pastoral theological roots for
understanding how Black shepherds find their way to care in these institutions. The Black sheep of Muslim women in prison deserve the best care
possible. I hope to continue working on this metaphor for a larger book
project as a Muslim pastoral theologian and caregiver.

---

4. Dykstra, *Images of Pastoral Care*, 4.

5. Marques et al., "'Black Sheep Effect," 1–16.

8

Phoenix Poetry in a Flammable World

— Melinda McGarrah Sharp —

Basketry: Intergenerational Wisdom, Story-Bearing, Future Story-Holding

"If you're invited into basket-making at midnight, say yes," a neighbor advised me before my Peace Corps service, explaining that invitations into cultural wisdom are sacred and should be carefully engaged, even around something trivial like basket-weaving. On the first point, I agreed. I honor the sacred nature of intercultural invitations, especially between strangers. Yet, I resisted rendering basketry as trivial, hearing echoes of the pejorative anti-intellectual, anti-indigenous phrase "underwater basket weaving," which emerged as early as the 1950s to diminish knowledge that does not count toward a degree or lead to a job, practices discounted as laughable, time-wasting distractions that avoid more pressing, profitable matters.[1]

In my view, no cultural practice is merely trivial; all intercultural invitations, whether sustained or hesitant, are miracles of hospitality. Whatever time of day or competing demands, carefully considering invitations into cultural wisdom practices, even as a silent guest, is sage advice. Further, negotiating invitations into literal and metaphorical basket-weaving is an intercultural pastoral care practice. Three elements of basketry inspire this claim. Basket-makers are intergenerational, intercultural wisdom-keepers. Baskets are sacred and resilient, communal story-bearers and future story-holders. Baskets are also highly flammable.

---

1. Kimball, "Magna Cum Nonsense," 68.

96

Basket-makers are cultural wisdom keepers. For several generations, I have had family in South Carolina. Although I have never lived there, I have often visited the lowcountry marshy coastal region. I recall as a child being beckoned to come near basket-makers in downtown Charleston's City Market, witnessing black women spin long grasses into fine basketry. I was drawn to moving hands at the exact point where straight lines of sweetgrass transformed into water-tight coiled patterns. South Carolina sweetgrass basketry, as Margot Theis Raven describes, is "circle on circle, coil on coil . . . when . . . fingers talked just right and the wet season came . . . basket held the rain."[2] As new generations have been initiated into Gullah and Geechee basket-making, sweetgrass baskets continue to embody intergenerational and intercultural wisdom. In *Talking to the Dead: Religion, Music, and Lived Member Among Gullah/Geechee Women,* Africana scholar LeRhonda S. Manigault-Bryant suggests sweetgrass basket-makers today are cultural wisdom bearers who "expect the dead to be present among the living," talking to the dead through the "painstaking, laborious, and delicate art" of lowcountry sweetgrass basketry.[3]

As a southern white family, we were basket-consumers and not makers, something that I must own and with which I continue to wrestle. Realizing separation between maker and consumer of making, as a child, likely contributed to my present—if slow—awakening as a racialized person in a nation of people whose identity is shaped by race. I like to think I come from generations of grateful consumers, invested not only in the economics of beauty, but also in story-sharing that deepen ties between material reality and human creativity, though I suspect the reality is far more complex.[4] Risks of commodifying, appropriating, romanticizing, exoticizing, and/or diminishing cultural histories held in sweetgrass baskets are always present, particularly for white lowcountry visitors, such as myself.[5] At the same time, I learned to value intergenerational and intercultural wisdom of sweetgrass baskets. Teaching me to revere basketry, my grandmother displayed Charleston sweetgrass baskets, using them for special occasions. Baskets stretch back in time past our holiday family meals and the Charleston City Market.

---

2. Raven, *Circle Unbroken,* 7.

3. Manigault-Bryant, *Talking to the Dead,* 114–15.

4. I engage this task in new ways as a faculty member at a school whose roots are entangled with institutions of enslavement and human trafficking in South Carolina. Fresh collective attention to this complicity both motivates and challenges healing and justice-oriented work of theological education today at my school and beyond.

5. Manigault-Bryant, *Talking to the Dead,* 182–90.

Baskets embody complex, painful, and beautiful histories. Enslaved Africans introduced sweetgrass basket-making into lowcountry rice harvesting, connecting skilled labor practices from Sierra Leone and other homelands to South Carolina and Georgia.[6] "Gullah/Geechee women have navigated histories that exclude them . . . that simplify their complex narratives and experiences," writes Manigault-Bryant.[7] Baskets bear survival stories; each evokes ancestral wisdom. Alongside technological and infrastructural changes, literal and metaphorical bridges from inland to islands increase access to basketry while displacing sources of sweetgrass and basket makers' homes. Yet baskets remain cultural wisdom-bearers.

Baskets are also sacred and resilient, communal story-holders and future story-bearers. Baskets are forms of art and transportation, holding and moving food, wood, cloth, and gifts. Materiality held in baskets represents cultural practices of planting, harvesting, fishing, feasting, fasting, bathing. Miraculously water-tight, baskets can float. Baskets move water from river to soup pot. From bearing Moses' infant body in radical biblical text to quenching the thirst of all we who still rely on moving rivers and streams for daily life in more and less visible ways, baskets bear the weight of stories across lands and waters. They hold future story ingredients, which pastoral theologian Andrew Lester describes as individual and collective visions of a future that shape human imaginations and practices.[8] Baskets carry food to market, weave buying and selling, facilitate meal fellowship. Even while being made, baskets already bear future stories.

In rural Suriname as Peace Corps Volunteers, my partner and I got to know a local basket-maker, Bakisiman.[9] Bakisiman's baskets were indispensable for daily life. Lodged in colonial patterns that threatened death for merely existing, village communities still plant crops many miles from dwelling places.[10] Baskets regularly transport food and wood long distances from field to cookfire. Baskets travel well-worn footpaths between village homes and the river–source for cleansing food and bodies, source of life. Baskets accompanied nearly every daily life practice and special ritual into which we were invited. Wherever baskets are present, there is life and life-future story. Before leaving Suriname, Bakisiman asked when we might need and wish we had baskets. We asked Bakisiman to make three baskets for future children we might welcome into our lives. These

---

6. Opala, *Gullah*.

7. Manigault-Bryant, *Talking to the Dead*, 201.

8. Lester, *Hope*. See also my *Creating Resistances*.

9. All names changed.

10. See my *Misunderstanding Stories*.

baskets link a shared past in intercultural friendship with Bakisiman to future stories that now include two living children who know the story of their baskets. Baskets bear future stories.

Baskets themselves are also storytellers. Accompanying seminary students to the US-Mexico border from 2011–2016, I encountered Tohono O'odham basketry. Across many revered patterns, O'odham baskets bear O'odham stories, "Desert People . . . formerly known as the Papago."[11] One prominent pattern addresses what it means to be human. With contrasting light and dark fibers made from bear grass, yucca, and devil's claw, a human-like figure stands at the basket's rim. Either entering or exiting an angular labyrinth, human "has no shortcuts, there are no dead-ends either, and the entire path must be followed in order to complete the journey."[12] Baskets bear stories of humans' life journeys, each twist and turn weaving growing wisdom and knowledge. Fascinated by O'odham baskets which range in size from a thimble to a building, my children and I sought to learn more, but found little O'odham representation in our local library or school history books. Such absences are pastoral care concerns.

Meeting O'odham peoples through interpersonal encounters, poetry, and readings, I learn that some O'odham baskets weave human figures side-by-side-by-side around the basket's outer edge, evoking a community whose interpersonal relationships, religion, economic practices, land relationship, histories and futures are border-crossing communal ventures. Figures move in one direction then circle back again. O'odham rituals also move, committed to "fixing the earth" through rituals, "drumming . . . on overturned woven baskets."[13] Today's geo-political international US-Mexico border cuts deeply through O'odham nation, now split into four tribes from one peoples. Both now and historically, "like many other Native American and indigenous peoples today, O'odham inhabit multiple ontologies, embodying different histories, and subscribe to multiple historicities."[14] Famously water tight, O'odham baskets move and depict movement, a key organizing principle of people who "move both within and between worlds, not always—or even ever—with ease, but in ways that generate and are generated by the 'friction' of encounter in the 'consumption' of the other, which necessarily involves the transformation of each by the other."[15] Students and I were moved at the

11. Zapeda, *Ocean Power*, 85.

12. "Tohono O'odham Baskets."

13. Zapeda, *Ocean Power*, 88–89.

14. Schermerhorn, *Walking to Magdalena*, 145.

15. Schermerhorn, *Walking to Magdalena*, 145–46.

O'odham museum where basketry walls respond to present guests, histories shared, and future encounters.[16] Baskets are story-tellers.

Yet baskets are highly flammable, tightly wound dried grasses that would kindle any fire. Basketry thus illustrates contexts of intercultural pastoral care practices in our contemporary postcolonial world. The world is aflame, not only from climate change, seething coals of white supremacy, settler colonialism, and imperialistic nationalism,[17] but indeed from colonial residue that burns indigenous lands, bodies, and cultural arts. Colonial violence seeks to destroy through assimilative policy and prejudice, erasing arts, histories, and, most extremely, peoples. Not only the work of grandmother's hands, but also grandmother is threatened. Ancestral connections represented in baskets weave land, people, shared stories, memory, and material reality to immaterial rituals throughout time.

Ashes that smolder in postcoloniality are laced with ancestral wisdom, contain charred fruits of tenacious making, and consume tender soul-food containers. Fire has also been used in response, such as when a colleague recently cried, "burn it down and start over," instead of repairing institutions built on the backs of minoritized peoples. Poignantly, in "An Open Letter to White Liberal Feminists," Manigault-Bryant decries, "Ashes to ashes, Dust to white liberal feminism."[18] Manigault-Bryant calls for "self-proclaimed white liberal feminists [to] interrogate racism, imperialism, capitalism, and sexism because they benefit from it and are too busy being protected by it."[19] When it comes to camping, I may "leave wood for the next person's fire,"[20] yet never know what will be burned in it. And do I reflect on what I pass by with water and yet leave smoldering? When it comes to basketry, am I an ash-maker? Do I value and seek to be in relationship with indigenous wisdom-bearers, the deeply troubling histories and liberating future stories that baskets bear? Do I seek postcolonializing practices that make intercultural creativity possible?[21] Have I interrogated

---

16. See my "Prelude to Decolonizing Immersion Pedagogy," 105–41.

17. Beaudoin and Turpin warn white scholars against placing themselves outside of white supremacy's snares and recommend instead interrogating its influence through partnerships of accountability (Beaudoin and Turpin, "White Practical Theology," 268, 256). Dismantling, they argue, involves listening more than positing and performing, increasing nonexploitative deep engagement with indigenous conversation partners, which I have attempted to begin to model here (264–65). See Beaudoin and Turpin, "White Practical Theology."

18. Manigault-Bryant, "Open Letter."

19. Manigault-Bryant, "Open Letter."

20. Kimmerer, *Braiding Sweetgrass*, 35.

21. Lartey, *Postcolonializing God*.

white normativity in theological, pedagogical, and care-participating commitments and practices?[22] Can we co-reside in both "joy for the being of the shimmering world and grief for what we have lost," as botanist and indigenous seer Dr. Robin Wall Kimmerer describes life that arises amidst fire?[23] Intercultural pastoral care practices can be imagined as collective phoenix poetry that arises from ambiguous ashes under foot today while destructive fires target baskets upon baskets.

Weaving basketry imagery with a paired image of phoenix poetry underscores transformative practices of intercultural pastoral care from disinterest to disconnected consumer to co-maker in collective creativity. Phoenix poetic creativity resides neither solely in pastors' vocations nor bound in stunning published poetry collections, but also in humanizing possibilities where life and love breathe together in air pockets unconsumed by colonial fires. Haitian-American author Edwidge Danticat shows how creating dangerously births transformation. Danticat's writings, teaching that resistance movements create dangerously, can resource intercultural pastoral care where phoenix poetry arises in a flammable world.

Phoenix Poetry: Persistent Joy, Prophetic Grief[24]

Healing impulses in intercultural pastoral care attentive to postcolonial realities recognize that my humanity can only be realized with mutual recognition of yours. Whoever is rendered *other* through histories, habits, and hatreds—where it is "[burned] into you that you do not count and that no provisions are made for the literal protection of your person" as Rev. Dr. Howard Thurman puts it—must be extravagantly welcomed as the author of life-saving, healing poetry.[25] Postcolonializing pastoral care connects mutual recognition to the life project of affirming our respective and particular deepest possibilities. This phoenix poetry arises in collective presence, that makes making possible, despite forces intending creativity's demise. Phoenix poets are resistance movements, policy reformations, decolonizing theologies, and collective affirmations that invite authentic participation in intercultural creative processes. I am in-process of becoming backdrop, phoenix, and more often ash-maker. And so are you.

22. Beaudoin and Turpin, "White Practical Theology."

23. Kimmerer, *Braiding Sweetgrass*, 248.

24. For this section of the paper, I am grateful to Brill for granting permissions to rework and expand portions of "Amplifying Phoenix Poets," chapter 4 in my book *Creating Resistances*.

25. Thurman, *Jesus and the Disinherited*, 39.

Differences between ash-making that assaults creativity and phoenix poetry that arises from and around campfires turn on the question, "Why care?" Why seek pastoral care images and metaphors accountable to intercultural life together? Learning and teaching empathy in this postcolonial world involves being moved by what is at stake enough to care within and across widely different contexts and human experiences. With basketry and phoenix poetry as pastoral care images, what does it look like to share the burden of being moved to care?

I cannot pretend to understand. Traveling reveals empathic limits, such as urges to imagine with certainty what I would do in a situation that is not my lived experience. Not all bridges empower intercultural care. Postcolonializing pastoral care fosters tiny connections that make empathy more possible than reading or resting in assumptions about neighbors. Authentic connections resist commodification and ash-making; creativity arises in sacred remembrance rituals. Ethically just intercultural pastoral care strives to build enough trust for mutual if guarded curiosities, believing and bearing to hear each other, and sustaining connection for a short or long time, while simultaneously daring to reflect on my practices to "interrogate [the] racism, imperialism, capitalism, and sexism" that work against intercultural care.[26] Such intercultural connections seek not to fish for experiential hooks to catch "the" meaning of an other from my own life (though this common strategy can support initial trust-building), but instead seek co-creative, mutually accountable partnerships.

Intercultural pastoral care practices transform understanding through deep listening that confronts systemic and personal desires not to be moved. Histories, habits, and hatreds that value invulnerability to movement and thus presume irrelevance to my life, must be confronted as part of moving from disengaged to transformative resistances. Intact structures of colonial bellowing target all who resist status quo destructivity. Collective phoenix poetry arises even here, especially here.

Today's postcolonial global habitat was built in part by limiting access to words, especially the humanizing words of poetry. Phillis Wheatley, already a prolific poet by her late teens in the 1770s in Boston, was met with disbelief that she, an enslaved African, could write anything relevant to people in power. Historian Henry Louis Gates imagines the scene where young Wheatley faces a panel of more socially respectable white male poets to defend the question: "Was a Negro capable of producing literature?"[27] Centuries later, today, bell hooks laments that academia still obscures and discounts many

26. Manigault-Bryant, "Open Letter."
27. Gates, *Trials of Phillis Wheatley*, 5.

voices, rendering "them" as "not good enough to be read or taught," while in fact "a world of poetry written by black folks . . . [is] just as wonderful, just as compelling as the work of my beloved Emily Dickinson."[28]

In the United States, the category of full person was historically legally restricted by race, gender, and class. Thomas Jefferson refused to consider anyone who did not count as a full person a rising poet. Contemporary Boston poet Clint Smith reminds publics: "Nor did Jefferson believe that black people possessed the ability to be creative or be artists. He refused to call Phillis Wheatley a poet."[29] Resisting from within colonial structures of asymmetrical power, on June 12, 1773, two political leaders, five judges, three lawyers, seven ministers, and "her master," all men self-identified as "the most respectable characters in Boston," published a public letter attesting that Wheatley not only could be, but already was an accomplished poet. These eighteen men attested that Phillis Wheatley in fact created the poetry that accompanied her name.[30] Wheatley's poetry stands on its own; she remains a qualified and inspiring poet in no need of any master's attestation.

Dehumanizing practices continue to impact poetry, art, music, leadership, and prophetic witness today. Intact colonial bellows will not call anyone to interrogate their ongoing harms. How does pastoral care respond to burning baskets in structurally colonizing fires as deeply wounding? Intercultural pastoral care can support phoenix poetry in a flammable world, calling forth poets willing to share creativity. Such pastoral care heeds, amplifies, and negotiates intercultural invitations into phoenix poetics that rise and rise again amid unfair, dehumanizing, sinful, hurtful obstacles. Whose voices are relevant to everyday life? Whose poetry do you attest to? Whose attestations assure you?

Deeply buried in collective and personal psyches, "you don't matter" is linked to "don't speak." In 2015, South Carolina poet laureate Marjory Wentworth, whose poetry engages the state's history of slavery and lingering racism, was uninvited from Nikki Haley's inauguration as state governor. Wentworth intended "One River, One Boat" to be read, which included:

> Because our history is a knot
> we try to unravel, while others
> try to tighten it, we tire easily
> and fray the cords that bind us.[31]

28. hooks, *Teaching Critical Thinking*, 104.

29. Smith, "Nor Did Jefferson Believe."

30. Wheatley, *Poems of Phillis Wheatley*, xi–xii.

31. Wentworth, "One River, One Boat."

When seeking to participate in creative healing as pastoral care, phoenix poets arise from such chaotic and dehumanizing fraying. Recognizing and amplifying phoenix poets as a postcolonializing practice can confront colonizing instincts to burn baskets.

Colonialism's lingering insidious effects dull imagination, creativity, and desires to be moved. In response, postcolonializing pastoral care tends the ground, bears witness to ash-making, and ritualizes remembrances where phoenix poetry arises in a flammable world and deepens possibilities of empathic creativity. Discounting phoenix poets feed fires that would consume baskets, basketry, and basket-makers. Invitations can expand spheres of voices and experiences that co-create healing, hope, and justice. Invitations reside in host-guest dynamics and can disrupt them. One cannot remain the issuer of empathy invitations for long without finding oneself also invited to participate. Intercultural pastoral care calls not only for some to participate, but instead cultivates reliable pathways of authentic participation for all creation.[32]

Intercultural pastoral care includes disciplined practices of listening into the heart of suffering, bearing to hear and believe what is shared by invitation and/or overheard while negotiating invitations, and responding in partnerships. Being moved to care interculturally across different experiences grounds practices. Both complicities and resistances intertwine through multiple layers of engagement: listening, inviting replies, bearing to hear, responding. For pastoral care participants, responsible practice invests in learning embodied empathy.[33] Studying complicity, I confront my complicities. Studying resistance, I more readily notice my moving into and retreating from both change-averse and justice-oriented resistances. I assess practices of listening, bearing to hear, responding, and co-participating in resistance movements in part by virtue of caring about learning and staying present to what is at stake.

Is your suffering relevant to my suffering, my joy to your joy? Persistent joy and prophetic grief co-reside in phoenix poetry that arises from costly ashes. These pastoral impulses inform practices of authentically participating in postcolonializing creativity that resists chaotic conditions and brush fires in lowcountry sweetgrass, desert bear grass, and Amazonian plants. Where are the weavers, the basket-makers the wisdom-bearers, story-bearers, and future story-holders? According to Haitian-American writer Edwidge Danticat, creating dangerously postcolonializes practice, particularly for displaced and moving peoples. Daring to read philosophy amid a long history

32. Lartey, *In Living Color*.

33. Capps, "Resistance in the Local Church," 588.

of orchestrated violence in Haiti, Danticat honors how people who move put their embodied creativity on the line and across lines. Creating dangerously is art-making that supports life within what Thurman names a "perpetual war of nerves."[34] "In the midst of both external and internal destruction," Danticat writes, creating dangerously is writing "as though each piece of art were a stand-in for a life, a soul, a future."[35]

Creativity resists the threat of annihilation through intercultural making. It is simple, yet profound. Radical. Art can restore humanization for all, including investors in ash-making, by holding profiteers of suffering accountable. Drawing on Toni Morrison, Danticat shows how creativity renews life at the "edge[s] of towns that cannot bear our company."[36] Such phoenix poetry attends to historical dehumanization, current events, national and international policies, and everyday microaggressions. Makers, including but not limited to basket-makers, are so well-informed about the world that art-making can leverage transformation. Where instruments are absent, creative visionaries schedule orchestra concerts. Muralists bend militarized walls into conversations. Film-makers and playwrights cast novel visions of leadership, power arrangements, and loves. Creating dangerously crosses borders between writer and writing (intrapersonal) and between writer and reader (interpersonal and intercultural). Much is at stake in crossing normalized borders. Danticat writes:

> How do writers and readers find each other under such dangerous circumstances? Reading, like writing, under these conditions is disobedience to a directive in which the reader, our Eve, already knows the possible consequences of eating that apple but takes a bold bite anyway. How does that reader find the courage to take this bite, open that book? After an arrest, an execution? Of course [they] may find it in the power of the hushed chorus of other readers, but [they] can also find it in the writer's courage in having stepped forward, in having written, or rewritten, in the first place.[37]

Immigrant artists and indigenous basket-makers respond into the question: "why care?" Danticat exposes writing as dangerous when papers serve both survival[38] and death.[39] Legal border-crossing documentation is made dif-

---

34. Thurman, *Jesus and the Disinherited*, 40.

35. Danticat, *Create Dangerously*, 20.

36. Danticat, *Create Dangerously*, 17.

37. Danticat, *Create Dangerously*, 10 (pronouns edited).

38. Danticat, *Create Dangerously*, 10.

39. Danticat, *Brother, I'm Dying*.

ficult to attain for phoenix poets.[40] Fires draw near to indigenous making even as ancestral wisdom persists in phoenixes' sacred feathers. Creativity unfolds as vocation of moving anyway, (re)creating family[41] in contexts that reduce productive work to undercompensated essential global labor.[42] Danticat writes, "the nomad . . . who learns something rightly must always ponder travel and movement, just as the grief-stricken must inevitably ponder death."[43] Writing, rewriting, studying, reading, and rereading dangerously become instances of and invitations into creativity.

Where phoenix poetry arises in a flammable world, four becomings unfold simultaneously: becoming phoenix, becoming ash-maker, becoming presence, and becoming bystander for whom the stakes are not yet moving enough to care. Sharing the burden of care—attending carefully and debriefing collectively—can mitigate urges to foist the burden of care always on the made-more-vulnerable party. Sharing also checks perfectionistic savior complexes that value care for all in theory while acting alone. Pastoral care is not a solo act. Wrestling with complicities through self-examination, action planning, and accountability partnerships inform rituals of remembrance that basketry is not irrelevant kindling available for the taking.

Intercultural pastoral care as phoenix poetry in a flammable world amplifies co-creators arising from ashes of death-dealing policies and closed hearts, accompanied by authentic co-participation in courageous self- and communal-awareness. Danticat describes being consulted after the 2010 Haitian earthquake to speak hope into conditions of grave loss. She writes, "'no poetry in the ashes south of canal street,' the poet Suheir Hammad had written. Would there be any poetry amidst the Haitian ruins?"[44] Before speaking, Danticat says she practiced what Haitians had always done amid death and destruction: read and listen dangerously. Does poetry arise in deserts, basket-maker spaces, burning rainforests? Who hears and heeds collective rising of phoenix poetry from these ashes? Intercultural pastoral care practices extravagant welcome in communities of phoenix poets through personal and communal courageous reflection on how I am becoming a presence, a phoenix, and more often an ash-maker.

---

40. Danticat, *Mama's Nightingale*, 30.

41. Danticat, *Mama's Nightingale*, 29.

42. Brubaker, *Globalization at What Price*.

43. Danticat, *Create Dangerously*, 16.

44. Danticat, *Create Dangerously*, 159.

Conclusion: Phoenix Poetry
in a Flammable World

A "mosaiculture" living art installation in Atlanta Botanical Gardens' "Imaginary Worlds" exhibit, a phoenix arises from the ground, made of thousands of living plants confronting the summer heat. This land was once inhabited by Creek Indigenous North Americans, by vibrant plantation slavocracy, was burned in civil war, once place of my childhood, today home to diverse peoples still wrestling to live well together. Collective joy and prophetic grief abide simultaneously here. Phoenix feathers are tiny coils of purple and gold vegetation. Gardener Amanda Bennett shares, "It looks like magic but there's a lot of dirty hard work that goes into it."[45] "Living sculptures are maintained daily by the horticulture team," explains garden caretakers, "to keep them thriving and healthy."[46] In this chapter, I propose basketry and phoenix poetry as images of pastoral care in a postcolonial world. Basketry reminds of what's at stake while phoenix poetry arises in creative possibilities that empower transformation. Basketry exemplifies the wisdom-bearing, story-bearing, future story-holding collective art that is flammable where intact colonizing bellows threaten to suck the life out of breathing, embodied human beings and communities. Where ash-making persists, phoenix poetry makes new life possible.

Basket-making and phoenix poetry are collective, intergenerational, invitational creative forms that consider well-being in a broader view: What is hope in a world of oppressive suffering? Who decides? What does it mean to practice pastoral care that joins possibilities of creativity with acknowledgements of complicities in harm? Can care cross dimensions of time and space, memory and dreaming, power and vulnerability? Where dehumanization threatens to burn ancient arts represented in basketry, phoenix poets co-create transformative possibilities while acknowledging wounding. Care is both individual and collective, historical and prophetic.

Years ago, my grandmother's treasured sweetgrass baskets were burned in an accidental fire and she found her way back to South Carolina seeking new baskets from James Island community basket-makers. Just recently, I returned to Charleston's City Market, surprised that upscale wares in air-conditioned aisles had replaced local artists' stalls. Outside, Miss Shirley beckoned me to hear stories of how she learned to turn sweetgrass into baskets from her mother who learned from her mother. She worries that people are losing interest in the making and lamented increasing scarcity of

45. Emerson, "'Imaginary Worlds.'"
46. Atlanta Botanical Garden, "Alice's Wonderland Reimagined."

basket-weaving materials. Sweetgrass and palmetto palm bundles are now harvested and sold rather than exchanged as gifts. A consumer still, yet one who tries to awaken to intercultural care and direct it into co-creativity of new rituals and possibilities, my son and I purchased a small basket and some roses made from coiled sweetgrass, thanking Miss Shirley, promising her to share about our encounter. Around the corner, we laid the sweetgrass roses at Mother Emmanuel AME church, read the "Emanuel 9" names, and affirmed the memorial inscription "love is stronger than hate," reigniting vigilance for recognizing and dismantling my complicities in hate while assenting to a persistent calling toward life. Prophetic grief at breath-extinguishing colonial bellows is past and present. Creativity and persistent joy are possible when grief and joy co-reside. Sit with basket-makers when invited, even at midnight, amid seemingly more important demands. Participate communally and interculturally in the possibility of phoenix poetry.

9

Humanist Chaplaincy as a
Kind of Midwifery for Secular
Connection and Meaning

Greg M. Epstein

What does humanist chaplaincy mean to me? The answer has evolved so much over the years that one could even say—with obvious and intended irony, but also with an earnest desire to imagine a secular version of a loaded theological concept with which I would not usually identify—that my own vision for my work has relatively recently been "born again." At the very least, the image I want to share in this essay is of my work as a kind of midwifery for a certain way of being human. This image, itself, was born only through experiences I have had in the process of doing chaplaincy work. In order to share my vision for my profession today, therefore, I first need to give you a sense of my own journey, and the journey that we humanist chaplains have taken over the years.

When I arrived in Cambridge, MA, in the fall of 2004, newly hired to take on the role of Assistant Humanist Chaplain at Harvard, I became one of only four people in the United States to formally hold the title "humanist chaplain." One of those four was my then boss Tom Ferrick, a former Catholic priest, who back in the 1970s, left the Catholic church and disavowed any theistic framework. He was *en route* to becoming the first humanist chaplain at any university in the world.[1] The other two were semi-retired

---

1. See, for example, Torpy, "Humanist Chaplains in the Dutch Military." The first-ever humanist chaplains anywhere emerged in the Dutch armed forces around a decade earlier; today, more than a third of the chaplains in Holland's military are humanists, and a humanist university, first established to train them, now educates hundreds of students.

volunteers who each spent no more than a few hours per week in unpaid humanist chaplaincy roles at Stanford and Columbia. My own job was to pay $15,000 for a year of what I overzealously imagined as full-time work. I had just returned to the States after a year-long fellowship to study Talmudic literature at the Hebrew University of Jerusalem, which had been the fourth year in a five-year process towards ordination as a secular humanist rabbi. This itself was a title which at the time was held formally by, at most, a dozen or two people worldwide. In other words, the sort of secular clergy work about which I write in this chapter was not exactly what one would describe as "well established" a decade and a half ago.

I was both honored and intimidated, then, to be asked to write about the growing phenomenon of humanist chaplaincy for a volume such as this. I feel honored because I believe in the importance and beauty of chaplaincy work by and for atheists, agnostics, and allies. I have enjoyed being something of a champion for this cause over many years now, as it has matured toward what might be called the "mainstream" of US chaplaincy. I would very much like to see a future in which any and every kind of institution which welcomes chaplains will fully include chaplains who openly identify as nonreligious, nontheistic, and humanist.

I am intimidated in writing for this volume because it is hard to assess exactly how established my profession is today at the time of this volume's publication. As of this writing, there have not been any formal academic studies to establish exactly how many humanist chaplains exist in the United States today. Informally, I am not sure I would feel comfortable describing whatever number there are of us now as "a lot." These days, I no longer take it upon myself to be some sort of academic authority on humanist chaplaincy. There was a time when I allowed myself to try to respond as such when faced with questions I was not fully qualified to answer from well-meaning religion and society journalists looking to write the latest "trend piece," but I would like to think I have matured in certain ways that will hopefully be more clear by the end of this essay. What I can say with some pride, for now, is that I have lost count. It seems to me that new humanist chaplains are cropping up just about every week, at universities, hospitals, hospice programs, and beyond. But I can no longer rattle off the names and institutions of everyone in the country who holds a title similar to my own, and that is a good thing.

What Is Humanism?

Humanism is the process of living well, of behaving ethically, caring for self and others, and attempting to be good stewards of this world which was created by a process of evolution that began with the Big Bang and continues to this day. The American Humanist Association defines it as a "progressive philosophy of life that, without supernaturalism, affirms our ability and responsibility to live ethical lives of personal fulfillment that aspire to the greater good of humanity."[2] Humanists International, the global representative body of the humanist movement, says in its "minimum statement" on the following definition:

> Humanism is a democratic and ethical life stance that affirms that human beings have the right and responsibility to give meaning and shape to their own lives. Humanism stands for the building of a more humane society through an ethics based on human and other natural values in a spirit of reason and free inquiry through human capabilities. Humanism is not theistic, and it does not accept supernatural views of reality.[3]

These are philosophically nuanced descriptions, written largely by academics, as parts of documents which have defined the word differently in previous iterations, in keeping with the idea that humanism is an evolving tradition which grows and changes as new evidence is uncovered, new data emerges, and new insights are gained. I have often found it simpler and more helpful, however, to simply explain that humanism is "good without god."[4] I do not mind, in other words, pragmatically referring to the popular notion that ethics are defined and enforced by supernatural forces, and offering humanism as an alternative worldview for people who treasure the idea of an ethical way of life but cannot or will not accept the idea of a conscious manager of the universe.

The term "humanist," as referring to the idea of an ethical and non-theistic lifestance, first came into use in the English language in the early twentieth century,[5] but under many other names, there have been humanists in every part of the world throughout recorded history. As early as three millennia ago, Indian philosophers from two schools of thought called the Carvakas and the Lokayatas became known for producing skeptical and irreligious statements such as this one:

2. American Humanist Association, "Humanism and Its Aspirations."

3. Humanists International, "What Is Humanism?"

4. Epstein, *Good Without God.*

5. Epstein, *Good Without God,* 169–71.

If a beast slain as an offering to the dead
Will itself go to heaven,
Why does the sacrificer not straightaway offer his father?
. . . If our offering sacrifices here gratifies beings in heaven,
Why not make food offerings down below
To gratify those standing on housetops?[6]

And in ancient Greece, three centuries before Christ lived to have his divinity debated, the Greek philosopher Epicurus said:

Nothing to fear in God;
Nothing to feel in Death;
Good can be attained;
Evil can be endured.[7]

Until the past hundred years or so, perspectives like these were adopted and expressed primarily by isolated individuals or by small groups of philosophers, social critics, and other intellectuals. But more recently, humanist communities and organizations of many and increasingly diverse varieties have emerged. Some of these have served primarily to argue against religion; others have adopted much more positive purposes such as serving the needy, building congregations to provide mutual support for secular people, or even sending chaplains to care for the nonreligious students at universities like Harvard. And why not? At Harvard College, nearly 40 percent of students now self-identify as either atheists or agnostics, which is more than *all Christians combined,* according to *The Harvard Crimson.*[8] At MIT, a 2012 study indicated that somewhere around half of all students may be atheists, agnostics, or nonreligious.[9] These statistics are entirely consistent with my experiences on campus as the Humanist Chaplain at Harvard since Tom Ferrick retired in 2005, and as the Humanist Chaplain at MIT (in addition to retaining my role at Harvard) since 2018. And they are resonant with, if perhaps slightly ahead of, general trends in US demographics more broadly. Recent studies conducted by the Public Religion Research Institute (PRRI) found that the number of Americans who claim no particular religious affiliation has more than tripled over the last two decades.[10] The numbers among Millennials were striking: 35 percent of Americans under the age

6. Madhava, *Sarva-Darsana-Samgraha.*

7. Murray, *Five Stages of Greek Religion,* 205. This saying, sometimes known as the Tetrapharmacon, does not appear in the extant writings of Epicurus but is an Epicurean formula generally considered to date to Epicurus himself.

8. See Damaraju et al., "Meet the Class of 2021."

9. Lloyd, "Religion at MIT."

10. Jones et al., "2012 American Values Survey."

of thirty described themselves as religiously unaffiliated, wit⌐
saying that religion was unimportant in their lives.

Religiously unaffiliated status, moreover, is often ac.
overall, 15 percent of Americans surveyed reported that they deliber.
left the religious tradition in which they were raised to become religiously
unaffiliated, and the PRRI's 2012 Millennial Values Survey reports, "Despite their relatively young age, Millennials report significant levels of
movement from the religious affiliation of their childhood. By far the
group seeing the highest increase in membership due to this movement is
the religiously unaffiliated."[11]

Of course, these sorts of numbers are often bandied about in secular
and religious circles alike, as part of an interminable debate about the future
of religion. Philosophers, theologians, activists, and assorted other intellectuals seemingly love to argue about whether such trends are good or bad for
society at large (a debate that will surely rage as long as we have societies at
all) as well as whether declining religious affiliation means similarly declining belief in God (answer: it really depends on how you ask the question and
how you define terms like "God").

But theological debates aside, the decline in religious affiliation in
America could be good news for chaplains, religious, and secular alike.
*People are disaffiliating, after all, but it is not because they do not want sup-
port, care, and meaning in their lives.* In fact, demand for such care has
skyrocketed. US and western society generally are more isolated and isolating than ever, and this is dangerous. Solitary rats will take nineteen times
more morphine (lab heroin) than rats living in a rat park with their friends.
Loneliness has been shown to be as big or bigger a factor than *medicine* in
recovery from stroke and heart disease. Men in Sardinian villages are ten
times more likely to live past one hundred—because they are not lonely. The
lack of close friendship has reached such epidemic proportions that Great
Britain recently established a Minister for Loneliness, to address its more
than nine million chronically lonely citizens.

Atheists, agnostics, and allies are not only among the fastest growing
population groups in this country, they are also among the most socially isolated, though they have got plenty of "company" in that category, from lonely
people who say they are religious or spiritual. In other words: Humanity is on
course to dramatically, almost exponentially increase its need for the human
connection that comes from the kind of well-trained and well-supervised
support, care, and meaning, that chaplains typically provide.

11. Jones et al., "Generation in Transition."

What Do Humanist Chaplains Offer?

There is far too little space here, and I do not know that I am the right person in any case, to offer any kind of how-to guide for humanist chaplaincy work. Hopefully many works of that nature will be produced in the future. For now, however, I want to offer a deeper kind of reflection on the "why" of humanist chaplaincy—not from a theological or political perspective, but as a meditation on our human potential for connectedness in a world in which we can be so disconnected from one another. It is that potential—that pregnancy with possibility—that I believe we work on when we humanist chaplains are doing our best and most important work.

A few years ago, I encountered a graduate student named Apurbo, a gifted young man in his twenties from Dhaka, Bangladesh, in Cambridge to study Computer Science. He was highly articulate and unusually emotionally aware for someone so skilled in a field often associated with cold logic and rationality. Perfectionism and the relentless pursuit of achievement (along with the completed suicide, a few years earlier, of a beloved girlfriend) had left him feeling alone in the world and unsure if there was anything that made human life worth living. He had come to me to discuss, he said, why there was so much loneliness and isolation among his fellow students, and in the United States in general.

Maybe you have heard the one, I told him, about how Eskimos have hundreds of words for snow. It may or may not actually be true, but in the Saami language spoken by people in northern Sweden, Norway and Finland, and in the northwestern-most parts of Russia, there are about one-hundred and eighty words related to snow and ice, and perhaps as many as a thousand words related to reindeer. Except whereas these rugged northern people have so many ways to speak about the experience of winter because it's so ubiquitous their lives, I have to wonder whether we modern western people have so many ways to speak about belonging and connectedness, because of how much we lack and long for it: *Community. Belonging. Mattering. Self-acceptance. Cameraderie. Usefulness. Networked. Feeling at home. Being cared about, noticed. Understood. Safety. Comfort. Taking part in something greater than ourselves.* I won't get into exactly how Apurbo responded, and indeed I have changed his name and some details about his identity in order to protect his privacy, but I will share what the fascinating conversation, which ended up continuing in various ways for a few years, brought up for me.

The alienation and despair that good and high-achieving young people regularly experience is a worthy challenge for religious and humanist chaplains alike (and may even be an excellent reason for religious and humanist chaplains to collaborate and support one another's efforts, despite theological differences), today. The chaplain's job, after all, is to help some-one whose life has been disrupted, such that they find themselves in our presence, to experience the feeling that life can offer both connection and meaning, even though we do not have the certainty or the longevity we wish we did, and whether or not we happen to believe connection and meaning come from the divine. How do humanist chaplains respond to this common but serious existential dilemma?

Whatever our response, it should start with some kind of recognition that human beings evolved from early, ape-like primates that evolved from other, earlier forms of life, over millions upon millions of years. As Carl Sagan famously pointed out, if the entire history of the universe were condensed into one of our calendar years, humanity would only have emerged on December 31, as midnight approached. Millions and millions of species preceded us here, setting the genetic stage for more of our behaviors and other aspects of our lives than we usually care to admit to ourselves. In the vast majority of pre-human species, our animal ancestors could not have survived by being loners. To anthropomorphize just a bit, ancient animals could not have imagined a fourteen-hour day in front of a screen in a cubicle at an office park, any more than they were planning on life in captivity in a cage at a zoo.

Looking at animal communities, we can see such incredible connectedness. Large groups of animals can actually be referred to, scientifically speaking, as "congregations." I like to reflect on some of the incredible photos of animal communities that one can find online: thousands of monarch butterflies, beluga whales, flamingoes, or African wildebeasts, moving in a common rhythm and a seeming ecstasy of togetherness that would put even the largest megachurch to shame. Or starlings, a stunning species of birds that fly in incredible formations, thousands collaborating at a time, sometimes looking as though they're all just one giant hummingbird. This is part of the human world, from which we humans have emerged.

One would think if we come from ants and birds and wildebeasts, a sense of connection would come naturally for human beings. And in a certain way it does: humans are certainly expert at collaborating to produce earthly achievement. Beavers never built the Hoover Dam, though MIT's students and alumni, known as "Beavers," have certainly constructed more than their fair share of such things. Ants have never erected anything as impressive as the World Trade Center, and when an anthill gets stomped out, the ants may rebuild, but nothing so ambitious as the Freedom Tower. No hive of angry wasps could ever have imagined weapons as complex or fearsome as our nuclear missiles. Bees create an extraordinary collaborative network in every hive, but it pales in comparison to the internet.

Each of these human achievements and so many more—cures for deadly diseases; agricultural techniques that allowed us to feed billions; men on the moon; a garbage removal system that actually gets our trash taken away on time, every week, every month, every year (almost)—require cooperation on an unimaginable scale, especially when we remember that in every one of our own bodies there are trillions of interconnected cells, each with a sort of agency of its own, each on some level similar to the original single celled forms of life of 3.5 billions of years ago, yet also communing with one another in the myriad ways that make us, "us," and only relatively rarely breaking down. In many ways, then, we are the spitting image of our evolutionary ancestors. Human beings represent connection and togetherness and collaboration on an unprecedented scale, at least on earth.

I have never met anyone, however, who wore glasses rose-colored enough to claim that human beings are perfectly connected creatures. We feel in our bones just as easily as we can evaluate through our social sciences, that human life can be lonely, isolating. On Hollywood Boulevard, in Piccadilly Circus, in Times Square or Red Square or Tahrir Square— in the midst of a crowd of billions, we so often feel alone. And it pains us. Why can it be so hard for us to connect? We need an answer for this question, not so much because the majority of those we help will want to discuss it with us—most will not. Rather we need an explanation for our own inevitable struggles in connecting, lest we pass on a message of despair, or hypocrisy, or some combination of both. If we are to base our helping work on the idea of connection, then we cannot afford to despair of our common ability to love and connect, even in the face of daily provocations, seemingly demonstrating the impotence of what Martin Luther King, Jr. called agape. And yet neither can we afford to forget just how disconnected good, well intentioned people can become from themselves, their loved ones, and indeed even their own humanity.

The writer and psychotherapist Alice Miller offered a profound explanation for the experience of disconnectedness among the forts of achievement-oriented people whom I tend to serve at Harvard and MIT— people who are are the products of an achievement-oriented culture. Miller highlights a catch-22 of modern life: the more we try to "escape" our evolutionary origins of connectedness and equality (along with, we fear, the *mediocrity* that comes along with it) the more we experience the terrible psychic pain that comes from cutting ourselves off from others.

In the introduction to her landmark book *The Drama of the Gifted Child,* a book I have felt compelled to recommend to my students perhaps more than any other, Miller writes,

> I sometimes ask myself whether it will ever be possible for us to grasp the extent of the loneliness and desertion to which we were exposed as children. Here I do not mean to speak, primarily, of children who were obviously uncared for or totally neglected, and who were always aware of this or at least grew up with the knowledge that it was so. Apart from these extreme cases, there are large numbers of people who enter therapy in the belief (with which they grew up) that their childhood was happy and protected.
>
> Quite often I have been faced with people who were praised and admired for their talents and their achievements, who were toilet-trained in the first year of their lives, and who may even, at the age of one and a half to five, have capably helped to take care of their younger siblings. According to prevailing attitudes, these people—the pride of their parents—should have had a strong and stable sense of self-assurance. But the case is exactly the opposite. They do well, even excellently, in everything they undertake; they are admired and envied; they are successful whenever they care to be—but behind all this lurks depression, a feeling of emptiness and self-alienation, and a sense that their life has no meaning. These dark feelings will come to the fore as soon as the drug of grandiosity fails, as soon as they are not "on top," not definitely the "superstar," or whenever they suddenly get the feeling they have failed to live up to some ideal image or have not measured up to some standard. Then they are plagued by anxiety or deep feelings of guilt and shame.
>
> What are the reasons for such disturbances in these competent, accomplished people?[12]

I think of my father as having lived his life caught in the web of social dynamics that Miller describes.

One day when he was a small boy during World War II, dad was drawing with chalk out on the stoop, surrounded by a few playmates. His father came home from work, observed the scene, and shouted at his little boy, eyes narrow and spittle flying, "where did you get that chalk?" Frozen in place, his son haltingly replied, "I . . . I bought it." "How much did you pay for it?" my grandfather shot back. "Two cents," my father told him. These were the years immediately following the great depression, and my grandfather snapped. "Don't you EVER spend two cents again without my permission!" he barked, snatching the small box containing several thin sticks of canary yellow chalk from my father's little hand. He snapped the sticks in half and threw them all in the trash for good measure. As he stomped up

---

12. Miller, *Drama of the Gifted Child,* 4–5.

the stairs and into their tenement building, his son was overcome by a fit of slow, heaving sobs, as his playmates looked down and away in silence. No wonder so many men of my father's generation were emotionally closed off, with few close friends and little trust that they could comfortably express warm love to their own children, let alone their neighbors.

This brings me back to my young student advisee, Apurbo, who had put his prestigious graduate degree at risk because he had begun to lash out in tears and anger, trolling others online and in person because he did not believe that his vulnerability and pain could possibly be received by others with anything but disdain. He had made a number of others around him, including his advisor and some of his female classmates, understandably angry. What they couldn't necessarily understand, however, was that the offensive comments he had begun to make about politics, gender, and religion were coming from an authentic place of pain and confusion, and the desire to find a way to communicate those feelings honestly in a world and especially in an academic culture that seemed to have little time for them.

My work with Apurbo, as I understood it, was to sit with him (occasionally—I am not a clinician) and help put him in a position where others could sit with him and provide a mutual safe space to process the authentic agony of existential despair, without losing track of the possibility of more positive emotional experiences. In other words, could there be a place, an environment, in which someone like Apurbo could talk about life as a whole, to hear others do the same, to laugh through tears, to be part of a murmuration, in pursuit of meaning? I do not know to this day, several years later, if I ever fully "succeeded" in my work supporting Apurbo, because through my work with him and hundreds of others like him, I found that I am limited in my ability to provide a congregational setting in which such work can take place. Congregations are just too expensive to maintain and manage, and as a parent I can no longer afford to work 80 hours a week to support one. But I take comfort in recognizing that the perfectionistic pursuit of being a helpful chaplain is itself a force of disconnection, to be avoided just as much as any other form of perfectionism. And I do know that while Apurbo has not (yet) found perfect answers to his own questions, he has bravely kept going, kept trying, kept talking, kept listening, all of which is, to my mind, not only enough but quite the point. Whether or not he goes on to fulfill the "potential" so many see in his intelligence and talent, my fondest hope is that he will continue genuinely connecting and reconnecting with others in his life, allowing his own sadness and anger and occasional hopelessness to be an opportunity to experience a sense of commonality with other human beings who experience such things too and who might even dearly value his willingness to articulate what they themselves might find too terrifying to speak out loud.

Humanism as Reclamation of Our Own Company

I was one of those "gifted children" of whom Alice Miller speaks: my father was taught that his only value as a human being lay in what he could earn, what he could do, what he could achieve. He lived his entire life believing he had not achieved enough and hating himself for it. He passed on to me the feeling that I had to achieve some kind of elusive state of greatness, not only to be worthy of his love or esteem but to redeem his life from that sense of failure he took to his death when I was a teenager. He could not express love or affection, because doing so required a kind of vulnerability he did not believe he deserved to possess. And while I learned to express myself differently than him, my inner experience was all too similar: I approached the idea of love, like so much else, as a kind of intellectual exercise where I could think about it, talk about it, research it, debate it, and even want it rather desperately, but I couldn't *feel* it because to feel love would have required me to feel loved, and that to me was something I could never quite *deserve*, no matter how much I did to try to earn the admiration of those around me.

Happily, something changed for me the day my son Axel was born in the fall of 2016. My wife ended up in back labor, with Axel's head face up in the birth canal, the back of his head jammed up against her sacrum. This resulted in an exhausting thirty-six-hour long process of delivery, culminating in painful emergency surgery that left her almost unconscious when the baby was removed from her uterus. When they took Axel out, I became self-consciously aware that I was the only parent who could see him as they went to cut the umbilical cord. I reached toward him instinctively, and he equally instinctively reached out and grabbed my index finger in his bloody fist, not letting go. And for the first moments in life, a certain combination of thoughts and feelings washed over me: here, I was encountering another human being whom I loved, without any reservation or qualification. I knew in that moment, and I still know in an almost perfect way to this day, that I would care for and treasure my son's very existence, no matter what he ever did or said or became or did not become. "Oh," I later reflected when I was able to begin to put the experience into words, "*that* is what people mean when they talk about unconditional love." Ever since, I have been re-imagining my own work (with myself and with others) as an attempt to sit with that insight and be present with it: that Axel is worthy of love, that I am worthy, you are, and we all are. And what should we do now that we know?

To me, humanist chaplains at their best are supposed to be a kind of midwife, or doula. Not to assist with the actual physical process of labor and birth, but in support of an emotional and philosophical process. Our job description is nothing more or less than to care for people who are learning to accept themselves and care for others the way I learned I could care for my son that day. In a world in which too much of human culture and religion teaches us to value one another only so far as we live up to expectations for proper belief or ability or success, we should strive to be a kind of counterweight, supporting and walking alongside people as they try to imagine living in a different way, even if only at the end of their lives.

My father never did say the words "I love you" to me, which was sad for me and even sadder, perhaps, for him. Even just those few words, stated once at the very end of his life, could have made a profound difference: they could have relieved my anxiety at not having heard them, and perhaps his at being unable to say them. More importantly, they might have opened up a moment of connection between us—one of those moments, called "peak experiences" by the humanistic psychologist Abraham Maslow, that can change the way we make meaning of our past and/or our future.

Though I did not get to have that kind of experience with my own father, I try to imagine its possibility as a reminder that every minute we are alive matters; that we can make a difference even when we are sick or weak or incapable of offering anything other than a moment of genuine humanity, of loving acknowledgement. And I try to make the emotional space for those moments with my own young son as often as I can, even if it means putting off other important work, even if that means achieving less, earning less, "doing" less of the sort of work my father and I once believed we had to do to earn the worth and dignity I now know is part of simply being born capable of love.

Team Human

This is what our students or our patients or our loved ones need from us, whatever kinds of chaplains we might be, and it is what we need for ourselves, because life is fleeting and unfair and the only thing any of us can reliably say about any of it is, "I'm here." I'm here for you, to listen in silence, and then maybe to share something of myself from that place of silence, with or without God. Recently, the author, technology ethicist, and spiritual seeker Douglas Rushkoff published a remarkable book called *Team Human*, in which he argues that even in an age where technology threatens to replace us all—religious people and humanists alike—what we need is to reassert our own common humanity, and the only way we can do so is by treating human connection as a kind of basic human right that we must continually offer and accept, defend and develop, especially in moments of pain, fear, and sadness. "We can't be alone," Rushkoff writes, "even if we wanted to. The only way to heal is by connecting to someone else."[13]

It seems to me that chaplaincy, whether humanist or religious, is ultimately no more and no less than helping others to experience themselves, in the face of whatever existential challenge that may bring them to the chaplain, as part of a team. We chaplains cannot save lives or cure illnesses any more than we can get ourselves to agree with one another about theology. But we can, in our hard-won ability to better understand our own disconnection, offer others a truly meaningful gift, even for the last time: the presence, sometimes best expressed through silence, of human caring.

13. Ruskoff, *Team Human*, 215.

10

Look for the Helpers

The Library as Sanctuary

———— NATALIE BERNSTEIN ————

Introduction

THIS CHAPTER EXPLORES THE ways that an elementary school library and the librarian help students, parents, and teachers. The space is welcoming and comforting, often a safe haven for children who are having a bad day or need a place to be calm—the solace of silence. It is also a space with a librarian who can provide help for curious, puzzled children seeking answers to their questions. Parents and teachers also drop in to read, work, and ask for help. The space, the librarian, as well as the children and the adults who use the library all work together in an organic way. Regularly scheduled classes of children from ages five through twelve visit the library for lessons in small groups, which allows for focused discussion on a wide variety of topics, ranging from cyber bullying to human sexuality to mindfulness. The relationship between the librarian and individual library users can be surprisingly intimate, with individual consultations about choosing a book that sometimes develop into personal confessions of fears ("Will I ever be a good reader?"; "How can I help my child become a better student?") and pain ("I'm having friendship troubles"). The subject areas that the library offers is wide-ranging, encompassing all learning, in many formats. At the heart of the library program, however, are books—especially stories—that create connections to personal experiences, deepen our understanding of the interior lives of others, help solve problems, build resilience, and, ultimately, nurture compassion. One sixth-grade girl wrote a note at the end of the year, saying "Thank you for this year. I didn't like reading before. I now feel like I *am* the person in the book. Thank you for opening my heart to books."

Sanctuary: The Librarian, Books, and Children

A six-year-old boy marched purposefully into the elementary school library. He was on a mission. "Where's the snake section?" he asked. I walked with him to the shelves, asking if he wanted information about a particular kind of snake. "No," he replied, "I just need to know how snakes mate." As an elementary school librarian at an independent school in Atlanta for twenty-five years, I have had the opportunity to help children in unexpected ways. Elementary school libraries are all different, and each reflects the culture of its school. The job involves mentoring teachers, developing curriculum and the collection, providing leadership in technology, managing circulation, programming special events, and being knowledgeable about children's reading development and children's literature. People occasionally question the need for a library when online sources can get us what we need at our doorstep. The library is more than a room filled with books; the library offers a real person, a librarian who listens intently, working to forge connections and create a sense of possibility for others. Here, I will focus on the personal and deeply meaningful interactions that have been the heart of my work as a school librarian as I share my emotional investment in the power of books to help readers. The books still move in and out of the library, and they move us. They nourish the entire community in ways we can never anticipate: they provide information, they build community when shared as a group, and they offer help to individuals confronting a dizzying array of problems and questions.

Most school libraries offer classes for children during the school day. These classes include instruction in research skills and cyber ethics. At the heart of my library program, however, is a focus on reading. When I read aloud to a group, I model my own thinking. I remind children that no one, including adults, is a perfect reader. We all get confused, and we all have to back up and re-read. I emphasize that a book is not about helping you become a better reader in the future; it is about speaking to you *now*. These conversations lead children to share their thinking and vulnerabilities, and here, I have offered reassurance. My goal is to create a culture of reading, where children read and adults share books with children, not to improve their standardized test scores but to enter into the lives of others and thus deepen our capacity for empathy. The most powerful moments of my work are when children share their own thinking: "I feel so sorry for her. I wish her mother was still alive."

One of the central themes that I highlight is the idea of *windows* and *mirrors*. We all look for ourselves in books, seeking a character that is just like us. It takes intentional work to make sure that the library collection is truly diverse. I share stories about social justice, immigration, ethics, families, moral justice, and LGBTIQ+ identities. I remember holding up the book *Amazing Grace* by Mary Hoffman, a story about a young African-American girl who wants to play the role of a white boy in a school play. A kindergarten girl shrieked, "Oh! Oh! She looks like me!" She had a mirror experience with a character. But we also need books that offer windows into the lives of others who are different. Learning to see the world from the perspective of another person has profound implications for prejudice, aggression, and empathy. A child who reads avidly is a child who gets into the consciousness of hundreds of characters; this is a child who understands what it is to be the excluded one, the shy one, the grieving one, or the hungry one. These readers may be the children who find the courage to stand up for victims and confront injustice, become less quick to judge, and more confident in entering conversations on civil and human rights. This has been my role at the library at its most profound level.

Because I have a sense of a library as a sanctuary, every year I share books with groups of children that affirm the place of the library and the librarian in our society. Many memoirs and autobiographies attest to the impact that a library had on a child, from novelist Richard Wright to Supreme Court Justice Sonia Sotomayor. Here are a few of my favorite picture books that I share aloud with children from ages five to twelve: *Ron's Big Mission* by Rose Blue. I open by noting that this book is the true story about a boy named Ron. As a nine-year old in the 1950s, he visited his local public library frequently in South Carolina to pore over books on airplanes and flight. He finally asked to borrow them but was told that only white library patrons could borrow books. He literally stood on the checkout counter and insisted on his right to check books out. The desk clerk called the police who told him the rules. Ron declared, "It's wrong. The rules are not fair. Why can't I check out books like everyone else?"[1] Mrs. Scott, the librarian, knew what she had to do: she went into her office and printed a library card for Ron. That boy was Ron McNair, who realized his dream: he checked out library books and he became an astronaut. Ron was aboard the space shuttle *Challenger* when it exploded in 1986. That same library is now dedicated to Ronald McNair. I wonder aloud, "Would I be like that librarian and do

---

1. Blue, *Ron's Big Mission*, n.p.

the right thing, even if the police told me not to?" We talk about our own opportunities to be brave, on the playground, in the classroom and in our homes. A book like this one, one that fosters the notion of civic participation, leads children to wonder aloud, "Could I ever be that brave? Would I stand up for what was right?"

Picture books that I share aloud prompt responses that help enrich children's moral development such as *A Bike Like Sergio's*, by Maribeth Boelts. I start by asking, "Was there ever something you really wanted? You ached for that thing? I remember desperately wanting something. Do you remember that feeling?" Lots of children nod as I begin reading aloud. A little boy, longing for a bicycle that his family can't afford, scoops up a dollar that has fluttered from a woman's purse in a store. At home, he realizes it's a one-hundred-dollar bill. What should he do? We ponder together the conclusion: the little boy finds the woman and returns her money. A conversation among seven and eight-year olds reveals the range of their thinking. For instance, one boy, Terence, exclaimed, "What an idiot! He could have had that bike! I can't believe he just gave the money back. He doesn't even know her. I would have kept the money." Another child, Charles, responded, "He did the right thing. But I think it was hard. I think his parents should buy him a bike." This was followed by Marcello's objection, "But remember, they can't afford it." A girl, Lenore, reflected, "Last year I found two dollars on the sidewalk. I told my teachers. They told me it was probably some other kid's money. And that I had a choice. I could keep it, since I found it, or I could give it to them. So I kept the money. But that was last year. This year I think I would give it to the teachers so somebody could get lunch." A first grader in another class insisted on sharing what she wanted most in the world, what she aches for most: "I want my Uncle Milton back. But we can't buy that with money because he died."

Other books help children make sense of troubling current news they may hear or read, stories about immigrant families who are rejected by, or welcomed to, the United States. *Dreamers* by Yuyi Morales is a poetic, autobiographical immigration story of a young mother and her infant who arrive in the United States, bewildered and frightened. At the public library, they find "a place we had never seen before. . . . Improbable. Unbelievable. Surprising. Unimaginable. Where we didn't need to speak, we only needed to trust. And we did! Books became our language. Books became our home. Books became our lives."[2] As classes talk about this book, they ask questions about recent news. They are distressed by stories of families, especially children, who are escaping violence and poverty in

2. Morales, *Dreamers*, n.p.

their home countries and seeking refuge in the United States. Children have borrowed this one, and others like it, and the connection between the library and home deepens as the books help parents frame stories that connect with both historical and current events. The students are full of indignation and sympathy: "I heard that little kids are in cages. That makes me scared for them. And it makes me so mad." "I wish everyone could be safe. It would be so hard to have to leave my home."

As with stories of refugees, I use books that help us tackle difficult topics together that children might not talk about at home. Such books help them see that they are not alone with their worries, pain, and loneliness. I share books with children in an effort to be inclusive to all kinds of families. Children live in a variety of family constellations: What's it like to grow up living with grandparents? What's it like to have two moms? Two dads? Young children are sometimes worried by the idea of divorce and struggle with terms like stepmother and stepfather. One simple picture book, *The Ring Bearer,* by Floyd Cooper, prompted responses from kindergarteners. In the story, a little boy is excited but nervous to be the ring bearer at his mother's wedding. "I was a flower girl!" exclaimed one child. Another asked, "Is her husband dead?" When one child noted, "My parents are divorced," several heads nodded in recognition. One little girl announced, "But stepmothers are evil!" and a little boy cheerfully replied, "No they're not. I have a stepmother, and she loves me so much!"

Some of the richest conversations in the classes have emerged after I share books on LGBTIQ+ topics. One of my favorites is the true story of two male penguins that hatch an egg at New York's Central Park Zoo, *And Tango Makes Three* by Peter Parnell and Justin Richardson. With young children, our discussion is simply all about families. With sixth graders, I trace the history of how people demanded that it be removed from American libraries because they objected to its positive treatment of homosexuality. I often do thematic book talks that include novels featuring gay, lesbian and transgender characters. A sixth-grade boy shared this memory:

> I was leaving summer camp and someone told me that my moms were here to pick me up. Another kid said, "Whoa, you have two moms? That's weird." But I felt good and I was so happy when I realized other boys were literally standing beside and behind me and one of them said, "No man, it's not weird," and the kid who said it just got very quiet and moved on. It was what you told us that Martin Luther King said: "What we will remember most is not the words of our enemies but the silence

of our friends." It's like what you said—we can be allies, standing up with somebody when we hear something mean.[3]

In recent years, there have been more children's books that deal with gender fluidity and include transgender characters. I shared the very simple picture book, *Julián Is a Mermaid* by Jessica Love with all the grades. In the youngest groups, we just talked about how there is no such thing as a boy color or a girl color, a toy that is just for boys or just for girls: anybody can wear anything they like, play with any toy and grow up to do any kind of job.

With the upper elementary classes, I included the word *transgender* and was struck by how much they already knew, from television, books, and social media. Their responses were full of both outrage and compassion. One sixth-grade girl burst out, "Halloween costumes! Why do girls have to be fairies or worse, be sexy, instead of being scary and fierce?" A fifth-grade girl chimed in, "I like dragons. I hate Target. The girls' aisle has pink dragons with *butterfly wings* that blow bubbles, while the boys' aisle has all the great, powerful, scaly fire-breathing dragons." A fifth-grade boy cited a common experience: "At my old school, if I said I liked a guy, they would make fun of me and say I was gay. I'm not gay but they made everybody feel like it would be a terrible thing." I was very careful when I responded to a reflection from a sixth-grade girl: "I think I disagree with my church. My church said that God made girls and boys . . . and that boys can't marry boys and girls can't marry girls." I needed to be respectful of her church and family values and I offered a possibility: "I don't know your church, but every church I know of, in fact every religion I've ever learned about, has as its central belief the idea of loving one another and being kind. So you have to figure out what the big message is, and what your own loving heart tells you is most important." She gave me a big smile and a nod.

The discussion continued with several classes, again centering on a national conversation about gender. One sixth grade boy noted, "I heard they are kicking transgender people out of the military," and another questioned, "What? They're ready to fight for our country and people say they're not good enough?" Finally, another sixth-grade boy, one who had never spoken up in library class, shyly offered, "I talked to my brother about this. I heard that teens who are transgender kill themselves a lot. It kills me that they do that. And it's probably because people are so mean to them." I was moved by the level of empathy they demonstrated as well as their critical thinking that contributes to social justice and the transformation of society. A parent who was nearby later said to me, simply, "You are saving lives."

---

3. Sixth-grade boy shared these comments with me.

The library is a physical space offering resources, quiet, comfort, and reassurance. My individual encounters with children over the years have been some of the most intimate, meaningful events not just of my career, but also of my life. Children come into the library just to have a quiet space to think or wander. One year, Katrina, a fifth grader, quietly slipped in each morning. I would smile and ask briefly if she wanted help or if she just wanted to browse. "I'll just browse, thanks." I realized that she was seeking the quiet of the library while her class gathered in the hall outside their classroom, waiting for the teachers to open the door. Many of her classmates enjoyed socializing during that time. Katrina did not quite know how to navigate that crowd. Like Katrina, there are always children who come to the library during recess. Recess can be like a big cocktail party. What if no one includes you? They are free to come to the library, browse, read and ask for help. The library is always open, welcoming and unthreatening. There is no grade, no score.

It never occurred to me when I started this work of connecting the books and children that the children also would create moments that transform me. Sometimes children notice my own reactions to books and come up to comfort me. I read aloud *Thank You, Mr. Falker* by Patricia Polacco, the picture book of a little girl who struggled to learn to read until a wise teacher figured out how to help her:

> The little girl learned to love school. I know because that little girl was me, Patricia Polacco. I saw Mr. Falker again some thirty years later at a wedding. I walked up to him and introduced myself. At first, he had difficulty placing me. Then I told him who I was and how he had changed my life so many years ago. He hugged me and asked me what I did for a living. "Why, Mr. Falker," I answered. "I make books for children. . . . Thank you, Mr. Falker. Thank you."[4]

This story brings me to tears every time. I sometimes hold the book up in front of my face, so the students do not see how overcome I am. But they hear it in my voice and they come and pat my shoulder; they offer reassurance and tell me that they sometimes cry too.

With sixth graders, I often wrap up the year by talking about the picture book, *Where the Wild Things Are* by Maurice Sendak. Max, a young boy, becomes furious at his mother and takes an imaginary journey to an island filled with monsters where he can dominate them all. This voyage of exploration, anger, and craving for power can be seen as a metaphor for European colonization, overpowering island inhabitants who are seen as

4. Polacco, *Thank You, Mr. Falker*, n.p.

less than human or at least uncivilized. Sendak, who grew up in a Yiddish speaking home in Brooklyn, once noted that the monsters were actually inspired by older aunts and uncles who came to visit, would pinch his cheeks and say, "I want to eat you up!" The relatives may have meant this in a loving way but it was frightening for a young boy, who was at some level aware that relatives in this immigrant family lost their lives in the Holocaust.[5] All children, like Max, get mad at their parents, but not all cultures allow children to act out their anger. In fact, Max is banished to his bedroom because he has violated the behavior expectations of his community. Like Max, children have inner monsters to which they can learn to say "no," and all of us long for forgiveness and nourishment.

I am surprised, over and over, by poignant moments in my encounters with children and adults. As a conclusion to this section of my paper, I share a few memories. One fifth-grade girl returned a book I had recommended and told me, privately, "I liked this book. Sometimes I have friendship troubles." I gave her more friendship novels. Later, she gave me a draft of her own novel, in which a girl with friendship troubles finds comfort with her librarian and just being in the library. For these children, it is a space of safety and comfort. Once I shared the library's sex education books with fifth and sixth graders, noting that the information in them is accurate. I told them that lots of young people run into pornography online and it shapes their notion of human sexuality in an unhealthy way. A sixth-grade girl asked if she could talk to me privately in my office: "I've seen pornography online. I'm scared. You said if you look at lots of it, you might have trouble growing up to be a sexually healthy adult. I'm afraid I won't be normal. I'm afraid it's too late for me." I was able to reassure her, and she borrowed one of the books, a safe resource. One day, I found seven-year-old Nathaniel intently poring over a big nonfiction book, *The Human Body*. I commented to him, "Oh, I see you are curious about the human body. Glad you found it!" and he replied, "I am reading it because I want to grow up to be a doctor so that I can help my dad get well." His father, I later learned, had a brain tumor. So, I bought more human body and brain books and made sure that they were on display whenever Nathaniel's class was due to come to in. The library was a comforting space that could speak to his needs because of books on display.

Sanctuary: The Librarian, Books, and Parents

One of my roles as an elementary school librarian is to try to help anyone who comes in the door, including parents. Once, during a two-week period,

5. Silverman, "Sendak's Legacy."

I talked to parents and gave them materials to help an eight-year-old who struggled with reading, a nine-year-old facing surgery for a brain tumor, an eleven-year-old whose parents were getting divorced, and a six-year-old whose father was going into hospice. My office, a sanctuary within a sanctuary, is the perfect spot to talk with parents. Once I even made an alphabetical list of subjects that parents come to talk to me about: adoption, anxiety, bullying, cancer, depression, divorce, dyslexia, death, eating disorders, friendships, guns . . . nightmares, obsessions, perfectionism. . . . I offer sympathy in the form of a concrete object—a book—featuring characters who struggle but are resilient. It is deeply moving to talk to adults who are utterly in love with their children but struggling to help them. They seem as vulnerable as their children.

Another hard topic that children are sometimes reluctant or frightened to talk about is death. Their parents struggle with these conversations and often come to the library to ask for books about death, most commonly because of the recent loss of a pet. But I believe it is important to share those kinds of books when there is no immediate death: they allow us to do the mental rehearsal of what it will be like when we do encounter loss, and how we can recover through the grieving process. One of my favorites to share with both parents and children is *Jasper's Day* by Marjorie Blain Parker, in which a family spends a whole day with their dying dog, visiting favorite spots and remembering Jasper as a puppy. After the final trip to the vet, the father returns home with Jasper's body. The little boy cries but also decides to make a memory book of Jasper. At the end, I ask children if they have ever lost a loved one. I took a practice from my synagogue, in which I invite anyone to say the name of the loved one and their relationship: "Scotty, my dog." "Goldie, my fish." I put tissues out and they are used. Parents tell me that they use the story to help children with a dying pet and feel relief as they guide them.

A father, married to a man, needed resources. "How do I talk to my ten-year old daughter about sex?" I handed him one of my favorites, *It's Perfectly Normal: A Book About Changing Bodies, Growing Up, Sex and Sexual Health* by Robie Harris. He came back a few months later with a very late book: his daughter had hidden it after they read some of it together, laughing about the shy little bee and the wacky, outspoken bird. He realized she had been privately reading and re-reading it. We both wished we had had a book like that when we were young.

I also work with parents who insist on pushing their children to read more advanced books. One little boy came in with a slip of paper; on it was written, in adult handwriting, *Tom Sawyer*. He looked disappointed and admitted, "But all I really want is books with little talking animals." Autonomy of choice, I tell parents, builds readers, because children can choose books not only to meet their personal tastes but also to address their longings.

A parent once told me that her eight-year-old son was in the hospital for surgery. The doctor asked, "So what's your favorite subject at school?" The parent was surprised when the child responded, "Well, you might not think of it as a subject, but my favorite subject is library." The doctor was surprised and asked him why. "Because I get to check out *Garfield*. *Garfield* always makes me laugh." I handed *Garfield* to the third grader who said to me, "I'm not a good reader. It makes me sad because I want my parents to think I am smart like them." That child later made his parents laugh with something he carried home—and he comes back often for more *Garfield*.

I have posted a weekly blog since 2009 to encourage parents to share books with their children, and to alert them to things that children are concerned about but might not talk about at home. One blog post told the story of how a parent picked up a bookmark, one I had made with silly jokes. This parent took the Halloween bookmark to the hospital where she works as a nurse. She gave it to a little boy who was waiting for a heart transplant. They read the bookmark jokes together and laughed. Word spread on the hospital floor, as hospital personnel, including janitors and surgeons, stopped by so that this seven-year-old could ask them, "Why didn't the mummy have any friends?" "He was too wrapped up in himself." The nurse told me that later got his heart and was happy to head home, carrying the bookmark with him.

In 2017, I invited children's illustrator Bryan Collier to visit with all the classes. One parent heard him read aloud Daniel Beaty's book, *Knock Knock: My Dad's Dream for Me*. In the story, a young boy wakes up one morning to find his beloved father gone. The child feels lost, but his father has left him a letter filled with advice to guide him. The story is richly illustrated, moving from bright, colorful collages to dark, torn layers and ending with hope as the little boy grows up and gives his own young children advice. The parent was overcome, left in tears, and then sent me this email:

> My emotions are flowing at this time. When Bryan Collier re-
> cited *Knock Knock* my own daddy issues of abandonment came
> to full surface. To hear the story of the boy wondering, I was
> immediately a little three-year-old wrapped up in family fables,
> court dates, a wedding, a new man to call daddy . . . with years of
> therapy, of repair. I was abandoned. I was told "why" but never
> by the man. He died before I became a woman strong enough
> to ask the why to him directly. . . . I got to be the little girl that
> hears an important person, a famous person, a big person tell
> her story and make it real. As parents, we want to make our

children feel okay when they hurt. As people sometimes what
we really need is just to be heard. I feel heard. I love what you do.
You are the thread between all of the books. You knit us together
into smaller groups, into tighter circles, into safe places. Your
gift of books is so vast. I imagine even you don't know quite how
far your reach truly is. You have gifted so many children today
and so many days. Today, I was the lucky child. I am so grateful
that my children will always have you in their minds. But today,
for a moment you healed me. . . . I feel heard. I love what you do.
I am so grateful to you. I hope you can bask in the glow this day
and every day. I am better in this world for knowing you.

I only hope that everyone, once in a career, gets a note like this. It is both unexpected but affirming that the reach of the library—and the librarian—can
affect a parent so profoundly!

Sanctuary: Librarian, Books, and Teachers

The library serves teachers in the community as well. In a society that often
questions what teachers are worth—for example, their low salaries—teachers are often vulnerable. They worry that they will not measure up and that
they will be evaluated solely on student test scores. The library is a safe,
nonjudgmental space where they can seek help. I talk privately with teachers, once again in the sanctuary of my office, about individual children and
their struggles in order to help them work together so that the child can
find reading success. Together we pull an assortment of books that the child
can explore in the classroom, tailored to that child's personal interests and
experiences. I work with teachers who are grappling with hard topics such
as how to teach about the history of slavery in America, the Holocaust, immigration, and climate change. These conversations are often emotional as
teachers share their doubts. I pull books that emphasize courage, optimism,
and solidarity—acting as an ally to help others.

Conclusion: Sanctuary as a Place
to Inspire Future Helpers

For the children I teach, I feel like I am the personal representative of the
consciousness of thousands of authors. I love looking at the faces of second
graders when I read aloud *The Story of Ruby Bridges* by Robert Coles. A
six-year-old, the first black child to attend her elementary school, had to be
accompanied to school each day by armed federal marshals because all the
white parents had withdrawn their children and many of them gathered on

the sidewalk each morning to scream at her. She was the only child in her class, alone with her teacher, for months. One morning, Ruby paused, even though the marshals urged her forward. When her teacher asked her why she had stopped to talk to the crowd, Ruby replied that she didn't talk to them. She just paused to repeat the prayer she said daily,

> Please, God, try to forgive these people.
> Because even if they say those bad things,
> They don't know what they're doing.[6]

Books are where we can turn when terrible things happen: they can give us a scaffolding around which to build a conversation and form connections. I will never forget the words of Mr. Rogers after the terrorist attacks of September 11, 2001:

> For me, as for all children, the world could have come to seem a scary place to live. But I felt secure with my parents, and they let me know that we were safely together whenever I showed concern about accounts of alarming events in the world. There was something else my mother did that I've always remembered: "Always look for the helpers," she'd tell me. "There's always someone who is trying to help." I did, and I came to see that the world is full of doctors and nurses, police and firemen, volunteers, neighbors and friends who are ready to jump in to help when things go wrong.[7]

I remind children, year after year, to look for the helpers. The helpers always come. The books in the library are full of stories of helpers. Children, too, can be helpers: when someone falls on the stairs, when someone forgot to pack a lunch, and when someone is being taunted or excluded. I am a librarian because I want to be one of the helpers too.

I have taught parents, teachers and children about the profound spiritual possibilities of books and stories, helping the community tell their stories to each other, and sharing my own responses to the stories. I work to build an environment of mutuality, trust, care and the wisdom to grow together. I work to help children have agency in their desire to learn, to cultivate interests, and to be vulnerable and loved. Many children at The Paideia School have learned to love reading because of the personal, intimate connection with the library and the librarian. I have walked with children and adults in their spiritual journey. I have helped them, and they have helped me.

---

6. Coles, *Story of Ruby Bridges,* n.p.

7. Rogers quoted in Mikkelson, "Fred Rogers—Look for the Helpers."

11

Intentional Rhythms and Organic Rituals

Urban Recipe as a Model of Care

————— JEREMY LEWIS —————

RHYTHMS AND ROUTINES HAVE a tremendous impact on our lives in the formation of who we are and who we continue to become. Activities of the day tend to be ritualistic. Individuals may arise at the same time each day, mindlessly consume the morning coffee, absorb the news from the previous day, shower and dress, and perform the required obligations of the day. Such rituals and routines eventually migrate into a workable rhythm in life. In much the same way, the care we give and the care we receive also takes place in the context of the ritual of life. These experiences have the possibility of becoming a workable rhythm in our lives and in the lives of individuals whom we meet. In this chapter, I explore the relationships formed—and the rituals established—at a food cooperative in the Atlanta area called Urban Recipe. I share the story of Karen's relationship with her co-op: how the relationship has been shaped and formed by the co-op, and how in turn, her co-op and organization have ultimately been changed. The spiritual care expressed in this co-op model provide helpful insights into the importance of how a shared need (food), patience, and relationships play in the dynamic care expressed by the co-op model. This particular care story that I share offers hope and encouragement to those who find themselves in an Urban Recipe Food Co-op, but also to those seeking to experience the meaningful positive by-products of life in community. The care provided is not expected or required. It truly comes, most appropriately, out of relationship.

Urban Recipe's co-op model has developed over the last twenty-eight years into what it is today. The model was originally launched and practiced by a United Methodist church in Tampa, Florida. This particular co-op did not last for very long. Fortunately, in the short period of time it was in operation, they created a manual for people who were interested in starting a similar model in their own community. An employee at the Atlanta Community Food Bank found out about the model and shared the manual with the Urban Recipe founder, Chad Hale, who was the pastor of Georgia Avenue Church at the time. The church had been seeking to find a different way to provide more food to their neighbors in need and to do so in a way that placed a great deal of value on the dignity and respect people deserve. Urban Recipe co-ops meet every other week throughout the year and are made up of up to fifty families in each co-op. The food co-ops are an alternative to food pantries and have the goal of creating food security for low income families. The amount of food that families receive creates abundance and allows families to move away from scarcity and "just getting by." As of 2018, a family of four will receive over six thousand dollars' worth of meals in a year.

History of Urban Recipe & Karen

I came to visit Urban Recipe as part of a class trip while working towards a Master of Divinity at the Candler School of Theology, Emory University. On the first trip, I was deeply moved by what I observed and how it contrasted with what I had seen in other settings that provided food to people in need. Every aspect of the visit raised questions of intrigue for me. I loved the power and agency that the co-op members exhibited and how they were in control of food distribution. There did not seem to be a false expectation that everything should run smoothly for the visitors, nor was there a need to put on a demonstration. The co-op meeting was authentic. The people were being real with each other, because they were among peers and friends. As an outsider, I felt challenged in relating to parts of their story, but the co-op members were a community of people who struggled with similar challenges. They supported and understood one another.

I decided to come back unannounced several times to observe the co-op in-action and to check to make sure people were not just putting on a performance for the visitors. Each trip was authentic and uniquely wonderful; and this authenticity continues to this day. Not too long ago, during a visit from a group of out-of-town people, a co-op argument started between two members. This was not rehearsed or planned but the co-op leadership responded as they always do. They worked through it and figured out a way for the co-op meeting to continue and for the members on each side of the confrontation to be able to continue. There is never a show for anyone. This is the reality of a good community: engaging in conflicts and working towards mutual understanding, communication, and care. I was so inspired by this model and its process that I applied and was chosen to be Urban Recipe's second Executive Director. I believe in—and want to help support—a model of creating food security in our communities that builds on this mutuality of care.

One individual who stands out is Karen. She was a larger than life figure in more ways than one. Upon first encounter, Karen appeared loud, stylish, and bossy; when she entered a room, everyone knew it. She had been a co-op member for about three years already when I started working at Urban Recipe. After getting to know her a little better, a different side to her personality began to emerge. She arrived on time or within minutes to the co-op meetings; helped out, usually in the kitchen as a hospitality helper; and demonstrated commitment, rarely missing a meeting.

However, it was not until Urban Recipe encountered a serious crisis that I learned more of Karen's story. On this particular occasion, all the co-ops came together to hear the news that Urban Recipe might be closing due to a lack of funds. Hearing the rather disturbing news, members began to respond openly. After a few co-op members shared words of encouragement and gratitude, Karen stepped forward and began to share from her heart. She explained to the group how she initially came to the co-op because she needed the food. Because she had been hurt by others over the years, she did not trust other people. In addition, Karen also did not trust God. Due to the lack of trust, Karen's method of survival involved getting in and getting out with her food as quickly as possible. As tears began to well up in her eyes, she related how the co-op had changed her over the years, something she did not think was possible at her age. She had grown to love her co-op family and expressed gratitude to them for loving her, even when she was hard to love. At this point, I scanned the room and noticed how moved many of the co-op members were to hear this story. Karen rarely spoke and certainly was not a source of encouragement when she did speak. On this day however, possibly, by the fact this co-op community might be coming to a conclusion, she was bearing her heart. Karen continued to share in her now shaky voice, that over these last few years, she had also begun to trust God a little. She was clear that this was just a start and she was tip–toeing into this "trust thing" again. After Karen sat down, she continued to listen as others shared their reflections on the co-op. It was a powerful day, filled with crying and singing and even an impromptu offering to try to save Urban Recipe and their co-op. Such a generous day on so many levels!

There is a happy ending to this story. Urban Recipe received two generous gifts that allowed us to continue. The co-ops resumed and everything seemed to be back to normal a few months after the crisis had passed. Everything was normal except that, now, Karen was behaving differently than before. Something had happened since sharing her heart during the co-op meeting that day. Now Karen seemed to have a constant smile on her face, walking around with her music blaring and with almost a skip of joy in her step. In addition to continuing to help in the hospitality area of the co-op, Karen began to be more involved in the general operation of the co-op. She took it upon herself to now welcome new members and make them feel at home. Something, indeed, had changed. The rhythm of Karen's life had changed!

Urban Recipe Co-op Structure

The Urban Recipe cooperative structure plays an important role in laying the foundation for the care that members receive and the manner in which members participate with other members. Before joining the cooperative, members must agree to a set of guidelines that have been developed over the twenty-eight years the program has been in existence. Individuals volunteer to join the co-op. They are not pressured or coerced to join, and that is an important and foundational principle of membership and participation in the co-op. Individuals receive many benefits by participating in the co-op activities. How much a person chooses to participate, however, is a personal choice.

Individuals know the time and location of their co-op meeting, and I have noticed a rhythm that develops over the months and years that someone is a member of the co-op. Over the course of the two–hour co-op distribution and meeting, taking place every other week, there are rituals that hold the space for collective care to occur. A typical person arrives about ten to fifteen minutes before the food distribution portion of the co-op activities commence. During that time, the individual may visit with another co-op member or even start helping to set up the room where the meeting takes place. Once the meeting officially starts and the truck carrying the food arrives, the members begin to assume their responsibilities. Individuals discern where their strengths are and then join in to complete the tasks of unloading the truck, as well as in the sorting and distributing of food, based on family size.

Of course, people do not necessarily engage in spiritual care for one another right away or every time they meet. A some-what predictable pattern of easing into getting to know each other occurs as individuals take on a co-op task together, share individual concerns, and then over time, begin to provide care. The care provided is not expected or required. It truly comes, most appropriately, out of relationship. Often the care comes in small ways. For example, a person may help another individual with a place to sit, knowing that the person is tired from staying up all night with a sick child. Another person may share a funny story when noticing that a fellow co-op member seems a little depressed or down. There are times when that care can also cause the entire meeting to stop while the group spontaneously, and without coercion, decides to take a moment to pray for a member of a family who is struggling with a particular concern. The immediate response of the co-op is impressive. While the care is not forced, it *is* rehearsed. These co-ops rehearse helping each other, working through disagreements, celebrating birthdays, attending funerals, and doing so much more—on a bi-weekly basis—which can last for years. For this radical form of spiritual care to thrive, communities need such an intentional and consistent rhythm of care.

Organic Care

It is in this communal environment that the ritual of hospitality and care leads to individual transformation and group formation. That formation is not prescribed or based on a set of guidelines or expectations from a book or a counselor. Such formation happens as the co-op members help each other. Through this process, they grow their relationships with one another. They are in service to and with one another. The care expressed in this setting reminds me of the interdependence and interrelatedness present in the mycorrhizal fungal network in the Pacific Northwest, said to be the largest living organism on the planet. Because of this amazing fungal network, trees in this section of the Pacific Northwest are able to share resources with each other to help trees survive when there is a drought or a forest fire. The trees are able to support the growth of a small baby tree, even when the canopy is so thick that getting the sunlight the small tree needs is virtually impossible. The trees thrive, however, because of their interdependence. If each of these trees was to stand alone, it would not survive. Even the weakest of trees is able to share its resources to help other trees survive. Every single tree is valued as an integral contributor to the survival of the entire fungal network.

I have observed similar powers of individual formation towards the strength of the community in the Urban Recipe co-ops. Every single person is valued and has to contribute in some way (whether it is active or not). The more interdependent the co-ops are, the more successful I have witnessed their growth. The sharing, caring, and living that takes place is transformational for everyone. Over 86 percent of the members share food with their neighbors (those who are not officially a part of the co-op). The fungal network and the co-ops are not anomalies. They are affirmations of the way the earth and humanity are meant to co-exist. Such similarities of the need for interdependence of people and nature are living testimony that we need to be in right relationship.

As the co-op continues to meet, members and their co-ops grow in the capacity it has to care for its members. The members' formation and change leads to the co-op's transformation and change. In this way, each co-op is unique and different based on the make-up of the membership. Some co-ops spend more time on holiday celebrations, some co-ops share meals with each other more regularly than others, and still other co-ops are more focused on creating support groups for their members. The unique qualities of each co-op are a natural by-product of the personalities of the members in each co-op. It is beautiful to watch this process emerge and morph over time—and as members come and go.

The co-op presents an alternative view of what spiritual care can and should look like in the context of community. Spiritual communities can learn a great deal from the co-op model. For example, in my Christian church community, ministerial staff have responsibilities to take the lead in the care of the needs in the fellowship. The size of the congregation determines how many staff and the assignments of the staff. A small congregation may only have one minister and they may assume all responsibility for care. As the size of the congregation increases, so the staff increases. Larger churches may have one staff person whose only responsibility is counseling, while another person is responsible for hospital visitation. Still other larger congregations may train lay persons in the church to be sensitive to the needs of the congregants. This is in stark contrast to the model discussed in this chapter. The care that each person needs and receives in the co-op occurs because of the community that has been shaped by a collective commitment and experience. Because there is a shared need around food at Urban Recipe, there is an increased likelihood that people will remain committed in spite of challenges they may encounter in the group or with individual personalities. Hence, food insecurity may initially be the reason a family might join a food co-op. Food becomes a resource that creates enough adhesiveness to the structure for community and relationships to form.

The special care that occurs in the co-op context takes place because people keep showing up to the co-op, in spite of the numerous obstacles that occur. These obstacles include personality clashes, transportation challenges, as well as normal situations of daily life. Individuals continue to be involved because there is a need for food that supersedes their need to just survive the day without being challenged or offended. I am not suggesting being offended is a good thing. I am suggesting that often, our desire to outsource or professionalize our care results in individuals missing out on the relationships that can be forged *in the midst* of adversity. Often, when a challenge surfaces, individuals choose an easier path to move on and thus by-pass the work that is necessary in developing deep relationships. Once that decision becomes the pattern in one's life, it becomes harder and harder to receive care from the community.

Conclusion

Prior to—and after—joining the co-op, individuals face the challenges involved in developing relationships. Not every co-op family is the paragon of relationship-building and care. Individuals come to the co-op from a variety of experiences and therefore their contribution to the co-op varies. The structure of the co-op creates the unique atmosphere where this radical form of spiritual care thrives. It is a place where the uniqueness of each individual can find a place to be expressed.

Urban Recipe co-op members have cultivated a model of spiritual care that can be described as radical communal love. Here are some of the key rhythms of each co-op:

1. *Shared experience*—Urban Recipe Co-ops are full of people who are from similar backgrounds and common life experiences and therefore the foundation of their relationship is based on some sense of a shared experience. For one, all the members have an expressed need for food. There may be many other commonalities, but at least, there is one need that is known among the co-op members. This has significant implications in the way in which co-op members can relate to one another. Members feel more empowered to be who they are, rather than how someone else expects them to be. In the meeting, there is usually one staff member from Urban Recipe, the co-op coordinator, but otherwise, the co-op is made up solely of co-op members, who share this common need.

2. *Voluntary sharing*—Urban Recipe Co-ops do not require a person to share or disclose anything about their personal or professional status or situation. If individual co-op members wish to share, they are encouraged to do so, within their own comfort zone. For some members, it may take months or years before being comfortable enough to share anything about their lives. Relationships are given opportunity to grow and develop naturally.

3. *Participation*—Urban Recipe Co-ops are driven by the participation of members. Each co-op can feel different and can operate a little differently depending on the unique members that make up each co-op. Some members participate by sorting cans, other members help set up a hospitality area before the co-op meeting time begins, and still others assist in the facilitation of each co-op meeting and serve on the steering committee, which is the elected leadership of each Food Co-op. A key tenant of the co-op structure is there is some way each person can and will contribute. To get the most out of the co-op, participation is highly encouraged. Participation also means that each member takes seriously their commitment to show up at each distribution meeting. These meetings happen every other week throughout the year and they are essential for the creation of the community.

4. *Cooperation*—There is a lot that has to be done at each Urban Recipe co-op meeting. These co-ops permit individuals to achieve tasks through collective action and cooperation. Individuals help one another accomplish the tasks at hand rather than taking on a burden by oneself. In this effort, co-op members figure out which activities they enjoy and those they prefer not to do. They also find other members who share a mutual interest. This shared activity or task may also be the foundational activity that begins to create a friendship or even a relationship.

5. *Rituals of care*—Urban Recipe Co-ops are built around rituals of care. New members are welcomed. Members' birthdays are celebrated at each meeting and each member with a birthday will receive a birthday cake and a card. Concerns can be shared, and announcements are made during the business meeting. Bereavement cards are given to families who have lost a loved one. Celebration cards are given at times of celebration. Each activity serves as a way for the collective group of the co-op to express care, but also create a window where other members may follow up more directly in the care of another member. In a recent meeting where a co-op member was recognized for her birthday, another member noticed that the person being recognized was not present. Consequently, the caring member reached out to

her fellow co-op member and found out that she was not feeling well and would love to have a visitor. A visit was arranged, and the two co-op members became closer because of the care and support that was being offered. This kind of action is so common in the co-ops, it feels almost like second nature. There are also many times when co-op members will hear about another co-op member who is sick and in the hospital. It is very common for a group from the co-op to find a way to go visit the person in the hospital. While this is a thoughtful gesture, it is often a challenging endeavor, since transportation can be a challenge for many of the members.

There are implications for each of us, whether we find ourselves in an Urban Recipe Co-op or not.

To experience a similar type of care, a person needs to find a group of people that share a similar need and commit to being with that group for a significant period of time like six months to a year. This group must have a reason for bringing them together. Maybe it is a support group or a volunteer group. The stronger the need in drawing the group together, the more likely people will be committed to staying together.

The next step is to find something to work on together. While working on whatever the group chooses, find a way of marking and celebrating the accomplishments of the group together, such as celebrating birthdays and other personal anniversaries. In the midst of all the work and celebrating, this group will become a safe space for a new form of spiritual care to emerge in the margins of relationships being formed. Rhythms and routines are all around us. In the co-op community of Urban Recipe, the rhythms and routines serve to provide stabilization and hope for individuals, facing the challenges of life. The combined care of the organization and the individual care of the participants provide hope and encouragement.

Just as the co-op example has been explored in this chapter, other opportunities are possible to influence individuals in a positive way, helping to change and improve life situations. The desire of this writer is to expand the care found in our co-op model to other institutions. Presently, Urban Recipe is expanding further in the community by engaging individuals in school settings. What a wonderful challenge to include and embrace the educational community while continuing to address the food needs of individuals that provide the dignity, agency, and love needed to create a robust community.

Part Three

Spiritual Care & Global Well-Being

12

The Cultural Broker

An Image for Prophetic Soul Care
in the Neoliberal Age

CEDRIC C. JOHNSON[1]

NEOLIBERALISM IS A CENTRAL framework through which to investigate the human suffering that has resulted from a growing economic divide that is now global in its scope. This chapter presents the *cultural broker* as a vital image for prophetic soul care in the neoliberal age. Caring for souls in the neoliberal age requires theoretical resources and strategies that attend to the complex connections between socioeconomic, cultural, and interpersonal dynamics. Understanding how certain capitalisms have been reorganized and rearticulated at different stages of their development is crucial to the effective provision of soul care in the twenty-first century. Historically, certain metaphors have served to inform the care of souls. The image of the cultural broker metaphorically structures soul care in the neoliberal age. It brings into view continuities among critical realms of practice that otherwise appear to be unrelated.

A *postcolonial hermeneutic* is employed in this examination of the cultural broker as an image for prophetic soul care in a neoliberal age. Post-colonial studies emerged as a way of engaging with the cultural articulations of societies disrupted by the historical reality of domination. It engages contexts where imperial projects have given way to societies whose makeup reflects the disjunctions of their specific histories of domination. The term does not signify a process that merely examines events and phenomena that

1. This chapter includes excerpts from my *Race, Religion, and Resilience*. I sincerely appreciate the publishers, Palgrave Macmillan, for the generosity in fair use of material from my book.

pertain to specific "postcolonial constituencies," nor does its prefix infer that the effects of imperial power have been surpassed. Postcolonial criticism also refers to a strategic response to contemporary contexts of domination, exploitation, and differentiation.

Postcolonial theory recognizes that race, gender, class, caste, religion, and ethnicity have all been employed by imperialist regimes at various times as tropes in the construction of "otherness" and the justification of imperial projects. It is attentive to the ways in which imperial encounters impact indigenous identities and how the subjugated develop strategies in order to articulate their own subjectivity and self-worth. Postcolonial criticism is deeply concerned with the psycho-cultural disruptions that lay in the wake of imperial histories. It is engaged in the formulation of frameworks within which "psychological decolonization" can occur. A postcolonial hermeneutic thus provides soul care practitioners, informed by the image of the cultural broker, with a helpful interpretive framework to analyze the traumatic and often debilitating impact of the neoliberal age on countless communities they serve throughout the world.

The Neoliberal Age

Neoliberal ideology is grounded in a privileging of the individual and the free market. Proponents of neoliberalism promote privatization asserting that markets are more efficient than governments in the provision of services. In the United States, neoliberalism is characterized by the fluid movement of capital, goods, migrants, and services across local, regional, and national boundaries. It holds that "the social good will be maximized by expanding the reach and frequency of market transactions, and it seeks to bring all human action into the domain of the market."[2] Neoliberal ideology "values market exchange as 'an ethic in itself, capable of acting as a guide to all human action, and substituting for all previously held ethical beliefs.'"[3] In too many instances, however, commercial interests and values have superseded concern for democracy, human rights, social justice, and the environment. As a result, low-wage local, regional or national economies attract capital and migrants, with jobs subsequently being moved from place to place, "leaving disarray and unemployment where jobs have vanished and dislocations and worker exploitation where those jobs are relocated."[4] In the wake of these dislocations, neoliberal ideology espouses the dismantling of the

2. Harvey, *Brief History of Neoliberalism*, 3.

3. Harvey, *Brief History of Neoliberalism*, 3.

4. Eitzen and Zinn, *Globalization*, ix.

welfare state and end of government sponsored social programs designed to address the effects of poverty. While the proponents of neoliberalism point to its perceived benefits, they tend not to emphasize that the net effect of these policies has too often been to benefit the few at the expense of the many, and the well-off at the expense of the poor.

The *neoliberal age* signifies a social formation that is far more complicated than the tenets of neoliberal ideology. The neoliberal age is characterized by the following: the subordination of democratic political power to unaccountable economic power; the marketing of Western culture and consumer-oriented ways of life; and advances in communication and information technologies capable of facilitating massive shifts in capital by investors unaccountable for social and environmental impacts. In addition, the neoliberal age entails the configuration of a matrix of interrelated systems of governance that are utilized: (1) to *maintain* the full reign of the free market; (2) to *contain* left-behind sectors of the population whose presence discloses the system's inequities; (3) to *control* segments of the society who pose a threat to the system's stability; and (4) to *secure* the continued contributions of those who are, in fact, indispensable to the system's operations.[5] To accomplish this, a "diffuse network of actors are positioned in quasi-market relations and charged with the task of bringing discipline to the lives of the poor and disenfranchised."[6] In the United States, this has included but is not limited to housing policy and the cordoning off of black and brown populations in public "housing projects," the militarization of the police, and the explosive growth of the prison-industrial complex. Different actors are employed, though, in different localities. In many rural farming regions, agribusiness is a prominent actor. In areas where oil or natural gas deposits have been detected, energy corporations are predominant actors. In cities where real estate properties are seized and demolished for private enterprise projects, the state functions as an actor. Finally, in "middle" America and white suburban communities, too often, doctors and pharmacists involved in the illegal sale of prescription drugs are actors. Neoliberal governance thus takes on distinctive forms depending upon the particular geopolitical context. Notwithstanding, in each location the neoliberal age has engendered *material violence*. The United States has witnessed unprecedented growth in economic disparities since the inception of the neoliberal age in the 1980s. Massive and fluid movements of capital

---

5. This framework, initially applied by Mark L. Taylor to the prison industrial complex, is broadened and similarly put forth here in the context of neoliberal governance. See Taylor, *Executed God*, 56–57.

6. Soss et al., *Disciplining the Poor*, 3.

have transformed some areas into "emerging markets," while others have been marginalized into socioeconomic "basket cases."

The neoliberal age has to do not only with economic and political relations, but also with the dissemination of a form of "mass culture." Though the concentration of capital has begun to drift to Asian countries, the narratives, values, and imagery of Western societies remains the "driving powerhouse" of this neoliberal mass culture. These movements involve *westoxification*—the imposition, in whole or in part, of Western worldviews and values on every culture they encounter. This neoliberally driven culture does not attempt to obliterate other local cultures. It operates through them, absorbing cultural differences. Countless communities in the United States and throughout the world thus experience the neoliberal age as a new mode of cultural imperialism. The neoliberal system that emerged in the United States, for example, is deeply racialized and reflects the legacies of North America's racial history. Racism did not end with the emergence of the neoliberal age. It has been redeployed as a component of a new socioeconomic configuration. The neoliberal age has subsequently also engendered *epistemic violence*. It involves the violent imposition of market-driven systems of cultural classification and the dislodging of indigenous cultural systems. The neoliberal age undermines cultural identities and traditions to the extent that it is able to supplant or commodify local cultures.

Prophetic soul care is an integrative approach which argues that understanding human functioning is not possible without comprehending the context in which it is formed as a subsystem within a matrix of interlocking historically situated systems. Prophetic soul care entails assessing interpersonal dynamics, family systems, sociocultural systems, economic systems, and political systems, as well as religious, spiritual, or other meaning-making systems. It is a multi-systems approach that considers the potential influence a matrix of forces may have on those who come for care. As a therapeutic modality, prophetic soul care integrates ongoing analyses of the disruptive ways in which capitalist forces are mediated through local cultures. It explores the traumatic impact these forces have on human flourishing and develops practices that facilitate healing, resilience, and social transformation. Strategies for prophetic soul care are thus derived from an ongoing assessment of where and how to intervene within a matrix of interlocking systems.

The Cultural Broker

The image of the *cultural broker* is a helpful metaphor for the practice of prophetic soul care. The essence of metaphor entails understanding and experiencing one kind of thing in terms of another. Certain enduring metaphors have informed the care of souls. Some of these metaphors include the *wounded healer*, *wise fool*, and *agent of hope*.[7] From this perspective, the concepts that govern our *thoughts* and *actions* are understood as thoroughly metaphorical.[8] One of the fascinating aspects of the employment of metaphor is its capacity to bring into view continuities among actions that previously appeared to be disconnected or unrelated. The use of any metaphor, albeit, provides only a partial understanding of the concept which it seeks to illustrate. "Metaphorical structuring" is always partial.[9] Any metaphor that brings into focus one aspect of a concept in terms of another will also necessarily mute other aspects of that concept. Interestingly, the image of the *cultural broker* metaphorically structures crucial practice realms of soul care in the neoliberal age.

A *broker* is usually defined as an intermediary, agent, interpreter, or messenger. The concept of *cultural brokering* can be traced back to the earliest recorded encounters between cultures. Anthropologists who observed that there were certain indigenous people whose role in their society was to act as a cultural intermediary first utilized the term cultural broker.[10] Cultural brokering is defined as the act of bridging, linking, or mediating between groups or persons of different cultural backgrounds for the purpose of reducing conflict or producing change. Cultural brokers also function *within* communities as guides, interpreting and negotiating complex processes. Cultural brokers can be understood as serving in four capacities: (1) cultural guide, (2) mediator, (3) liaison, and (4) catalyst for change.[11] These four functions are not mutually exclusive. Each capacity, however, illumines key practice realms of prophetic soul care in the neoliberal age.

Cultural Guide

Cultural brokers function as *cultural guides*. Cultural guides facilitate the enhancement of cultural awareness and competence to manage cultural

7. See Dykstra, *Images of Care*.

8. See Lakoff and Johnson, *Metaphors We Live By*.

9. Lakoff and Johnson, *Metaphors We Live*, 13.

10. NCCC et al., *Bridging the Cultural Divide*, 2.

11. NCCC et al., *Bridging the Cultural Divide*, 3–4.

change. Within any culture there are cultural guides that disseminate symbolic representations within the collective. These are individuals or groups working in the community who give voice to the community's concerns. The poet, preacher, activist or artist may be among those who re-present significant events. They have the task of identifying or developing systems of symbolization that best give expression to the community's experiences. They function as cultural guides within the community, giving voice not to their own ideas and interests, but rather articulating ideas to and for the collective.[12] For prophetic soul care practitioners, this includes educating traumatized and threatened communities about the dynamics and impact of the neoliberal age.

The role of the cultural guide is reflected in this author's contention that the Western psychiatric industry serves as one of the structures of governance in the neoliberal age. The uncritical employment of Western psychological frameworks has, too often, served as a deterrent rather than a facilitator of soul care. Current diagnostic instruments do not identify economic exploitation or racism explicitly as potential precipitating factors in traumatic stress and other challenges in human functioning. Traditional psychodynamic approaches do not give sufficient consideration to the person in context and tend to disregard the needs of the collective, and the complexities of the total situation.[13] Too often these approaches are characterized by "psychoanalytic functionalism." Psychoanalytic functionalism divorces its study of the subject from the historical and political contexts in which they were formed. It privileges intrapsychic dynamics over the social and historical contexts in and through which such dynamics are constituted. Conflict, oppression, exclusion, subjugation, discrimination, and other forms of "social terror" are typically consigned to the intrapsychic world.[14] As a result, the challenges of human functioning in the neoliberal age have largely been defined in terms of individual pathology or cultural inferiority. Those who express appropriate rage or realistic fears in response to experiences of injustice are often criminalized or pathologized. The etiology for appropriate rage or realistic fear is situated within the individual or group, rather than a problematic neoliberal system that fosters feelings of inferiority, material deprivation, dissociation, emotional repression, ruthless competition, and narcissistic self-concern.

As a corrective, I propose a diagnostic category that informs the practice of prophetic soul care in the neoliberal age. Here, the diagnostic focus

---

12. See Mora and Christianakis, "Feeding the School-to-Prison Pipeline."

13. Nader et al., *Honoring Differences*, xviii.

14. Brickman, *Aboriginal Populations in the Mind*, 158.

is not on the formulation of individual psychopathology, but rather on how populations are positioned and position themselves within the context of what might be characterized as a "pathological" racially driven neoliberal society. For practitioners serving in African American and other marginalized contexts I posit the concept of *estrangement*. Karl Marx understood estrangement to be a debilitating condition in which the human capacity for meaning making and self-reflection are undermined by a situation that reduces people to objects and commodities.[15] Estrangement is manifested as human beings and their products are turned into commodities to be exchanged on the market. What is pointed to is the experience of estrangement from one's self and other human relations. The psychiatrist and activist, Frantz Fanon, I believe, extends Marx's notion of estrangement beyond the economic realm. For Fanon, estrangement entails the systematic negation of a people that results in the feeling that they are "the living haunt of contradictions . . . without an anchor, without a horizon, colorless, stateless, [and] rootless."[16] Fanon recognized that encounters with oppressive regimes of representation could lead to the inner expropriation of cultural identities that cripple and deform. It is a conception of estrangement that is cultural and psychological, affecting every area of life. Erik Erikson similarly notes that if a group is systematically excluded from full participation in a society, individuals in the excluded group will feel "estranged."[17] These ideas integrated together point to a conception of estrangement that contributes to our analysis of the impact of the neoliberal age. Estrangement, employed here as a diagnostic category, points to the fact that the systematic exploitation and exclusion of people of African ancestry from full participation in American society has undermined their opportunities for meaning-making and disrupted attempts to develop a positive sense of self. This conception of estrangement disavows the tendency to pathologize or criminalize the individual victims of the neoliberal age. Rather it situates the etiology of many of the challenges to human functioning in the neoliberal age firmly at the doorstep of an oppressive pathological anti-democratic society. The experience of psychocultural dislocation is a *violent* act that impedes, distorts and disrupts human "being." For African Americans and other disenfranchised communities, it is tantamount to an act of *psychocultural terrorism*. This discussion of estrangement seeks to educate traumatized and threatened communities about the dehumanizing impact of the neoliberal age.

15. See Marx, "Economic and Philosophic Manuscripts of 1844"; "Grundrisse."

16. Fanon, *Wretched of the Earth*, 218.

17. Erikson, *Identity*, 309.

The work of Liberty Church in New York City can also be viewed within the context of serving as a cultural guide. Liberty Church is a non-denominational faith community comprised of several multicultural congregations. In response to ongoing incidents of racial injustice in New York and elsewhere, the church convened a "Forum on Race, Justice and Unity." Held on a weeknight, the forum drew a racially mixed audience of approximately three hundred people. The program included live music, spoken word performances, and reflections from an African American female member who shared her encounters with racism *within* their church. Many of those encounters had to do with inappropriate responses from white members of the church to her natural hairstyle. The evening also included expressions of lament, small group discussions, and a transparent conversation about race between the church's lead pastor, who is white, and an African American pastor. On another occasion, Liberty Church sponsored a viewing of the documentary "13th." The film's title references the thirteenth amendment to the United States Constitution that made it illegal for someone to be held as a slave. The documentary explores the emergence of the prison industrial complex in North America and its historical intersections with race and economics. It argues that the prison system functions as a modern form of slavery. The viewing was followed by a discussion of the film with a panel comprised of activists, advocates, authors, artists, and pastors. Approximately two hundred people were in attendance for the viewing of the film and panel discussion. Both the work of Liberty Church and this author's discussion of estrangement illustrate the way in which individuals and groups can serve as *cultural guides*, facilitating the enhancement of cultural awareness in the neoliberal age.

Mediator

Cultural brokers function as *mediators*. Mediators facilitate the grounds for negotiation and pave the way towards the resolution of a conflict in a way that is beneficial to all sides. Practitioners of prophetic soul care serve as mediators, working as intermediaries that diffuse conflict or distrust between entities. Working as intermediaries, practitioners of soul care also enable groups to access mediating structures. Mediating structures are safe spaces that promote healing and aid in reframing past traumas and future possibilities. They are environments that support personal and political efficacy. Mediating structures are communal sites of alternate ordering where the material and epistemic harm done by the neoliberal age are rectified. These structures function as sites of resilience and resistance that mediate relationships of power and provide opportunities where subjects can make creative use of these "third spaces" for formation of the self.

The American film, *The Best of Enemies* (2019), portrays the way in which practitioners of soul care work as mediators and enable groups to access mediating structures. The biopic explores the issues of racism and segregation in the town of Durham, North Carolina in 1971. It does so largely through the lens of the real-life, initially antagonistic, relationship between civil rights activist, Ann Atwater, and the local Ku Klux Klan president, C. P. Ellis. Racial tensions in the town are intensified when a local school that African American children attend is set on fire and almost burned down. Rather than allow the dislocated black students to attend a nearby school for white students, the mayor of Durham orders that the black students must finish the year in their half-destroyed school building. The mayor's ruling outrages the African American community. In an effort to appease Durham's black community an African American mediator, Bill Riddick, is summoned to convene a town forum known as a charrette to diffuse tensions and vote on several community issues connected to race relations. Riddick surprisingly nominates Ann Atwater and C. P. Ellis to serve as co-chairs for the charrette.

Bill Riddick's efforts as a mediator, working to diffuse the conflict between Durham's black and white communities, is a central focus of the film. Riddick employs various techniques as a mediator—instructing blacks and whites to sit next to each other in the cafeteria; making his co-chairs, Ann Atwater and C. P. Ellis, eat meals together; and taking all the participants of the charrette to visit the school that was set on fire. In addition to Riddick's work as a mediator, the film highlights how the charrette functioned as a mediating structure that diffused distrust and aided in reframing future possibilities. *The Best of Enemies* climaxes with a scene in which C. P. Ellis, the former local Klan president, surprisingly, casts the deciding vote to end desegregation in Durham's schools. In the film, Bill Riddick facilitates the grounds for negotiation and paves the way towards the resolution of a conflict between the black and white communities in Durham. The charrette serves as a mediating structure that supports personal and political efficacy. *The Best of Enemies* thus provides a poignant portrayal of the way in which prophetic soul care practitioners might function as mediators in the neoliberal age.

Liaison

Similar to the role of mediator, cultural brokers serve as *liaisons*. Whereas the goal as a mediator is to effect reconciliation, settlement, or compromise, a liaison acts as a link to facilitate communication or cooperation. The neoliberal age, as indicated, entails a matrix of interrelated systems of governance utilized, among other things, to control segments of the society who pose a threat to the system's stability. Rather than serve and protect, the police too often function as a core component of neoliberal governance. In the United States, encounters with local police have led to countless cases of black men and women being brutally beaten, sexually violated, and inexplicably killed. In these contexts, prophetic soul care practitioners also function as liaisons.

One of these inexplicable encounters with local police occurred on August 9, 2014, when Michael Brown Jr., an unarmed eighteen-year-old African American male, was shot and killed by Ferguson, Missouri police officer Darren Wilson. In a spectacle akin to a modern-day lynching, Brown's body was left exposed on the pavement in the middle of a residential neighborhood in Ferguson with his blood streaming down the street for over four hours. This horrific incident shocked the world, fueled weeks of protest, and catalyzed the #blacklivesmatter movement. The city of Ferguson would become a site of both cultural trauma and collective resistance. In *Ferguson & Faith: Sparking Leadership & Awakening Community*, Leah Gunning Francis provides a frontline account of the experiences of young activists and clergy in the aftermath of Michael Brown's tragic death. Among other issues, *Ferguson and Faith* explores how activists and clergy use their skills, experiences, and resources to serve the Ferguson community and engage in transformative social action. One of the clergy staff highlighted, Willis Johnson, pastor of Wellspring United Methodist Church, functions as a cultural broker.[18] Johnson leverages his proximity and community status to serve as a liaison between the protestors and the Ferguson police.

As Gunning Francis states, Willis Johnson lived near the Ferguson police station. On the evening of August 9th, as news of Brown's death spread, Johnson could hear the demonstrators protesting at the station. He decided to walk over. The group of young protestors wanted answers and was preparing to rush the police station. Concerned that the police would not respond well to that strategy, Johnson suggests an alternate approach. He shares that he lives and pastors in the community and offers to serve as a liaison with the police. The young demonstrators eventually agreed. Because someone at the

18. Francis, *Ferguson and Faith*, 19–22.

front desk knows him, Johnson is buzzed into the police station. He is eventually able to speak with the captain on duty. Johnson shares again, now with the police captain, that he lives and pastors in the community. He asks if the captain would be willing to talk to the protestors. After navigating significant resistance, Johnson is able to broker a brief conversation between the captain and a small contingent of the protestors. Though the police share nothing in detail, the protesters feel that they were at least heard. The crowd of approximately a hundred demonstrators soon dissipates, at least for that night. Reverend Johnson, functioning as a liaison, successfully facilitates communication between the protestors and the police. Again, the goal was not to effect reconciliation per se, but to facilitate communication and cooperation. Willis Johnson thus models the way in which practitioners of prophetic soul care might serve as liaisons in the neoliberal age.

Catalysts for Change

Acting as a *catalyst for change*, the cultural broker advocates for and facilitates transformation. This entails facilitating interventions that address not only interpersonal impediments but also structural hindrances to human development. This includes interrogating any system aligned to maintain the hegemonic hold of the neoliberal age on the lives of disempowered and exploited groups. Here, prophetic soul care critiques and confronts social forces inhibiting human flourishing and undermining human worth. The deployment of strategies that enable people to resist the debilitating impact of the neoliberal age is also considered.

Maisha Sapp is a community activist and advocate in New York City who functions as a catalyst for change. She is an African American single mother and parent of a ten-year-old son who attends a public elementary school in the Boerum Hill section of Brooklyn. Maisha serves as cultural broker largely between black parents with school-aged children and the public school system. In the neoliberal age, the public school system too often initiates black youth into, rather than liberate them from, systems of disempowerment. Research regarding the so-called school-to-prison pipeline concurs,

> The increase in prisons and the policing of schools are both rooted in the convergence of neoliberalism, conservatism, and penal populism. This convergence criminalizes minority youth and reinforces the school-to-prison pipeline. . . . Law enforcement and school officials compound the matter by implementing zero-tolerance policies in the name of public safety. The

result is that minority youth who have been suspended, expelled, or adjudicated in the juvenile justice system will likely be
fed into the school-to-prison pipeline and be further excluded
from our neoliberal society.[19]

In addition to the implementation of zero-tolerance policies, gentrification
has heightened tensions in many public schools. The influx of the children of
wealthier, predominately white, families into public schools that previously
served significant percentages of working class black and brown students have
shifted the priorities and relationships of power in those schools. Those shifts
have frequently been detrimental to their students of color.

As a catalyst for change, Maisha works in various capacities in the
cultural spaces between public schools, parents and their kids. She serves
as the co-chair of the Social Action Committee at her son's school. The
mission of the Social Action Committee is to organize events and lead
the parent community to build relationships across difference so they can
support each other and engage the school more effectively. The committee coordinates workshops where parents can learn and collaborate on
parenting issues related to racial and social justice, communication, and
identity development. Parents build relational power with each other to
change the school system so that it betters serves their children. Strategies
are used to engage families to support both their own children as well as
all the children in their community.

Maisha also creates family-dedicated spaces outside the school. She
convenes a Parent Healing and Empowerment group on Monday morn-
ings scheduled right after parents drop off their children at school. This safe
space for families helps cultivate new relationships and networks between
parents and connects them to the school. These meetings attend to the traumas that parents experience as well as coaching them on how to advocate
for their children and influence decision-making in the school. These strategies build on parent strengths and knowledge of their own children, and
communities to support the students' success. As a catalyst for change, Maisha seeks to facilitate interventions that address interpersonal impediments
and structural hindrances to parents and their school-aged children. She is
a tireless advocate for parent rights who critiques and confronts issues in the
public school system that inhibits the flourishing or undermines the worth
of black students and their parents. Maisha Sapp models what it means to
be a cultural broker and is an inspiring example of what prophetic soul care
looks like in the neoliberal age.

19. Mora and Christianakis, "Feeding the School-to-Prison Pipeline."

Conclusion

The practitioner of prophetic soul care is called upon to critically engage structures of oppressive power and employ interventions that facilitate healing and hope. This includes building bridges of communication, managing the dynamics of cultural difference, helping groups mediate those differences, and advocating for interpersonal and social transformation. To this end, four capacities are identified as key realms of practice for soul care in the neoliberal age: cultural guide, mediator, liaison, and catalyst for change. The image of the cultural broker "metaphorically structures" these four functions. It brings into view continuities among these care practices that may appear to be unrelated. In light of the global expansion of neoliberalism, countless communities struggle to live their lives in a world that increasingly escapes their grasp. It is my hope that the image of the cultural broker will serve as a useful metaphor that informs the practice of prophetic soul care with populations traumatized or threatened by the material and epistemic violence of the neoliberal age.

13

Caring for Souls within the Dark Web

As the Internet began to emerge, many observers hailed it as an instrument of equality and democracy. It would, some asserted, finally enable the masses to push back against monopolies. Unfortunately, the opposite occurred. During the 1990s vast international corporations established control over the Internet, transitioning it "from noncommercial oasis to capitalist hot spot."[1] This happens to coincide with the period when capitalism shifted into its neoliberal phase, distinguished not by a free market but by the dominance of gigantic monopolies and a global governance by financial institutions.[2] This amounts to a transformed colonialism. The Internet has proved immensely useful for this system. It as a network of pathways upon which neoliberalism establishes and extends its control over politics, economics, and culture. Rather than an equalizing force, the Internet "is starting to resemble maps from centuries past, when empires ruled vast swaths of land, engulfing independent villages and smaller kingdoms. Think the Roman Empire in the second century or the British Empire in the 19th."[3] The Internet today is an instrument of neoliberal colonization.

---

1. McChesney, *Digital Disconnect*, 20.
2. Birch, *Research Agenda for Neoliberalism*; Lynn, *Cornered*.
3. Bivins, "Digital Colonialism."

The Living Human Web:
A Colonial Imaginary?

These developments complicate the image of "the living human web" that has guided pastoral theology for the last twenty-five years.[4] We have usually deployed this metaphor in accordance with philosophical idealism. In other words, we tend to neglect the material political economic context of this social imaginary. In hindsight, it is surprising that we have generally overlooked the embeddedness of this image in the evolution of the Internet. It is no coincidence, perhaps, that pastoral theologians began espousing this metaphor at precisely the historical moment when the Internet was rapidly expanding and coming under the control of neoliberal interests.[5] In fact, the image might not have garnered such widespread appeal had this not been the case. I am not suggesting that we have intended to support neoliberal governance. I simply propose that this metaphor would not have achieved such currency had it not been a sublimated manifestation of the dominant political, economic, and cultural power of our age. That said, to continue utilizing this image as an abstract signifier for "the interconnection and interdependence of all life," as in effect an ontological descriptor, could be politically dangerous.[6] Using the metaphor in this way might lead us, paradoxically and unwittingly, to accept the faith system of neoliberalism, to value what it values and see what it sees, and also to render invisible whatever threatens its hegemony.

My reflections extend the critique that Hellena Moon has levelled at the living human web imaginary. She attempts to historicize this web, astutely interpreting it as an instrument of colonialism and capitalism. Seen this way, the living human web "becomes a metaphor for predatory behavior."[7] However, Moon does not suggest that we dispose of this image, and neither do I. Rather, I propose that we utilize this imaginary *dialectically*. We must re-ground this symbol in the material political economic context of the Internet itself. If we see the living human web as analogous to what is available whenever we peruse the Internet, using the search engines and server hubs owned by monopoly corporations (Google, Apple, Facebook, Amazon et al.), we begin to comprehend the colonizing quality of this web. This is a web that, as Moon indicates, exploits the vast majority of human beings, as well as life on the planet itself, for the sake of increasing wealth for a few.

---

4. Miller-McLemore, "Living Human Web."
5. Miller-McLemore, "Human Web."
6. Miller-McLemore, *Christian Theology in Practice*, 27.
7. Moon, "'Living Human Web' Revisited," 22–25.

However, the web that is visible through corporate search engines is not the entire web. There remains what popular discourse identifies as the *dark web*. Usually, mentioning the dark web conjures associations to criminal activities. Indeed, some people do use the dark web to conduct illegal pursuits. But in this respect, it does not differ much from the visible web. What does distinguish users of the dark web is the desire for anonymity, the evasion of surveillance and control by the dominant order.[8] For many of its participants, the dark web provides cover for political dissent and subversive conversation. Gabriella Coleman observes that dark web activities "can also enable a positive, constructive ethics of interacting and of being-in-the-world that runs counter to state, corporate, and colonial interests."[9] Robert Gehl concludes that "we lose a valuable means of political speech and dissent if we shut down the Dark Web."[10]

I wish to employ the web imaginary to evoke the tension between the living human web and the dark web. The living human web is a neoliberal global network where the atmosphere is decidedly optimistic, a place that celebrates never-ending progress, ever-expanding knowledge, wealth production, and individual meritocracy. This dominant part of the web is designed to exploit the vast majority of human beings and the planet itself. The dark web, meanwhile, offers an opportunity for resistance within the hidden interstices of this global network. Though much smaller than the visible internet, it signifies by far the largest mass of human beings. This invisibilized throng of humanity, Frantz Fanon's "wretched of the earth," occupies coloniality, the space Walter Mignolo has portrayed as the dark side of modernity.[11] The atmosphere of this realm is not celebratory. Rather, it is saturated with humility, despair, hope, and grief. For reasons that will become apparent, I propose that this web may best be imagined as the *dying human web*.

From here I proceed in two additional moves. The following section describes what happens to human subjects under the new coloniality. While Anton Boisen once described the focus of care as the "living human document," I perceive that caring for souls today is perhaps better understood as attending to *dying human documents*, those who are colonized and infected by the dominant web.[12] In the last section I will attempt to reimagine the contours of spiritual care within the dark web.

---

8. Gehl, *Weaving the Dark Web*.

9. Coleman, *Hacker, Hoaxer, Whistleblower, Spy*, 426.

10. Gehl, *Weaving the Dark Web*, 17.

11. Mignolo, *Darker Side of Western Modernity*.

12. Boisen, *Exploration of the Inner World*.

Dying Human Documents

Astute observers of colonialism have long noted that it impacts not just geographical spaces, but also individual subjects. Examples include classics such as Frantz Fanon's *Black Skin, White Masks*, but also more recent works such as Kelly Oliver's *The Colonization of Psychic Space.*[13] There is now an abundant literature on how neoliberalism has transformed culture, yielding what Randy Martin has called "the financialization of daily life," which entails particular understandings of what it means to be human.[14] So, what is the character of individuals colonized by neoliberalism? For my purposes here I will follow the lead of a team of psychologists in the United States directed by Glenn Adams.[15] These researchers group the psychological effects of neoliberalism into four categories: *radical abstraction* of persons, *entrepreneurial self, growth imperative*, and *affect management*. They refer to these four features as "neoliberal selfways."

First, neoliberal selves idealize a "freedom from constraint" that mirrors the deterritorialization and fluidity of money in financial capitalism. Neoliberal selves thus undergo a *radical abstraction*: "Standardization erases local identity . . . as it transforms cultural patterns for ease of consumption and contributes to the cultural dominance of hegemonic global forms."[16] Prizing mobility and fluidity influences us to see connections to others as free choices. This "contributes to conditional identification that can undermine collective solidarity and community participation."[17] Moreover, such a radical freedom from constraint requires a spatial and temporal displacement. Spatial displacement "happens when affluent communities outsource violent production practices and harmful byproducts to impoverished communities."[18] Temporal displacement "happens when present consumers mortgage the future, passing financial debt and ecological consequences to future generations."[19] The negative consequences of "unconstrained freedom" are simply passed off to another place or time. Finally, people are expected, *and expect themselves*, to "overcome" their limitations and achieve this freedom even when they do not have the resources to do so. This is so because individuals are also abstracted from their *material context*.

13. Fanon, *Black Skin, White Masks*; Oliver, *Colonization of Psychic Space*.

14. Martin, *Financialization of Daily Life*.

15. Adams et al., "Psychology of Neoliberalism."

16. Adams et al., "Psychology of Neoliberalism," 5.

17. Adams et al., "Psychology of Neoliberalism," 5.

18. Adams et al., "Psychology of Neoliberalism," 5.

19. Adams et al., "Psychology of Neoliberalism," 6.

Second, neoliberal subjects are under pressure to see themselves as enterprises, as *entrepreneurs* of the project that is themselves. This is nothing short of "radical self-authorship." This sort of project "marks a tendency to develop oneself as a product or brand in response to demands of the social and economic marketplace."[20]

Third, individuals colonized by neoliberalism are primed to pursue interminable *growth*: "Being well in neoliberal systems requires selves that are fluid, changing, and growing. They take risks; seek new opportunities; and acquire new skills, talents, interests, and preferences."[21] Such a notion of wellness depends entirely on personal willpower and making good choices. This is not an option. It is required. Adams and his team notes, however, that this advice works best for people who are socioeconomically privileged, and not so much for others. Coupled to a narrative of personal responsibility, individuals who fail to achieve personal growth blame themselves, engendering shame and depression.

This brings up the fourth neoliberal selfway—individuals are expected to engage in diligent efforts aimed toward *affect management*. In everyday life neoliberal systems emphasize feelings more than reason. This leads one geographer to explore the "structures of feeling" within neoliberal societies.[22] Cultures differ as to "ideal affect." In the United States cultural leaders promote "high arousal positive" (HAP) states, such as enthusiasm, excitement, elation, and happiness.[23] Neoliberal individuals must assiduously nurture HAP affective states in themselves, while avoiding low-arousal "negative" states, such as sadness. In the precarious and isolating atmosphere of contemporary capitalism, this becomes a virtually impossible task. Ironically, escalations in the incidence of depression become inevitable when positive affects are idealized. One meta-analytic study suggests that negative judgements toward depressed moods significantly contribute to depression.[24] Global increases in the incidence of depression throughout the neoliberal era have been amply documented.[25]

Besides depression, empirical evidence that neoliberalization is causing an astonishing rise in general psychological distress is now abundant. In the United States deaths from suicide and drug overdoses have increased

20. Adams et al., "Psychology of Neoliberalism," 6.

21. Adams et al., "Psychology of Neoliberalism," 7.

22. Anderson, "Neoliberal Affects."

23. Tsai, "Ideal Affect."

24. Yoon et al., "Are Attitudes Towards Emotions Associated With Depression?"

25. See, e.g., Hidaka, "Depression as a Disease of Modernity"; Rogers-Vaughn, "Blessed Are Those Who Mourn"; Walker, *Depression and Globalization*.

exponentially since the 1980s, and the number of people reporting they are lonely is unprecedented.[26] The same is true globally, leading experts on international health to conclude that we now have a "worldwide epidemic of mental illness."[27]

In summary, I submit that everyday life for individuals pursuing neoliberal selfways is characterized by a deadness that is simultaneously overwhelming and subtle. When I refer to deadness, we must of course not forget that neoliberal practices result in literal physical death for countless people.[28] Even for those not killed, however, existence becomes a living death, a progressive deterioration of soul. This is a zombie suffering: "We are hollowed out and going to pieces, but hardly awake. The horror of this age is that we are not horrified."[29] In our neoliberal times, the vast majority of humanity has joined the company of those Fanon called "the wretched of the earth" (*les damnés de la terre*).[30] And, as Nelson Maldonado-Torres has concisely stated: "The *damné* exists in the mode of not-being there, which hints at the nearness of death, at the company of death."[31] And this is why, in our times, those who would care for souls are part hospice chaplains, part revolutionary activists. We are actively striving toward the life of a new age. But in the meantime, we are also attending to the dead, and to *dying human documents*, those Eric Cazdyn has called "the already dead."[32]

Caring for Souls within the Dark Web

These reflections deepen our comprehension of existence within the dark web and what it suggests for spiritual care. The dark web is not to be taken literally, a mere signifier of a portion of the Internet. Like the living human web, it is a metaphor for where we now find ourselves. Elsewhere I have portrayed neoliberalism as a virus that has contaminated the whole fabric of the living human web.[33] The dark web is a way to imagine the concealed recesses of this altered existence. It is a pathway for understanding today's

26. Cigna and Ipsos, *Cigna US Loneliness Index*; Katz, "Drug Deaths in America"; Storr, "Metamorphosis of the Western Soul."

27. Tucci and Moukaddam, "We Are the Hollow Men," 4–6; Walker, *Depression and Globalization*.

28. Klein, *This Changes Everything*; Leech, *Capitalism*.

29. Rogers-Vaughn, *Caring for Souls*, 169.

30. Fanon, *Wretched of the Earth*.

31. Maldonado-Torres, "On the Coloniality of Being," 257.

32. Cazdyn, *Already Dead*.

33. See chapter 3 in Rogers-Vaughn, *Caring for Souls*.

coloniality. Walter Mignolo observes that coloniality "is constitutive of modernity—there is no modernity without coloniality."[34] Just so, there is no living human web without the dark web. Going further, Mignolo argues that modernity, which he identifies with capitalism, entails "a rhetoric of salvation." But, it just "so happens that not everyone believes in the salvation being proposed."[35] Those residing within the dark web do not desire a kinder, gentler neoliberalism, but long for an alternative salvation altogether. I do not wish to provide a blueprint for reaching this salvation. Rather, I will identify just four sorts of experience that typify what is practiced within the new coloniality. My assumption is that these ways of being are not only alternatives to neoliberal selfways, but guide caring for souls within the dark web.

This means I will not focus here on *who* lives within the dark web, a critical exploration in its own right. Saskia Sassen has demonstrated that, whereas industrial capitalism was a system of expansion, today's capitalism is a system of *expulsion*. In the age of financialization, fewer people are needed as workers or consumers. The consequence is that multitudes of people are simply expelled, warehoused in deserted spaces, slums, prisons, and in the growing masses of migrants.[36] These are people who are evicted from present-day capitalism, those Zygmunt Bauman has described as "human waste."[37] They are the castaways of capitalism. We might imagine these as among the principal residents of the dark web. However, I want to focus here on *what types of human experience* have been expelled from, or rendered invisible by, neoliberalized cultures. These practices live in the gaps, recesses, and interstices of the living human web, and thus within the dark web. From Mignolo's perspective, they are markers of decolonization. Many of these could be described, but here I will identify only four: hope, humility, love, and mourning.

I have noted that neoliberal selfways require "high arousal positive" (HAP) affective states. Prominent among these is optimism, which assumes that if we try hard and follow the designated "best practices," success is assured. Residents of the dark web are decidedly not optimistic. They have lost faith in the system. Rather than optimism, they practice *hope*. And, ironically, despair is a precondition for hoping. "The truth is," Gabriel Marcel asserts, "that there can strictly speaking be no hope except when the

34. Mignolo, *Darker Side of Western Modernity*, 3.

35. Mignolo, *Darker Side of Western Modernity*, xxiv–xxv.

36. Sassen, *Expulsions*.

37. Bauman, *Wasted Lives*.

temptation to despair exists."[38] Today, hope feeds off the rot and decay of neoliberal excess. Sorting through the debris, hope is a hope-against-hope that arises from staring into the abyss. "The abyss," says An Yountae, "conveys the unspeakable: both the unspeakable pain of the colonial wound *and* the unspeakable state of the self who lives in the suspended present, awaiting for the unforeseeable future to unfold."[39] This waiting is not, however, a paralysis. Hope is an active waiting not unlike that portrayed in the Hebrew scriptures: "But those who wait for the Lord shall renew their strength, they shall mount up with wings like eagles, they shall run and not be weary, they shall walk and not faint" (Isa 40:31 NRSV). Moreover, in contrast to neoliberal optimism, hope is not for the sake of "me myself." As we shall see, it dwells on the plane of love. It is a relational activity. It's "most elaborate expression," says Marcel, is "I hope in thee for us."[40]

This interdependent activity suggests something that could easily be missed: *humility*. The spirit of neoliberalism is boastful, arrogant, optimistic, self-assured. It believes progress is irresistible. Technology and innovation will bring infinite growth and prosperity. "There is," it screams, "no alternative!" "Capitalism," China Miéville opines, "is catastrophe, exhausting, brutal, quite unrelenting, it just will not give us a minute, and it is too fucking loud."[41] Those who are colonized, who live within the shadows of the dark web, know that all of this is a lie. But they do not counter arrogance with arrogance. They are aware that their knowledge is partial: "For we know only in part, and we prophesy only in part" (1 Cor 13:9 NRSV). Their hope makes them utopians, but they are not "blueprint utopians" who have meticulously drawn out and thus know the path to the future. Instead, they are "iconoclastic utopians" who refuse to "inventory the future."[42] Ever suspicious of the seductiveness and danger of imagery, they expend energy breaking images rather than making them. They trust their ears more than their eyes. "Like the future, God could be heard but not seen. 'Hear, O Israel!' begin the Jewish prayers."[43] Iconoclastic utopians are an apophatic bunch who are peculiarly fitted for our time. Russell Jacoby contends that the opening lines of Ernst Bloch's *Spirit of Utopia* is a credo tailored for them: "I am. We are. That is enough. Now we have to begin."[44] This humility

---

38. Marcel, *Homo Viator*, 36.

39. Yountae, *Decolonial Abyss*, 12.

40. Marcel, *Homo Viator*, 60.

41. Miéville, "Silence in Debris," 144.

42. Jacoby, *Picture Imperfect*, xiv–xvii.

43. Jacoby, *Picture Imperfect*, 33.

44. Jacoby, *Picture Imperfect*, xvi.

means that residents of the dark web resist a politics of certainty. Opting out of the "Left versus Right" binary of today's political landscape, an ethic of love even for one's enemies leaves them listening for truth wherever it appears.[45] Rejecting the objectifying and commodifying knowledge of neoliberal colonization, the thoroughly relational knowledge appearing within the dark web appears as a sort of "unknowing."[46]

The relationality of hope and humility points to their grounding in *love*. William Davies has observed that neoliberal logic "gets stuck when it comes to love."[47] Advocates of neoliberalized systems will object that love is central to their positive psychology and native to high arousal positive (HAP) affect states. Adams and his research team, however, explore their understanding of love and conclude that relationships simply become "another site for self-expression, self-expansion and pursuit of personal fulfillment."[48] Love is something one enters into as a personal choice and out of self-interest. This perspective is not reflected in classical understandings, such as those in most religions, where love is not a personal choice and is not limited to private, intimate relationships. Here love arises as an ethical demand, an *obligation*. It is not chosen. It is *already there*. Moreover, it is essentially non-utilitarian, and thus is not in the service of self-interest. Robert Johann has contended that authentic love is *disinterested*. "When love is interested," he states, "when the attraction is based on a motive of profit or need, it has no difficulty in finding words to justify itself." This sort of love, he concludes, is "technically only desire." But, he continues, there is a love that cannot explain itself: "Why do I love you? Because you are—*you*. That is the best it can do. It is indefensible."[49] This love is inexplicable by the logic of neoliberalism. It simply cannot exist. Thus, it has immigrated to the interstices, into the dark web. This love, whenever it occurs, is an act of resistance, defiance, even rebellion. *One way to oppose present-day colonization is to cultivate relationships that are, according to the logic of neoliberalism, absolutely useless.* Moreover, love is not simply an individual act. It may inhabit a whole community or society, or even manifest an ontological status. For example, the relational world indicated by the Pan-African term *ubuntu* points to a decolonizing reality that exits the neoliberal paradigm entirely.[50] Often translated "I am because we are," *ubuntu* opens up a world

45. Hamid, "Resist the Lure of Theological Politics."

46. Keller, *Cloud of the Impossible*.

47. Davies, "Democratic Critique of Neo-Liberalism," 90.

48. Adams et al., "Psychology of Neoliberalism," 17.

49. Johann, *Meaning of Love*, 19.

50. Dreyer et al., *Practicing Ubuntu*; Nyengele, "Cultivating Ubuntu."

where individuality is made possible by the social surround. In this world we could no more choose to be in community than we could choose whether to breathe air. The community precedes us, and creates the possibility for our existence, including our individual agency.

Love contradicts not only the logic of neoliberalism, but its ideal affects as well. The feelings associated with love are not unambiguously positive. As Miguel de Unamuno has observed, to love is to suffer.[51] Why? Because the beloved is subject to alienation, disease, pain, exploitation, and death. To love is to bear the other's distress or absence. There is no escape from this. Love leads inevitably to *mourning*, the last dark-web practice I will consider here. I have remarked elsewhere: "Grief is essentially love under the condition of absence."[52] If our love extends to Fanon's "wretched of the earth," then we live our lives in the shadow of death. Being among *les damnés* means attending to dying human documents, to the already dead, and thus to be infused with mourning. This makes no sense to neoliberal inclinations. Johann Baptist Metz observes: "When it comes to the dead there is no exchange relationship, no *do ut des*. The love that mourns for the dead is that form of love . . . that cannot be taken up into a consumer society's exploitation structures." Capitalist modernity erodes such a love. "A symptom of this," Metz continues, "is the fact that . . . men and women are forbidden any mourning or melancholy."[53] By contrast, a Christian praxis manifests a "pathic structure." This grounds a community in which mourning becomes "a category of resistance against the proscription of mourning in a society of success and victors." The solidarity of this community "looks backward." It is "a solidarity with the dead and the vanquished."[54]

It is utterly critical to realize that mourning is the root motivation for resisting and overturning neoliberal systems. Revolution against the proud optimism of these structures begins not in the head but the heart. Referring to the humility of an "apophatic Marxism," China Miéville asserts: "With such humility should come grief appropriate to the epoch. 'Don't mourn,' goes the Left injunction, 'organise.' A bullying disavowal. How can we organise except through mourning?"[55] Knowledge is necessary, but it is not enough to know. Speaking is essential, but it is not enough to speak. Organizing is indispensable, but it is not enough to "rise up." First, we grieve. We grieve for those who do not know the way, who cannot speak, who are too exhausted to

51. Unamuno, *Tragic Sense of Life*, 132–55.

52. Rogers-Vaughn, "Recovering Grief," 40.

53. Metz, *Faith in History and Society*, 51.

54. Metz, *Faith in History and Society*, 67.

55. Miéville, "Silence in Debris," 116.

rise up—in other words, for all of us. We grieve for those who have come before us, and for the already dead. Exiled upon the dark web, we are as Rachel, "weeping for her children; she refuses to be comforted for her children, because they are no more" (Jer 31:15 NRSV). So, we must first weep. Weep until the confluence of our tears become rivers of justice. Weep until the swelling of our tears become tides of steadfast love. Then our knowledge will become wise. Our words will come to us, but spoken in humility. Our actions will be prudent. And the paths before us will become clear.

14

The Aporias of Freedom and
the Immured Spirit

———— HELLENA MOON ————

Introduction

IN 2017, BONNIE MILLER-MCLEMORE delivered a twenty-five-year retrospective lecture on the image of the "living human web" in South Korea.[1] The "living human web" is a phrase Miller-McLemore coined twenty-seven years ago to describe the state of the field of pastoral theology. The web metaphor not only conveys the shifting, constantly changing, amorphous nature of the field itself. It also illustrates our creativity as human beings—we are constantly creating, weaving, and re-weaving the web of our own lives.[2] Re-weaving can come in the form of daily processes and practices in our lived reality. It can also come in the form of re-weaving or revising our historiographies and creating new theories based on critical epistemological formation. I argue such a historiographical critique of spiritual care is essential for the decolonizing work needed in the field of pastoral theology.

Miller-McLemore's twenty-five-year retrospective lecture in South Korea serves as a timely beginning for my chapter on critiquing the historicism of Western thought and its impact on spiritual care. I share the following paragraph of the Enlightenment ideals of freedom and rights as it pertains to what I shall describe as the aporias of the "living human web" of pastoral theology.[3] Miller McLemore states:

1. Miller-McLemore, "Living Human Web," 337.
2. Keller, *From a Broken Web*.
3. I want to express gratitude to Bonnie Miller-McLemore for the creative

> A basic premise of the human web—that how we understand pastoral care is deeply shaped by our historical and cultural contexts—suggests that Americans and Koreans will understand the idea of the web itself in different ways. Broadly speaking, for at least three centuries Westerners have emphasized ideals of individual autonomy. Some historians credit the European Enlightenment's promotion of human freedom and civil rights; other scholars look further back to Reformation in the 1500s and its emphasis on the individual as justified by faith without mediating priests or religious institutions. . . . Whatever the source, people in the United States have prized *individuality* and personal freedom for a long time and have been rightfully criticized in the last century for our extreme individualism and neglect of the wider common good in pursuit of our own selfish interests.[4]

Koreans (in Korea) and UnitedStateseans[5] *do—and did*—understand the European Enlightenment ideals of human freedom and civil rights in different ways due to many factors. The differing understandings and experiences of the web are not just between the two nation-states or its peoples, "Americans" and "Koreans." Within the United States itself, people have experienced and interpreted the "living human web" in vastly different ways due to the liberal, neo-liberal, colonial underpinnings of how human freedom and rights were interpreted for, and practiced by, its people. For a vast number of people, freedom and rights were denied altogether.

According to historian Niall Ferguson, the United States "is a direct descendent of the British Empire," a "dysfunctional descendant."[6] Our theories and practices of freedom emanate from the same political economic philosophical genealogy of Locke, Rousseau, Nietzsche, Hegel, Hayek, etc. What gave human freedom to the white Christian privileged European man or UnitedStatesean translated into the oppression, abuse, slavery, discrimination, and exploitation of non-whites (Christians or not) and wo/men.[7] Sartre states, "There is nothing more consistent than a racist hu-

---

springboard she has provided with this metaphor. Like a good piece of art that has many critiques, interpretations, debates, and discussions, we can all have a different perspective on what the metaphor can and does mean to us based on our histories and lived experiences.

4. Miller-McLemore, "Living Human Web," 337.

5. Janet Halley's neologism. See Halley, *Split Decisions.*

6. Ferguson, "American Democracy," 3.

7. Wo/men is a neologism of feminist liberation the*logian Elisabeth Schüssler Fiorenza. It signifies the limitations of a sex/gender identity because we are not a unified social group. Wo/men are a heterogeneous category, fragmented by our multiple

manism, since the European has only been able to become a man through creating slaves and monsters."[8] In other words, Europeans achieved their "humanity" and freedom via the de-humanization, oppression, massive colonization, and economic exploitation of others and the environment. Indeed, the European and Western notion of freedom has had very different meanings for white heterosexual men than it has for Africans, Asians, people in the Americas, the LGBTIQ+ community, and certain classes of white wo/men. White UnitedStateseans gained their freedom via slave labor, indentured servitude, immigrant low-wage labor, as well as prison and migrant labor.[9] The quasi-extirpation of indigenous peoples and their cultures helped solidify the land on which the Europeans then branded and claimed as their own property.

In this chapter, I argue that there is not just one meaning of the living "human" web. Just as there is not one meta-colonialism, but fragmented colonialism(s) and hierarchies of power; so too, there exist multiple, conflicting, interlocking human and non-human webs within the dominant neo-liberal, neo-colonial, imperialist web.[10] I explore the variegated meanings of freedom, "human," and spirit in the neo-liberal state—historically as well as presently. In part one, I describe the current warped situation of neoliberalism in our society. Political theorist Wendy Brown argues that the present-day global, politico-economic climate of neoliberal fascism is a distorted new chapter of neo-liberalism from the original vision of its founders. In critiquing Brown, I argue that what is current in our society is a pathological desire to *maintain* the racial, sexual, spiritual equilibrium that has sustained the socio-politico-economic hierarchies and inequalities envisioned via liberal and neo-liberal ideologies.

Part two is a critique of Lockean liberalism, Hayekian neo-liberalism, and Hegelian thought that have shaped our ideals and practices of freedom and rights. I explore the omitted narratives within theories of liberalism and neoliberalism that have justified violence against infrahumans and the environment.[11] The desire by infrahumans to be free from colonization and

---

subject positions due to ethnicity, race, class, gender, religion, education, colonial historiography, family roles, and so on.

8. Sartre, "Preface," 26.

9. The year 2019 commemorates four hundred years of the first slaves who were forced from their homes in Africa to the Americas.

10. Moon, "'Living Human Web' Revisited."

11. Infrahumans refer to those who were considered "sub" human by the standards of Western "civilization." Who was categorized as infrahuman has changed and shifted over the centuries. Paul Gilroy states, "The extensive critique that was required demanded attention to the life of the nonhuman beings with which Africans and other

domination, as well as to benefit from—and be part of—the capitalist projects promised in liberalism and neoliberalism has only further locked them/us into a dependence on our marginalization and subjugation. This is the paradox of rights discourse: "Certainly, rights *appear* as that which we cannot not want."[12] The heuristic I use for such aporias of freedom and its implications for the spiritual care of infrahumans is the "immured spirit."[13]

As a conclusion, I ponder the "non-human" web in trying to come to terms with the fragmented meanings of being human in our world today and in coming to terms with our freedom. Human beings, *homo economicus*, are seen as economic actors in the age of neoliberalism. We have also come to be seen, collectively, as a geological force in climate change, what Dipesh Chakrabarty refers to as the "non-human" human.[14] Since the Age of Enlightenment, Chakrabarty notes there has been little discussion of freedom with any awareness of our geological agency *in* the acquisition of freedom.[15] I explore the aporias of the immured spirit and the future of our freedom as a species. Given our dependence on fossil fuels and the earth's natural resources, how free are we?[16] Our freedom is not only confined by the historicism of Hegelian spirit and the parameters of injustices created by neoliberalism. Our freedom is also tethered to—and immured by—our relationship to nature and our ongoing intimate relationship with fossil fuels that sustains our material lifestyle. In that regard, most of us should be concerned about the problems of neo-liberalism and society's unfettered use of precious natural resources that endanger our existence.

Philosopher Walter Benjamin was rightly concerned that 'the state of emergency' in which we live is not the exception but the rule. We must attain to a concept of history that is in keeping with this insight.'[17] In response, Homi Bhabha suggested,

> State of emergency is also always a state of *emergence*. The struggle against colonial oppression not only changes the direction of Western history, but challenges its historicist idea of

---

racialized or infrahuman peoples were regularly associated" (Gilroy, "Suffering and Infrahumanity," 24). In this paper, I use infrahumans to refer to non-whites, non-Christians, most wo/men, the LGBTIQ community, immigrants of color, refugees, asylum seekers, and the impoverished.

12. Brown, "Suffering Rights as Paradoxes," 231.

13. This chapter is part of my larger book project. See Moon, *Mask of Clement Violence*.

14. Chakrabarty, "Climate of History."

15. Chakrabarty, *Crises of Civilization*, 174.

16. Chakrabarty, *Crises of Civilization*, 192.

17. Benjamin, *Illuminations*, 59.

time as a progressive, ordered whole. . . . If the order of Western historicism is disturbed in the colonial state of emergency, even more deeply disturbed is the social and psychic representation of the human subject. For the very nature of humanity becomes estranged in the colonial condition and from that 'naked declivity' it emerges, not as an assertion of will, nor as an evocation of freedom, but as an enigmatic question.[18]

I use the context of Bhabha's "state of emergence" for humanity in critically reflecting on the historicism in the field of spiritual care, as well as for incorporating the insights of "emergence" into decolonizing our theories and practices of spiritual care and its ongoing relationship to the paradoxes of freedom. At this particular juncture of politico-economic and environmental abyss, such explorations of emergence and enigmas are crucial for the liberative work of our immured spirit.

Part One: The Neo-Liberal Web and the Aporias of Freedom

Political theorist Wendy Brown argues that the intellectual founders of neoliberalism—Friedrich Hayek and Milton Friedman—had not envisioned the current conditions under which neoliberal ideals have flourished. She alleges that what is occurring today is a strange mixture of politics and economics, plaited with "racism, nihilism, fatalism and *ressentiment*" that would be scorned by the original architects of neoliberalism.[19] Wendy Brown describes the current neoliberal situation in the United States today as such:

> the new hard-right populism was bled directly from the wound of dethroned privilege that whiteness, Christianity, and maleness granted to those who were otherwise nothing and no one. . . . Thus were the causalities of neoliberal economic policies mobilized by the figure of their own losses, mirrored in a nation lost. This figure drew on a mythical past when families were happy, whole, and heterosexual, when women and racial minorities knew their place, when neighborhoods were orderly, secure, and homogenous, when heroin was a black problem and terrorism was not inside the homeland, and when a hegemonic Christianity and whiteness constituted the manifest identity, power, and pride of the nation and the West. Against invasions

18. Bhabha, *Location of Culture*, 59–60.

19. Brown, *In the Ruins*, 9.

by other peoples, ideas, laws, cultures, and religions, this was the
fairy-tale world right-wing populist leaders promised to protect
and restore.[20]

According to Brown, the architects of neoliberalism who gathered at Mount
Pelerin Society in 1947 would have been shocked to see the metamorphosis
of the original vision of neoliberalism to its current model. She argues that
Hayek and Friedman would have eschewed the involvement of politics in
markets and economic interests in policy making, and they would have been
horrified by the overzealous abuse of power by political leaders.

Brown argues that what is occurring globally in terms of a neoliberal
fascism is not a regression or return to past eras. Rather, it is a new narrative, a new chapter of global history. We need to look beyond the economic
calculation of humans, *homo economicus*, as many neoliberal narratives have
painted. I agree that we need to think beyond the mainstream analysis of a
neoliberal framework that justified such an economic and political exploitation of humans and the destruction of our natural environment to maximize
self-interest and private property. In light of the original intentions of the
founders of neoliberalism, we need to further examine how the underpinnings of freedom via the "markets and morals" vision of Hayek have been
pragmatically manipulated to the grossly twisted version of conservative
neoliberal fascism that has become the "living human web" of today.[21] Brown
argues that the warped transformation of neoliberalism's original framework is the complex result of the exploitation of ideals of markets, freedom,
Christian morals, and the ongoing abuse of white Christian heteronormative
privilege and power that is not seen as socially produced but as normative
and natural. She refers to it as the transmogrification of what constituted
the original values of neoliberalism as a mixture of markets and morals
(i.e., traditional Western Christian values). Freedom of the marketplace has
been strangely imbricated with legal interference in upholding "traditional"
Christian "values" in society, markets, and the political arena.

While Brown states that neoliberal framers would be shocked to see
what is going on politically today; I argue that such benevolent theorizing
on the part of Brown is a disavowal of responsibility to which we should
assign the original framers of liberal and neo-liberal thought. While the
architects of liberalism and neo-liberalism may not have prophetically
determined such an outcome of our current political-economic systems
on a global level, I argue that analyzing the current neoliberal fascist political era as a *new chapter* of the genealogy of freedom can be problematic.

20. Brown, *In the Ruins*, 5.

21. Brown, *In the Ruins*, 7.

Such an interpretation elides the profoundly entwined historicism, racism, Christocentrism, sexism, heterosexism, anthropocentrism, and patriarchal power that were rooted in—and extant throughout—Western economic and political history, but specifically in the works of Locke, Hegel, and Hayek as part of a genealogy of Western freedom and its imbrication with liberal thought. I refer to this as the "Christian hubris of the zero point." Walter Mignolo succinctly describes the phrase coined by Santiago Castro-Gómez, "hubris of the zero point," denoting the arrogance that the European "knowing subject maps the world and its problems, classifies people and projects onto what is good for them."[22]

In a previous article, I argued that Bonnie Miller-McLemore's web metaphor is a precarious one for those who have historically been marginalized by dominant society. While the metaphor of the web was constructed to imagine our inter-connected nature as persons and as a community; it has instead revealed images of solipsism and individualism, as a web is typically woven and occupied by only one spider.[23] Such an interpretation speaks realistically of our neoliberal society and the institutions that were never meant to cultivate democracy, care, or equality. The spider of the web is the neo-liberal subject: the white, Christian, privileged male in society whose status and social power provides protection from institutional and societal inequalities. The "living human web," then, is an apt metaphor for our global community—with its obstacle courses and entanglements specifically designed to marginalize non-whites, non-Christians, most wo/men, immigrants of color, refugees, asylum seekers, etc.

Just as only one spider can realistically occupy a web, so too, does the neoliberal project promote the values of individualism and autonomy. Autonomy of the web meant protection for the privileged white man and his property, while creating pitfalls of exploitation and oppression for infrahumans. The web has become a metaphor for predatory and Darwinian survival-of-the-fittest, individualistic behavior that depicts US society well. The web metaphor accurately depicts the vision of the original founder and architect of neoliberalism, Friedrich Hayek. His vision of freedom meant the acquisition of private property; and justice referred to the protection of the white man's private property. The job of a government was to protect that private property. The web of our neoliberal "community" has been one of exploitation and domination, whereby democracy and equality were

22. Mignolo, "Epistemic Disobedience," 2.

23. This paragraph was modified from my article, "'Living Human Web' Revisited," 22–23. I thank the editors of *Sacred Spaces* for the use of portions of my article to be republished here.

never part of the original vision. In fact, a robust, healthy democracy could be deleterious to the "advancement" of civilization.[24]

Friedrich Hayek was resolute in thinking that society needed to be disbanded in order for us to have true freedom via the market. According to him, the phrase, "social justice" was a "semantic fraud" because justice referred to the protection of private property, not to "altruistic" practices that would harm and deter civilization to its fullest potential.[25] He saw social justice advocates as false "lovers of freedom," and he lamented their "anti-capitalist ethic."[26] Hayek firmly believed that in order for neo-liberalism to survive, social justice projects needed to be eliminated and dismantled. He was apprehensive that socialism could lead to totalitarianism. He feared power in a socialist state and felt that the most secure method of guaranteeing freedom was through a system of private property.[27] Hayek agreed with the work of Adam Ferguson and Adam Smith, who both stated that ownership of private property signaled progress and civilization, which was to be maximized under a neoliberal society.[28]

Today's neoliberal fascism is rooted in the liberal trajectory; it is a nostalgic turn to the vision of freedom—which also entailed a spiritual and racial equilibrium—that was initially envisioned under Lockean liberalism. When we call this Orwellian dystopic phase a "new chapter" of a transmogrified Hayekian neoliberalism, we continue to neglect and dismiss some of the core problems in Western political philosophy, economic theory, and spiritual thought that was part of the idealistic vision of white patri-kyriarchal freedom.[29] We, infrahumans, thought we could be a part of the liberal project of freedom and did not critique the historiographical fine print of the liberal and neoliberal contracts. White Christian supremacy is not exclusive to fringe, ultra conservative right-wing thought relegated to KKK men in white

24. Hayek, *Constitution of Liberty*.

25. Hayek, *Fatal Conceit*, 117–18.

26. Hayek, *Fatal Conceit*, 119.

27. Hayek, *Road to Serfdom*.

28. Hayek, *Fatal Conceit*, 35.

29. I use Elisabeth Schüssler Fiorenza's intellectual framework and category of analysis that addresses the dualistic conceptualization of gender oppression. Kyriarchy is derived from the Greek words for "lord" or "master" (*kyrios*) and "to rule or dominate" (*archein*), in order to redefine the analytic category of patriarchy in terms of multiplicative, overlapping structures of domination. "Kyriarchy" means the domination of the lord, slave master, husband, the elite freeborn educated and propertied man over all wo/men and subaltern men. Patri-kyriarchal oppression refers to the multiplicative and complex ways in which oppression occurs, not simply along the binary of male/female. Patri-kyriarchy more realistically addresses complex situations of power and "control over." See Schüssler Fiorenza, *Jesus and the Politics of Interpretation*.

hoods. In my next section, I explore the elisions and omitted contracts in the genealogy of freedom within Western political theory.

Part Two: Neo-Liberalism and the Infra-Human

For to survive in the mouth of this dragon we call America, we have had to learn this first and most vital lesson—that we were never meant to survive. Not as human beings. And neither were most of you here today, Black or not.[30]

In this section, I "postcolonialize" and interrogate the Christian hubris of the zero point in our theories of liberalism and neoliberalism.[31] I argue that we have failed to thoroughly analyze the problems of Christian hubris within a supposedly secular state from which liberal theories about markets arose. A postcolonial critique of Western ideas of freedom argues that forms of violence against wo/men, people of color, and the environment were coeval with concepts of freedom and liberalism that were imagined in the fictive social contracts. In addition to the physical violence experienced by infrahumans, I want to highlight the imbrication of clement and curative forms of violence that were coterminous with the writings and theories of Locke, Hayek, and Hegel. The desire for freedom and the goods of liberalism sanctioned (and still causes) many wo/men and people of color to endure, tolerate, and even accept certain forms of violence that are seen as part of the norm of daily life. We believe we have to accept certain types of violence as part of the conditions of freedom because "normative society" operates at the Christian androcentric hubris of the zero point. Christianity became a tool of Locke and other contract theorists to justify patri-kyriarchal rule as the framework that would advance the propertied self-interests of white men.

Spiritual care was an important part of the framework of Lockean liberalism and Hayekian neo-liberalism that have shaped our ideals and practices of freedom and human rights. Situated at the Christian hubris of the zero-point, clement violence refers to the condoning or pardoning of micro-aggressions and practices of white supremacy by people of color, non-Christians, and the LGBTIQ+ community (i.e., the infrahumans). Curative violence denotes the assimilationist practices or the physical and psychic spiral declivity of our dignity for the sake of being accepted by the dominant white society.

---

30. Lorde, *Sister Outsider*, 42.
31. Lartey, *Postcolonializing God*.

Our dignity and self-respect are obliterated within the ordinary, quotidian violence of the infrahuman experience, such as invisibility, spiritual erasures, and racial microaggressions. The historicism of Western civilization (i.e., notions of progress and our quest for freedom) has led the majority of the global community to accept the conditions of liberalism under which non-whites were colonized and wo/men were subjugated. People bought into (or were forced into accepting) the European/US narrative of the superiority of white, Christian, heterosexual "civilization." Postcolonial theorist Gayatri Spivak speaks of liberal individualism as a "violating enablement," and liberalism as "that which we cannot not want."[32] The immured spirit refers to this historicist Hegelian understanding of Spirit in political and economic theory that justified the denial of freedom and property to people of color. The immured spirit signifies the chasm/gulf between that desired freedom and the psychic and spiritual violence we experience, endure, or tolerate in order to attain that freedom. In other words, our spirit and dignity have been imprisoned in our desire to be part of the discourse of freedom.

Spiritual care, therefore, has been intricately and intimately tied to concepts of freedom and liberation—whether in denying a people their freedom and humanity or in helping white Christians obtain theirs. Engaging in spiritual care certainly is not just an individual or devotional matter, relegated to the private sphere of the home or in religious spaces. Spiritual care has been integral—and imbricated—in shaping our political, economic, and social web of life. Yet, spiritual care is rarely addressed outside of theology classes, seminaries, or chaplaincy programs, where "care" is still predominantly seen through a paternalistic lens of Western "arrogant perception."[33] Hegelian theories of the inferior spirit of wo/men, non-whites, and non-Christians have been central to the justification of our/their subordinate subaltern status.[34]

Race, gender, and religion have been coeval determining social constructs in establishing privilege in the political system of white supremacy in the contract theories, as well as in the work of neoliberal architect, Friedrich Hayek. Liberalism and neoliberalism are premised on Christian underpinnings of society (the spiritual care contract is coterminous with the sexual and racial contract). Here, I interrogate Wendy Brown's assertion that our current politico-economic state is a warped, transmogrified neoliberal system that would shock its founders. Our current twisted state of neoliberalism

---

32. Spivak, *Outside in the Teaching Machine*, 230.

33. Gunning, "Arrogant Perception."

34. Hegel, *Phenomenology of Spirit*.

reinforces the historicism of Hayek, Hegel, and Locke, as well as the Christian hubris of the zero point. Infrahumans are exploited for the sake of the white European/UnitedStatesean man's vision of freedom of the right to maximize private property and self-interest under a liberal and neo-liberal ideology that has produced forms of violence against wo/men, people of color, non-Christians, the LGBTIQ+ community, as well as the environment.

John Locke

John Locke's ideas, especially his *Second Treatise of Government,* had a huge influence in American ideas of a limited government, unlimited private property, and the right to revolution.[35] Lockean liberalism is premised on a mythic social contract, which established and upheld modern patri-kyriarchy. The Western myth of freedom describes how white Christian men left the state of nature and entered into political and civil society. To transgress from the state of nature to a "civil society," theorists such as Rousseau, Hobbes, and Locke constructed the quintessential metaphor of freedom for humans as the white, European, Christian man whose rational minds would guide them to maximize their self-interests in the market. The synecdoche for freedom was the secular-but-Christian, autonomous liberal subject who lived outside the perimeter of "nature." This theoretical project of universal Western liberalism justified forced domination, subordination, and assimilation of people's identities, religions, spirits, and cultures. The state of nature is metonymic of barbarian, savage, child-like people of color whose animistic spirits were not truly worthy of human dignity. Homi Bhabha describes the ways in which a colonial regime drives the colonized to mimic the ideals of whiteness.[36] Even when infrahumans accepted the terms of liberalism and freedom via colonialism, assimilation, Christian normativity, and self-hatred; they could only attain the status of "*almost the same, but not quite*" white.[37] Infrahumans are products of the mimicry of the Western liberal subject.

Locke's social contract theory also established modern patri-kyriarchy that legitimized rule by white Christian men as "natural" and part of the path to civilization. Political philosophers Carole Pateman and Charles Mills have challenged the androcentric, white privilege of the social contract with a sexual and racial contract, respectively. Pateman argues that the social contract tells only half the story of the original contract that

35. Locke, *Second Treatise.*
36. Bhabha, *Location of Culture.*
37. Bhabha, *Location of Culture,* 127.

established modern patriarchy. She argues that the sexual contract has been neglected, thereby granting men the right to domination and subordination of wo/men. Given the historicism and deep paternalism of the social contract, to build an argument of universal freedom on such patriarchal myths is problematic, and therefore, "a political fiction."[38] The sexual contract is ignored and men's patriarchal right over wo/men is not told in the story of the social contract; wo/men were left out of the contract to form or govern the political state. The premise of a Lockean liberalism of the right to property and patriarchy, therefore, is no path to freedom or equality for wo/men. Pateman warns of the limits of using contractarian theory for progressive use, securing false gendered and sexed narratives of not only patriarchy but also of heterosexual relations.

Political philosopher Charles Mills also critiques the limits of Western philosophical discourses in the elision of "White supremacy" as the "unnamed political system that has made the modern world what it is today."[39] Mills refers to the social contract as a contract that mattered between people who counted, i.e., white people. This elision of race, i.e., the racial contract, critiques the epistemological, political, and moral aspects of the social contract. Contract theories have justified patri-kyriarchal rule and white racial privilege. While the Lockean social contract theory is presented as a story of freedom; it is one of subjection for wo/men and people of color.[40] For infrahumans, then, contractual freedom is based on subjection and subordination to elite white Christian men.

In the same vein of Carole Pateman and Charles Mills who have pointed out the omissions of the sexual and racial contracts, I argue that a spiritual care contract has been left out of the original social contract. While Locke's A Letter Concerning Toleration could be read as a prescription for religious pluralism, it was actually a Western Christian reformulation and interpretation of spiritual practices and what was considered to be "religion" as defined by Christian categories. The Letter, in describing a tolerance for "religion," was referring to Christianity and Christian denominations. Locke's "truth" of religion actually led to the undermining of the plurality of spiritual intellectual ideas in other parts of the world. Here, he was referring to toleration of varying Christian beliefs and interpretations. He assumed his readers to be Christian. Despite his support for secularism in public life, Locke disdained atheists in a civil society. He stated,

---

38. Pateman, Sexual Contract, 18.

39. Mills, Racial Contract, 1

40. Pateman and Mills, Contract and Domination.

> Those are not at all to be tolerated who deny the Being of a
> God. Promises, Covenants, and Oaths, which are the Bonds of a
> Humane Society, can have no hold upon an Atheist. The taking
> away of God, tho but even in thought, dissolves all.[41]

This understanding of secularism (based on Christian principles) was a historicist concept imposed on non-Western countries, as most countries did not perceive a secular/sacred divide in the way that Locke, as well as Western political philosophers or theologians, categorized. Confucianism or Buddhism would be considered atheism in a Lockean mindset and were categorized as "religions" by Western scholars to study other cultures. A postcolonial analysis of the Christian hubris of the zero-point critiques how Western scholarship constructed religion as a hierarchical category in objectifying other peoples in relation to Christianity. Timothy Fitzgerald argues that liberal ecumenical theologians have constructed "world theologies" as part of a "wider historical process of western imperialism, colonialism, and neocolonialism."[42]

Locke argued that belief (i.e., Christian belief) was important to keep civil rules and that there are no atheists who can keep promises of civil grounds. Christians—as Locke has reinterpreted—would serve a new role in civil society, and atheists were not to be tolerated. He contradicts himself when he states, "Obedience is due in the first place to God, and afterwards to the Laws."[43] Yet in another place, he argues that first one needs to obey civil laws. At the same time, he emphasizes in several places that religion is private and should be up to the individual. A secular, civil society, then, is one that is governed by "Christian" principles and ethics. Just as he has zero tolerance for atheists, there is no tolerance for non-Christians (he categorizes Muslims and Jews together) to be seen within his framework of care and civil society.[44] At the same time, he states, "But there is absolutely no such thing, under the Gospel, as a Christian commonwealth."[45]

As much as there is confusion for Locke in compromising a Christian hubris of the zero point; it becomes the standard for the principles of Western political, economic, and social civilization. While the devotional aspects of religion (i.e., Christianity) are private and society should be secular, Locke still believed a society needed to be Christian. I am not sure how he reconciles splitting Christianity and civil society if he strongly believed

41. Locke, *Letter Concerning Toleration,* 51

42. Fitzgerald, *Ideology of Religious Studies,* 7–8.

43. Locke, *Letter Concerning Toleration,* 48.

44. Locke, *Letter Concerning Toleration,* 43–45.

45. Locke, *Letter Concerning Toleration,* 44.

atheists and non-Christians were unhealthy *for* a civil society. Gender is also part of the discourse of secularism. Feminist historian Joan Scott argues that secularism helped promote gender inequality by arguing for separate spheres of religion and secular, private/public, thereby justifying inequality by relegating wo/men to the margins.[46]

Friedrich Hayek

Friedrich Hayek shared similar views with Locke on private property, self-interests, and the Christian foundations of a neoliberal market. By "liberal," he was referring to the original nineteenth-century term of the property-owning man who denied all privileges. He equated conservatives with paternalistic, nationalistic, and power-clinging defenders of established privileges who leaned on the power of government to protect their privileges. Writing on the heels of the great depression and seeing socialism gain strength globally, he warned Europeans (and later, UnitedStateseans) about the dangers of big government, care, and altruism. His central concern was the power acquired by leaders in a socialist state. He believed that a system of private property was the most secure guarantee of freedom. He saw the importance of Christianity, individualism, and the free market. Christianity was the signifier of civilized Western society, which he linked to individualism and the free market. He believed,

> Individualism, in contrast to socialism and other forms of totalitarianism, is based on the respect of Christianity for the individual man and his belief that it is desirable that men should be free to develop their own individual gifts and bents. This philosophy, first fully developed during the Renaissance, grew and spread into what we know as Western civilization.[47]

While Hayek did not think the displacement of various groups of people *needed* to be bloody, acts of violence and displacement of savages were justified if it meant progress towards greater ideals of Western civilization by advanced people.[48] This underlying justification of violence within the neoliberal project seems to contradict Wendy Brown's assertion that Hayek would have scorned the neoliberal fascist "Frankensteinian" creation of our current global political situation. Hayek would possibly see the necessity of fascist-like polities if the white Christian androcentric neoliberal subject were

46. Scott, *Sex and Secularism*, 4.

47. Hayek, *Road to Serfdom*, 42.

48. Hayek, *Fatal Conceit*, 121.

to maintain and maximize "his" property to the greatest extent (the original canonical vision of neo-liberalism) and secure "his" freedom to do so.

Contractarian theories have elided the sexual, racial, colonial, and spiritual care contracts. Such elisions in the social contract can be interpreted to mean that all of these "other" contracts of being "human" were not important *if* it interfered with the maximization of white Christian men's private property. This is the Christian hubris of the zero point with regard to freedom for Britain and its dysfunctional descendant, the United States. Georg W. F. Hegel's racist understanding of spirit continues to reverberate and shape our understandings of freedom and civilization. Europeans or whites became the very paragon of freedom and rationality and it emanated from their spirit. Hegelian thought privileged European white modern thought (modern but secular meant Christian) as the model of universal freedom. This historicist misunderstanding of Hegelian spirit largely informed European/American racist understandings of the inferior status of people of color, thereby justifying the enslavement of Africans, colonization of lands, and the economic and cultural exploitation of people of color. Hegelian thought privileged European/white subjects as a model of freedom. The Hegelian view of Asia and Africa as static, despotic, and irrelevant to world history—as ignorant and superstitious—has shaped how people's spirit was seen. Neoliberalism upholds this framework of the elision of the sexual, racial, colonial, and spiritual contracts.

Clement and Curative Violence

If we do not define ourselves for ourselves, we will be defined by others—for their use and detriment.[49]

The "markets and morals" that framed the original neoliberal framework is directly connected to the Christian hubris of the zero point, the scaffold for the fascist neoliberal political economic system in which we are living today. The construction of the modern citizen was part of the legacy of colonialism and European historiography.[50] It was this aspect of the civilizing projects of the Europeans (as well as the Japanese towards their Asian neighbors) that justified oppression of the Other. It was also under colonialism that subjects engaged in discourses and practices that led to the formation of the "modern citizen." The discourses of the liberal subject, rights, modernity, nation, and identity are fragmented discourses that presuppose Western

49. Lorde, *Sister Outsider*, 45.

50. Chakrabarty, *Provincializing Europe*.

assimilation or a colonial contract as a precursor to attaining such rights. The aporias of freedom—according to Western liberal discourse—is that without colonialism, assimilation, and the internalization of androcentric European superiority; infrahumans could not be part of the liberal project of Enlightenment. Assimilation, civilization, and imperialism were necessary to lift us out from the place of backwardness, stagnancy, dependency, and our child-like state. Infrahumans were, and are, circumscribed by the very discourses from which they sought liberation.[51]

I refer to this concept of spiritual erasure, identitarian violence, and psychic colonization as clement and curative violence. Disability studies scholar Eun Jung Kim refers to curative violence as the desire by mainstream society to "fix," "change," and "cure" someone because they think they need normalizing, curing, or altering. Kim describes the desire of disabled people in Korea to belong and society that pressures this desire. In depicting the propagandistic scenario of how the disabled are depicted in Korea, Kim shows the uncannily similar representation of Darwinian-era evolution of humans who turned from ape to human in different stages. Here, Kim shows a 2005 postage stamp showing the "evolution" of a man in a wheelchair, whereby each scene shows he is a little more upright until he is jumping and hugging another able-bodied human. She writes, "This process captures how curative science enables intimate relations, making visible the assumption that normative functioning is the precondition of social inclusion."[52] Similar to a linear Western progress of civilization, she shows how Korean society disavows disability to the extent that they depict those with disabilities as being less intimate, less social, and less able to be part of the nation-state. The curative violence coeval with neoliberalism conveys a similar message: in order to belong and be part of Western civilization means "curing" the primitive and hyper-religious self and assimilating into a recognizable and palatable almost-white Christian subject.

Clement violence is a metonymy for the quotidian violence of racial micro-aggressions that have been woven into politico-economic, social, and cultural structures and have become part of the demos of society.[53] Clement violence is tolerated and seen as "mild," in opposition to direct physical forms of violence. Sue and Sue coined the term, "marginal man," referring to the Asian American subject who desires to assimilate into mainstream

---

51. This paragraph was adapted from my article "Fictions of Liberation." I thank the editors of *Journal of Pastoral Theology* for the generous use of this paragraph in this chapter.

52. Kim, *Curative Violence*, 2.

53. Clement violence is a concept that I develop more fully in my book, *Mask of Clement Violence*.

society at any cost. The marginal man denies racism and the heinous acts that occur because to admit racism would mean he is joining a racist society.[54] I extend this concept of the marginal being to apply to all people of color who have to live in a world of code switching—wary that their true selves have to be cloaked in order to be accepted as part of white European civilization.[55] Such structures of white Christian privilege have created bipolar identities of racial melancholia for people of color. By that, I refer to the inability to blend into an assimilated "melting pot" of Christian America—it is unattainable and virtually impossible for people of color and non-Christians, thereby being seen and labeled as "pathological to the nation."[56] We are imprisoned in our own identities because we are seen as negligible or treated as marginal in society.

The clement violence of the immured spirit is the violence to which people of color are exposed on a daily basis. They are willing to overlook, disdain, or grant such violence amnesty/clemency—whether in the workplace, in schools, community spaces, and in interpersonal encounters—because of the Christian hubris of the zero point that normalizes such violence. People of color fear that they/we *look* "pathological" if we do not grant amnesty to the micro-violence. We, therefore, endure further pathological treatment and inhale the invisible poison of racial microaggressions, thereby perpetuating the toxicity of racism on which liberalism and the freedom of this nation were founded.[57]

Curative violence, in reference to spiritual care, is part of the assimilationist colonial-era violence that robbed infrahumans of our dignity and humanity. Curative violence of the Christian hubris of the zero point further refines this understanding of what constitutes "pastoral" care. The heuristic of an immured spirit signifies much more than the colonization of the infrahuman mind or our impaired freedom. The immured spirit is a synecdoche for the curative and clement violence that impales and pierces the very entelechy of our identity. We cannot envision or theorize religion or spiritual care without incorporating—and tending to—the colonial wounds that were inflicted and continues to dictate who has power to control what is

54. Eng and Han, *Racial Melancholia*.

55. Frantz Fanon describes this in his *Black Skin, White Masks*—accepting an inferiority complex.

56. Eng and Han, *Racial Melancholia*.

57. Derald Wing Sue refers to microaggressions as comparable to carbon monoxide—"invisible but potentially lethal" to the person of color, who is the target of the microaggression, while invisible and benign to the perpetrator. It is easily dismissed and explained by the perpetrator and left unaccountable. See Sue et al., "Racial Microaggressions in Everyday Life."

(and is not) spiritual care today. Spiritual care (and its colonial wounds) has to be theorized more critically in discourses about religion. Further, the theories need to examine the entangled forms of power—physical, structural, and discursive—that have shaped how spiritual care has been understood in US society, as well as how it is practiced.

What we are currently witnessing in the even more perverted neoliberal fascist United States (and other places) are the roots of the traditions and morals from which neoliberalism grew. White Christian men were supposed to profit from this and preserve their property. Those of the "lesser" civilizations were benefiting and gaining from the ideals and visions reserved for white Europeans and "Americans." Hayek makes a discomforting statement about Asians *profiting* from the ideas of the whites (who were superior), yet, they were not really changing in their customs.[58] This underscores the curative and clement forms of violence that have been coeval with neoliberalism. We are expected to assimilate to "normative" white Christian society if we are to profit and be part of "civilized" Western neoliberal society.

From such structures of clement and curative violence, we have seen the "emergence" of "postcolonializing" spiritual care. Those of us involved in this book project desire to address the "colonial wounds" that have immured our spirits. We need to re-theorize clement and curative violence and its imbrication with spiritual care. The quotidian violence of micro-aggressions situated at the Christian hubris of the zero point is overlooked and tolerated for the sake of belonging in a neoliberal material world. In this regard, we are reifying the ideologies that have perpetuated colonial hierarchies in hospitals, universities, schools, the markets, as well as other public spaces. If our work is involved in public institutions and public spaces, we need to critically examine our complicity in the structures of quotidian violence at the Christian hubris of the zero point and critique how we reproduce clement and curative violence in the daily practices of care. We continue to excuse the quotidian spiritual violence that seems mild and is tolerated; but this "descent into the ordinary" circadian violence has helped create the Frankenstein transmogrification of neoliberalism we experience today.[59]

---

58. Hayek, *Constitution of Liberty*, 52.

59. Das, *Life and Words*.

Conclusion: The Climate Care Contract

Economist Thomas Piketty lays out the grave problems of a neoliberal market and the extreme inequalities that result.[60] Markets generate capital accumulation at a greater rate than they generate growth. Increased wealth at the top means a larger impoverishment gap at the bottom of society, creating a stagnant economy. With such extreme inequality, a neo-feudalist, oligarchic class will emerge, rather than a growth-based economic development. Free markets are not generating growth to its fullest potential, signifying the end of equality of opportunity. Given this trajectory of a neoliberal economy, there are limited options for liberative social justice, given our Frankensteinian neoliberal state. The idea of freedom and *individual* freedom to which Bonnie Miller-McLemore referred in her twenty-five-year retrospective of the "living human web" is no longer tenable in such a trajectory of a neoliberal market society. This leads me to address one commonality of the variegated meanings of freedom in the neoliberal living human web of the United States and Korea: our extreme profligate use of fossil fuels and the accumulation of material goods.

The founders of liberal and neo-liberal theory also omitted a climate care contract. We are not free. There is no *individual* freedom; we are dependent on collective communities and resources for our care needs. That is, we are not really free and independent—no one is immune from the dependence that we, as humans, have on the fossil fuels that drive our neoliberal society.[61] Not only are we *not* just human economic actors; we are also geological agents, trenchantly and abidingly contributing to the global climate crisis. The ground zero of anthropocentric hubris begins with imprudent fossil fuel use: the locale to which our freedom is tethered.

The living human web, therefore, is also a metaphor for our geological agency in the age of the Anthropocene.[62] The geophysical force of the "non-human" human, whereby conventional understandings of nature and human collapse and are blurred, reinforces our connection to the nonliving and the non-human.[63] The collective force, being neither "subject nor object," has become responsible for the climate crisis and global warming

---

60. Piketty, *Capital in the Twenty-First Century.*

61. Chakrabarty, "Climate of History."

62. The term, "anthropocene," was coined by US biologist Eugene Stoermer and Dutch geochemist Paul Crutzen. It refers to the geological force of human activities that has transformed the planet's atmosphere due to the burning of fossil fuels, accounting for climate change.

63. Chakrabarty, "Climate of History."

in a neoliberal age from which we cannot escape.[64] Our freedom, in that regard, has equal bearing on seeing our extreme dependence on fossil fuels. This non-human geological force of our own human creation has resulted in the Frankensteinian climate crisis that is now part of the genealogy of Western "progress," neoliberal ideology, and Western Enlightenment ideals of freedom. It is what Timothy LeCain refers to as the "Great Ontological Collapse"—we have been taught to believe by Western Enlightenment thinking that European society was superior to the natural world and the infrahumans of Asia and Africa.[65]

In conclusion, I critically reflect on the aporetic tensions of power and the paradoxes of freedom in a neoliberal economizing of the state, its people, and its natural resources. In this chapter, I have described some of the ongoing discursive shifts of what constitutes the "human," freedom, and spiritual care. I described the dehumanization of peoples who played a liberating role for elite white Christian people. The poor and disenfranchised infrahumans that were exploited to give white androcentric Christian supremacy its power, once again, have given wealthy, elite humans our freedom in the current era. Chakrabarty notes the irony that if socialism had succeeded, we would have had greater climate change problems.[66] It is because the poor and marginalized do not have as much access to material resources that we are actually in a better position with regard to climate change. Because neoliberalism as a mode of capitalism succeeded, we have less of a climate crisis than if socialism had provided greater resources of capital for the poor.[67] The living human web—human and "non-human" human—has become a force for our liberation, but also paradoxically has been the source of our collective immured spirit. As we have acquired freedom and liberation, we have oppressed and exploited the environment to such absolute declivity that it has contributed to our own ontological downfall. We are all utterly dependent on nature and fossil fuels for our survival, our pleasure, our work. We are *all* immured by the very structures that gave us our freedom.

A neoliberal society disavows providing structures for care. Neoliberalism destroys and takes over the political process of democracy and civic participation. It remakes the soul, the citizen, nature, and the demos.[68] Yet, we have seen from the contributors in this volume that humans and the

64. Chakrabarty, "Climate of History."

65. LeCain, "Heralding a New Humanism," 16.

66. Chakrabarty, "Climate and Capital," 10. He states there are only twelve or so nations (about one-fifth of humanity) that are responsible for the majority of greenhouse gas emissions.

67. Chakrabarty, "Climate and Capital," 11.

68. Brown, *Undoing the Demos*.

environment *are* in need of care, as well as in a position to *create* structures of care. Despite all of the barriers to social justice in a neoliberal world, this volume shows the commitment that people and their communities have made to overcome such demoralizing structures that destroy humans and nature. The "rhythms of care"[69] pulsate as part of our internal biological clock, challenging the ongoing quotidian violence against humans and nature. The practices of care reveal, "not an ascent into the transcendent, but a descent into the ordinary."[70] Such "rhythms of care" help to humanize our neoliberal world that disavow structures of care. These are the aporias of our freedom and the ongoing emergence of subversive powers and practices of spiritual care in a neoliberal age.

69. Lewis, "Intentional Rhythms."
70. Das, *Life and Words*, 15.

Epilogue

Beyond "Classic Readings"
in Pastoral Theology

— BONNIE MILLER-MCLEMORE —

WHEN ROBERT DYKSTRA PUBLISHED *Images of Pastoral Care: Classic Readings* almost fifteen years ago, I doubt anyone raised a question about a leading term in the title—*classic*.[1] Since then, however, the very meaning of classic has undergone considerable revision. While working on a comparable anthology, *The Wiley Blackwell Reader in Practical Theology*, I encountered the dilemma head on.[2] The intent of the *Reader* was to collect pivotal or classic essays from practical theology's renaissance as a discipline in the twentieth- and twenty-first century. But what, indeed, defines a "classic?" And who gets to determine that classification? Few of us avoid neglecting key scholarship in our research, but "omission is especially egregious when it comes to a reader," as I note in the *Reader*'s preface. Given the "proprietary spirit" of white practical theologians, which has fostered an obliviousness about the racialized nature of conventional scholarship, a reader today demands an "active rereading" of the so-called classics, to borrow the words of Tom Beaudoin and Kathryn Turpin.[3] This raises a crucial question when compiling a volume that collects key scholarship and recounts a discipline's history: How has the term *classic* not just preserved valuable work but also perpetuated exclusion and discrimination?

1. Dykstra, *Images of Pastoral Care*.
2. Miller-McLemore, *Reader in Practical Theology*, 7.
3. Beaudoin and Turpin, "White Practical Theology," 268.

Fortunately, other authors and books disturb the status quo, and you have just such a book in your hands. By contrast to Dykstra's collection that inspired it, *Postcolonial Images of Spiritual Care* turns the comfortable discipline of pastoral theology wonderfully upside down. You cannot read these chapters without seeing care of others and the world anew. The book before you, raises crucial questions about colonialist and imperialist presumptions within pastoral theology and pushes scholars and care practitioners toward fresh horizons of care for all those wounded by the toxic fallout. In a word: what a significant and energizing collection of essays!

I am honored to add a few words of closure, even though my own work has sometimes contributed to the problems that these essays explore. I am grateful to see ideas corrected and fresh proposals projected. Indeed, even as I worked on this epilogue, I benefited immensely from the constructive feedback offered by Hellena Moon, Sumi Kim, and other authors on places where my own oversights reemerged. Although I began teaching when neither white women nor people of color had much of a place, I have affiliated with the ruling class through association, whiteness, wealth, education, Christianity, heterosexuality, and world and language location. Habits of distortion and misunderstanding are difficult to overcome, especially when we adopt the scholarly mode and tone that we inherited from our white forefathers. I and colleagues in similar places have missed much that we should have noticed along the way, leaving reverberating wakes of harm behind us. We need to stand corrected (and re-corrected). The grace and benefit of the doubt extended to me and others throughout this book despite our transgressions models the kind of kindness that all of us will need if we are to flourish together within and beyond the discipline of pastoral theology.

Critique: Subverting Eurocentric Pastoral Images

So, what did I learn and what do I imagine readers learning as we read the book? Whereas Dykstra's *Images of Pastoral Care* looks back, *Postcolonial Images* looks forward. In turning back, *Images of Pastoral Care* surveys an imposing terrain of white Protestant Christian men predominately from the United States (e.g., Anton Boisen, Seward Hiltner, Charles Gerkin, Henri Nouwen, James Dittes, etc.) and includes only a glimpse of the turn-of-the-century-present—one African American man and five white women out of nineteen contributors. By contrast, *Postcolonial Images* opens out into the brightness of a new day and turns our attention toward a daunting future, imploring us to consider where we are going. It offers at once a stunning array of scholars from diverse positions, *and* it constructs a remarkably coherent vision. I group my remarks around three common diagnostic arenas to which the authors contribute: critique, reconstruction, and transformation.

When it comes to critique, Hellena Moon's labor on this volume and her own chapter on the hypocrisies surrounding individual freedom deserve special mention. *Postcolonial Spiritual Care* offers a formidable critique of top-down Christocentric pastoral care. Drawing on political philosophers Carole Pateman and Charles Mills in her own essay, Moon reveals the hidden contracts within the liberal social contract.[4] When John Locke advocated for the inalienability of human rights, and Friedrich Hayek supported the free market, they procured freedom for their recognized subjects—educated and equipped white men—while limiting it for all others. "While the Lockean social contract theory is presented as a story of freedom," Moon argues, "it is one of subjection for wo/men and people of color," and as she says elsewhere, of land itself.[5] Three hidden contracts turn freedom into a specter: the *gender contract* presumes that women will serve men; the *race contract* ranks people from light to dark; and, too often overlooked in my view, the *climate contract* hides the devastation spewed by Western "progress."

A dominating metaphor for the subject matter of pastoral theology, the living human web, reflects its Euro-centric origins. Even though the metaphor arose to "confront systems of domination"[6]—the personal as political, illness as located within wider systems, and repression of minoritized voices in the discipline—the living web inherits the pathologies of its context and has inevitably covered over patterns of colonial erasure. We must "reground this metaphor" in its "material political economic context," argues Bruce Rogers-Vaughn in his chapter. How do we "care for souls" in the midst of the "dark web" or the "gaps, recesses, and interstices" of contemporary capitalism, including the entrapping market web of the Internet? Cedric Johnson goes further in his contribution. The problem is not simply neoliberal ideology; we live in a *neoliberal age* "that is far more complicated," he says. To counter the "interrelated systems of governance" of a neoliberal age, we need a "multi-systems approach that considers the potential influence a matrix of forces may have on those who come for care."

Events in the United States in the last several years—police and civilian murder of people of color, the 2016 US presidential election, and publications internal to pastoral and practical theology on white racism—make a book

---

4. See Pateman and Mills, *Contract and Domination*.

5. Please note: all quotes without citation, here and below, come from the chapters above.

6. Miller-McLemore, *Christian Theology in Practice*, 35. See also Miller-McLemore, "Human Web"; "Living Human Web."

like *Postcolonial Images* absolutely requisite. As I observe in the *Reader in Practical Theology*, intolerance, xenophobia, chauvinism, ultra-nationalism, and colonialism remain prevailing problems of our time.[7] In fact, in the United States white supremacy and misogyny have gained an alarming level of acceptability. The self-reflective essay by Alexander Brown, written by an undergraduate student, offers one of the most compelling critiques in the volume precisely because the author takes us inside the embodied struggles created by exclusive norms that reject the complexities of human identity. Although to a certain extent these problems are unique to the United States, white nationalist and patriarchal movements here have parallels in other so-called developed countries and in countries where democratic efforts struggle against brutal regimes. As the powerful words of Brown attest, overcoming white supremacy, patriarchy, and heteronormativity cannot be done by an act of will or contrition or even consciousness-raising. As we have seen in pastoral theology and beyond, assertions, confession, and learning are not enough. Progress requires spiritual discernment, disclosure, pain, and persistent self-scrutiny that goes beyond words, uttered or written, and transforms interior, interpersonal, and political spaces. The very organization of *Postcolonial Images*—from personal to communal to global—reflects this dynamic movement. Rehabilitation—a reconstituting of bodies, minds, souls, and politics—is no small agenda, especially for those who have inherited four centuries of colonialist mis-self-perception and dis/advantage.

Two questions arise as we listen to the critique in this volume: First, what *do* we do about modernity? Modernity puts us into a double-bind. We cannot live without it, but we can no longer live within it. Selling a book on neoliberalism via the US market and social media is a trite example of the Catch-22. I encountered a more ingrained instance last year while attending an international conference in Brazil. In its beginnings, the International Academy of Practical Theology necessarily but unselfconsciously adopted English as its working language.[8] The decision seemed self-evident. Members needed a lingua franca to communicate across multiple language differences. Yet, English has the honor of worldwide dependence as a result of Western imperialism and global markets. It is a language of aristocracy and conquest. However, in South America where Spanish and Portuguese predominate, there is less need to master English. Even though Portuguese has its own ambiguous colonial legacy in Brazil, people experience English as a colonizing language, capable of fostering a sense of inadequacy and misperceptions about intelligence. Meanwhile, native English speakers

---

7. Miller-McLemore, *Reader in Practical Theology*, 1.

8. See Miller-McLemore, "Tale of Two Cities," 8; *Reader in Practical Theology*, 11.

fail to recognize the advantage wielded or the harm done through English dominance. *And yet*: English allows for international conversation, association, and even friendships.

In other words, can we "reject historic Western models of research" as a panelist on the future of practical theology remarked at a 2018 session of the American Academy of Religion, an institution that itself perpetuates a Western model of intellectual interchange?[9] Is rejection possible? Contest, modify, and transform, yes; reject, not really. Minimally, individual and collective healing from historical trauma cannot occur, as Cedric Johnson argues in his book on resilience in a neoliberal age, without cultural memory and processes of "commemoration."[10]

This puzzle raises an important sub-question: *are* there *any* goods that remain within modern European Enlightenment, such as the worth and dignity of each person? Even as liberalism sustained structures of oppression for women, for example, it also laid the grounds for women's inherent value and liberty. Or to take a lesser instance, even as the Internet exploits, as Rogers-Vaughn asserts, it also provides a means for connection and even resistance. Has neoliberalism "contaminated the *whole* fabric of the living human web," as he argues, or just significant parts? Greed, patriarchy, bigotry, and other oppressions existed before modernity in and beyond Europe. Modernity paradoxically provided fresh means to challenge such oppressions, even as it imposed further tyranny through colonization, color codes, the cult of domesticity, obsession with technology, idealization of abstract rationality, and so forth.

It is worth noting as an aside that pastoral and practical theology's white male Christian founders faced their own kind of academic ostracization.[11] In one of the first international volumes in the 1990s, for example, faith stage scholar James Fowler describes the 1980s "revolution" in practical theology as a move from the "basement" of departments housed "as though they were afterthoughts."[12] Seward Hiltner, heralded as a founder and advocate for study of living documents, littered his *Preface to Pastoral Theology* with testy footnotes about the "antipractical bias" in academe.[13] These stories do not diminish the biases and distortion in our own history, but they should help spark a spirit of generosity among ourselves.

9. Hong, "Teaching Practical Theology De-Colonially."

10. Johnson, *Race, Religion, and Resilience*, 2, 101–26. See also Herman, *Trauma and Recovery*.

11. See Miller-McLemore, "Theory-Practice Binary."

12. Fowler, "Emerging New Shape of Practical Theology," 75.

13. Hiltner, *Preface to Pastoral Theology*, 218.

In addition to modernity's ambiguities, a second question arises. Are there times when global or totalizing language gets in our way? For example, is the Internet really "an instrument of neoliberal colonization," as Rogers-Vaughn argues, or is it more complicated than this? Is the living human web really "a neoliberal global network . . . that celebrates never-ending progress, ever-expanding knowledge, wealth production, and individual meritocracy," or does this depiction distort the modest meanings of a term that merely describes the discipline's subject matter? Code language and overstatement are dangers worth avoiding. Temptation toward polarization and the reduction of complexity into good-evil binaries characterizes early infant development, the tenor of Mao's Cultural Revolution, and the political era in which we live.[14] The danger of global denouncements and abstractions is that they can leave people, especially those minoritized, more disempowered than before, obscuring understanding, diminishing a sense of agency, and skirting concrete tactics for resistance and change.

If I could change anything in my own writing, it would be to diminish overstatement and extend charity more abundantly.[15] Adopting a "visionary" rather than "castigating" tone, as Sumi Kim suggested in personal correspondence, invites a more inspiring and enduring reading. Academia trains us to castigate; this volume summons us to imagine. Such generosity of spirit toward others and ourselves contests the colonizing ideologies that we have inherited and undergirds both sound work and the wider common good.

Reconstruction: Fostering New Postcolonial Images

Even more important than critique, authors in *Postcolonial Images* offer a virtual banquet of fresh pastoral images grounded in the mandate to "love one another as we are," in Omid Safi's opening words. Emmanuel Lartey reclaims an African spirituality that stands in sharp contrast to modern conceptions, reconnecting persons with other animate and inanimate beings and imbuing all reality with a *relational sacrality* that is woven into and through interconnection. Kim turns to the Buddhist image of the *flower of interbeing* to enhance personal agency while "feeling trapped in large-scale political, economic, and social systems." Mindy McGarrah Sharp paints a beautiful portrait of *basketry* and *phoenix poets in a flammable world*. Especially groundbreaking, Bilal Ansari draws on his experiences of Islamophobic and racist acts after 9/11 to overturn negative connotations of *black sheep* and reclaim *black shepherding* as a metaphor that builds on Muslim traditions

14. See Thien, *Do Not Say We Have Nothing.*
15. See Miller-McLemore, "Hubris and Folly."

of care. Equally powerful, Greg Epstein recalls a finger grasp with his newborn son as their first act after a harrowing birth and suggests *midwifery* as an image for care that reaches the religiously disaffiliated, a population that has "tripled over the last two decades." Lori Klein and Cedric Johnson both suggest the image of the *cultural broker* who counters the forces of a neoliberal age, "bridging, linking, or mediating between groups" and "*within communities*" in Johnson's words. Rogers-Vaughn encourages us to confront the *dark web*, the unnoticed but debilitating dimensions of the market that pervade the Internet and every dimension of daily life. Amani Legagneur proposes the *healing welcomer* that reconstructs healing as non-imposed, collaborative, dependent on reception, and temporary (death comes to all, Legagneur says, even those Jesus raised and healed). Jeremy Lewis describes an on-the-ground or living metaphor of *urban food* that models a cooperative response to food deprivation, empowering people locally to counter wider global forces of environmental stress.

Most unexpectedly and a special favorite for me, Natalie Bernstein depicts one of the finest models of good pastoral care that I have ever seen described in such intimate detail—*elementary school librarian*. She sees children's needs, provides sanctuary space, and dispenses lived truth through fiction for children and the wider community of teachers, staff, and parents alike. One sixth grader tells her, "Thank you for this year. I didn't like reading before. I now feel like I *am* the person in the book." The counsel interspersed throughout Bernstein's chapter is brilliant and her inclusion of children unique. She alone in the book addresses one of the most overlooked prejudices in the theological academy—adult-centrism. Moreover, her chapter brings the readers back full circle to where the book started, as Hellena Moon shares in her Acknowledgements, with her children and their profound questions, observations, and conversations.

I do not mean to pick frontrunners, however. Johnson reminds us that a metaphor merely provides "a partial understanding of the concept which it seeks to illustrate" and cannot help but "mute other aspects." Metaphors are "always partial." Given the particularity of any metaphor and the complexities of pastoral care today, the plethora of images contained within this book seems both mandatory and remarkable.

At least two constructive themes appear across the multiple metaphors: *interconnection* and *humility*. Despite the difficulty of debunking the binaries and the separateness with which modern humans regard themselves, many authors try. The interconnection of the web reappears here but in entirely fresh forms—*hourglass, basketry,* and perhaps nowhere more profoundly than in Kim's exposition of a *flower*. A *flower*, if studied closely, discloses that all of its parts—stem, leaves, bud—come from and through other substances; the flower is, in other words, nothing on its own and only fully constituted through its deep interconnection. A flower is "empty of a separate, independent self," observes Vietnamese Buddhist monk Thích Nhất Hạnh, and so also is all of life, humans included. We only look like a solid substance set apart from other selves and bodies. In reality, "you cannot be, you can only inter-be."[16]

Ellison's *hourglass* also contains paradoxes. In the hourglass, a circle becomes a triangle, the self flows into community, and divine influence anchors the whole. As he puts it, "the hourglass, complete with two circles and two triangles spiraling into an identifiable center" serves as a "practical metaphor for pastoral caregiving," spinning together wholeness, awareness, care, and hope. Both Kim and Ellison point to the connection between "my center" and the "center of all things," as Ellison puts it.

The art of *sweetgrass weaving*, sustained by enslaved Africans and First Peoples, also connects generations, transfers wisdom, and holds basic material goods. Sharp first encounters the power and deeper meanings of basket-weaving on advice received before her Peace Corp work in rural Suriname: "If you're invited into basket-making at midnight, say yes," a neighbor told her; such "invitations into cultural wisdom are sacred and should be carefully engaged." Here and in Lartey's work, readers should notice a complete shift in worldview and in how humans situate themselves in the world that makes colonialist exploitation for personal profit difficult, if not impossible. For Lartey, pastoral reorientation comes down to language itself and the difficulties of grasping in English realities implicit among the Akan peoples of West Africa where the term of person itself—*nipadua*—literally means "person-tree."

In addition to the theme of fluidity within both subjectivity and divinity, several authors gravitate to a second theme: humility. Many authors question what Klein describes as the aspiration for "cultural competence" and instead lift up, as Klein, Rogers-Vaughn, and Legagneur suggest, the place of "cultural humility" as an "antidote to supremacy," in Legagneur's words. Such a stance is not easy. Both Rogers-Vaughn and Sharp insist on the inevitable co-existence of joy and grief, hope and mourning. Sharp captures the complexity of hope well: "Phoenix poetics . . . rise and rise again" in a "flammable world" of "unfair, dehumanizing, sinful obstacle." Creativity must defy destruction, and our own stories must dispel lies. We must write with commitment *and* desperation, says Haitian-American

---

16. Nhất Hạnh, *Heart of the Buddha's Teaching*, 147, cited by Kim.

author Edwidge Danticat, "as though each piece of art were a stand-in for a life, a soul, a future."[17]

Transformation: Seeing the Earth and Global Context

The stories and theories in these essays radically transform the boundaries and aims of the discipline. The volume takes Dykstra's observation that pastoral theology has a disruptive history of instability—"insanity," "insecurity," "outside the mainstream, off the beaten path," "fragmented identity on the margins"—and pushes it further than he and most of the authors in his original collection ever anticipated or imagined.[18] Even if pastoral theologians cannot "get over" the colonialism and imperialism that mars our history, the authors in *Postcolonial Images* offer multiple ways that we can transform the damage that these pathologies inflict. Contributors show that pastoral theology possesses distinct practices and proficiencies needed by the theological academy and our conflict-ridden times of listening, attending, mediating, fostering safe space, cultivating and sustaining respect, exuding humility, and so forth.

Postcolonial Images makes major inroads on three growing edges that I acknowledge as limitations of the *Reader in Practical Theology*, places the next *Reader* must counter and correct: Western/northern hegemony; progressive Christian biases; and Christian-centrism.[19] *Postcolonial Images* especially pushes beyond Christian-centrism, and the effort is long overdue. Several years ago, in her entry in *The Wiley Blackwell Companion to Practical Theology*, Kathleen Greider urged scholars to broaden the religious parameters of the discipline.[20] Pastoral and practical theology have "been too untroubled in [their] Christian confidence," as Tom Beaudoin suggests, often excluding the "religious other" and "nonaffiliated/secular persons." In the introduction to the *Reader*, I observe that the book is, "in actuality, a *Reader* in *Christian* practical theology." Looking ahead I conclude, "When more scholarship with religiously diverse representation appears in practical theology, it will be a sign that the current *Reader* has outgrown its shelf life."[21]

17. Danticat, *Create Dangerously*, 20, cited by Sharp.

18. Dykstra, *Images of Pastoral Care*, 1–3.

19. Miller-McLemore, *Reader in Practical Theology*, 11.

20. Greider, "Religious Pluralism and Christian-Centrism," 454.

21. Miller-McLemore, *Reader in Practical Theology*, 11.

Postcolonial Images provides just such a sign. It is the most religiously inclusive collection in pastoral theology available today, from the Foreword by Sufi Muslim scholar Abdullahi An-Na'im, to key explorations into cultural humility by Jewish Rabbi Lori Klein, the imaginative imagery of Theravada Buddhist Sumi Kim, the invitation to include Islam from Muslim chaplain Bilal Ansari, the protest against essentialism and gender binaries offered from the Muslim-Christian Alexander Brown, the intimate rapport with invisible forces in African spirituality of Emmanuel Lartey, and the plea for the non-religious believer from humanist Greg Epstein. Quite simply, Epstein explains, *humanism* means "good without god" or, in more formal terms, "an ethical and nontheistic life stance."

When faced with the epistemic violence of selecting essays for the *Reader in Practical Theology*, I resorted to the creation of a rationale for selection: I looked for essays that advanced the steady *epistemological insurgency* that has characterized both pastoral and practical theology for at least a half century, unsettling conventional boundaries that define where theology is located and how it is done.[22] Unsatisfied with theology as an abstract cognitive exercise performed by an elite cadre of thinkers in academy and ecclesia, practical theologians have gradually resituated the study and practice of theology more immediately within bodies, time, action, and community. Especially innovative contributions have emerged in the last decade as diverse scholars offer fresh approaches, and *Postcolonial Images* is no exception. All of its authors contribute in one way or another to the "epistemological provocation" that I describe.[23] Ellison, for example, invites "full-sensory pedagogy" within the classroom and "pilgrimage pedagogy" outside the classroom. The volume itself locates theology in the midst of practice and includes as many professionals in ministry (chaplain, rabbi, minister, librarian, etc.) as professionals in the academy. The very fact of including authors from religions besides Christianity opens up new worlds of reflection and sets this volume apart from typical collections in almost all areas of theological study.

One important epistemological insurgence hovers around the edges of this volume and invites a virtual third volume of spiritual care imagery that extends the boundaries of pastoral theology once again: the earth's wisdom and demise in our Anthropocene age. This horizon has only impressed itself on my own research and teaching in the last several years. But it seems like a vital next step for efforts like the *Reader* and *Postcolonial Images*. The postcolonial efforts of this volume are on the right track,

---

22. Miller-McLemore, *Reader in Practical Theology*, 1.

23. Miller-McLemore, *Reader in Practical Theology*, 4.

Moon's chapter in particular. Colonization means taking land, occupying ground, and exploiting it. Within this Western proclivity for possession and exploitation, this volume subtly implies, lies an even more formidable assault of calamitous proportions, and we are running out of earth and ecological time to right the wrong.

Moon, Kim, Lewis, and Lartey are singular in *Postcolonial Images* in considering the land, earth, climate, and environment. And their essays plant important seeds for further growth. Our own survival depends on the "earth's ecological web," Kim notes, although for her the earth's web is only one among many crucial interconnections. Human ties with animate and inanimate beings forbid, Lartey argues, degradation of the earth. Food is a powerful place where ecology comes home to roost, as Lewis demonstrates. The problem is even more central for Moon. The liberal subject lives "outside the perimeter of 'nature,'" she insists, "superior to the natural world," exuding a heedlessness and hubris exemplified in the "profligate use of fossil fuels and material goods." The earth itself forces us to rethink modern conceptions of freedom: "Given our dependence on fossil fuels and the earth's natural resources, how free are we?"

Putting the earth front and center remains a difficult agenda, even in *Postcolonial Images*. Sometimes the non-human takes a necessary backseat because of our valuable disciplinary focus on caring for humans and the dire importance of attending to other postcolonial challenges. I understand the dilemma. In my own work, I have wondered how I failed to notice the nearly exclusive emphasis on *human* when speaking of *the living web*? Why has the wider web of life or what scientists call the "wood wide web"[24]—and not merely the "living *human* web"—remained a nearly absent theme for pastoral theologians, including in my own use of the term?[25] Why do people (myself included and especially white westerners) disbelieve and miss the intelligence of the nonhuman and, as a consequence, resist the ecological disaster wrought by our cherished obliviousness? There are important exceptions, of course.[26] But sometimes our writing and teaching remains incredibly anthropocentric, perhaps because we have focused on personal and social suffering, perhaps because patriarchy and imperialism likes us to keep oppressions separate, perhaps because of a disciplinary emphasis on the concrete rather than matters of theological reconstruction. We write church curriculums on environmentalism, join earth movements, preach climate sermons, and head outside.

24. Simard et al., "Net Transfer of Carbon."

25. See Miller-McLemore, "Trees and the 'Unthought Known.'"

26. See, for example, Graham, *Care of Persons, Care of Worlds*; Helsel, "Loving the World"; LaMothe, "This Changes Everything"; Rowley, "Practicing Hope"; "Intersystemic Care."

Nonetheless, even if we have not yet foregrounded the earth or contributed extensively in our publications to discussions about ecology and climate crises; that reality, I would wager, is about to change. Now more than ever, climate violence and earth justice weigh heavily on our minds, especially for emerging scholars with young families.

Ironically but perhaps not surprisingly as a pastoral and practical theologian, my own wakeup to the land has come more through a confluence of environmental novels, collegial conversation, and my own anxiety bordering on despair about the state of the earth than through didactic argument. Two novels in particular have compelled me: Annie Proulx's 2017 historical masterpiece *Barkskins*, an epic tale spanning 300 years of massive deforestation of the Americas, forests long gone from Europe that enterprising merchants assumed inexhaustible in the New World; and Richard Powers's 2018 *The Overstory*, an ode to trees, their hidden inner life, complexity, mystery, power, and wisdom.[27]

Proulx does not take sides, overtly at least; she simply offers thick description of intergenerational greed, ignorance, and hubris. By contrast, Powers's novel conveys disruptive convictions (one review even describes it as "browbeating," but I am a convert).[28] The novel reveals our utter blindness and redirects our attention to life above *and* below ground, revealing so many ecological and arborist oversights that they threaten to overwhelm readers. He reminds humans that we are a blip on the evolutionary screen. "*People aren't the apex species*" we think we are, one of his characters asserts. "Other creatures . . . call the shots, make the air, and eat sunlight. Without them, *nothing*."[29] And again: "*This is not our world with trees in it. It's a world with trees where humans have just arrived*."[30] Most Westerners fail to grasp the limits of human knowledge and the wisdom within the natural world, unknown, untapped, unprotected, and disrespected. "Your kind never sees us whole," the trees say, "You miss the half of it, and more. There's always as much belowground as above."[31] Contrary to assumptions about social constructivism, Powers implies that we do not *construct* reality, we *evade* it—"by looting natural capital and hiding the costs. But the bill is coming, and we won't be able to pay."[32]

---

27. Proulx, *Barkskins*; Powers, *Overstory*.

28. Jordison, "How Could *The Overstory* Be Considered."

29. Powers, *Overstory*, 285.

30. Powers, *Overstory*, 424.

31. Powers, *Overstory*, 3.

32. Powers, *Overstory*, 320.

These insights raise a critical question for pastoral theologians: Is hierarchy of "man over nature" the deadliest binary of all, even a linchpin binary?[33] The planet's imminent demise is not our only woe to be sure. Many issues demand attention today—white supremacy, immigration, women's body rights among the most perverse and pressing. The harm perpetuated by exploitation of the nonhuman world reflects the intersecting consequences of these other challenges and presses upon us with a unique urgency. Earth and climate upheaval almost always have the worse consequences for those with the fewest resources. Reversing the harm to woods, water, air, fish and fauna is likely beyond our present reach; and a different kind of response, one we have yet to imagine, will be required. But as I consider the road ahead, I ask: What do tree wisdom and ecological unrest require of our teaching and learning? If coloniality meant taking land and displacement, what does decoloniality require from pastoral theologians as a countermeasure and counternarrative when it comes to the earth? What do pastoral theologians have to say not just about humans, but about land, rocks, trees, plants, animals, rivers, oceans, sea creatures, and their voices and meaning?

33. Ecofeminists, black theologians and scholars, and womanists are among those who have argued about an intersectionality that actually includes the earth. See, for example, Ruether, *Gaia and God*; Gebara, *Longing for Running Water*; Cone, "Whose Earth Is It Anyway?"; Spencer, "Environmental Racism and Black Theology"; Harris, *Ecowomanism*.

Bibliography

Adams, Glenn, et al. "The Psychology of Neoliberalism and the Neoliberalism of Psychology." *Journal of Social Issues* 75.1 (2019) 1–28.

Alcoholics Anonymous. "Frequently Asked Questions about AA History." Online. https://www.aa.org/pages/en_US/frequently-asked-questions-about-aa-history.

American Humanist Association. "Humanism and Its Aspirations: Humanist Manifesto III, a Successor to the Humanist Manifesto of 1933." *American Humanist*, 2003. Online. https://americanhumanist.org/what-is-humanism/manifesto3.

An, Yountae. *The Decolonial Abyss: Mysticism and Cosmopolitics from the Ruins.* New York: Fordham University Press, 2017.

Anderson, Ben. "Neoliberal Affects." *Progress in Human Geography* 40.6 (2016) 734–53.

An-Na'im, Abdullahi. "The Individual and Collective Self-Liberation Model of Ustadh Mahmoud Mohamed Taha." In *Beyond the Secular West*, edited by Akeel Bilgrami, 45–75. New York: Columbia University Press, 2016.

——. "It's Time to Decolonize Human Rights." *Abdullahi Ahmed An-Na'im* (blog), April 4, 2016. Video. Online. https://scholarblogs.emory.edu/aannaim/2016/04/04/its-time-to-decolonize-human-rights-video.

——. "The Spirit of Laws Is Not Universal: Alternatives to the Enforcement Paradigm for Human Rights." *Tilburg Law Review* 21 (2016) 255–74.

Anzaldúa, Gloria. *Light in the Dark/Luz En Lo Oscuro: Rewriting Identity, Spirituality, Reality.* Edited by A. Keating. Durham: Duke University Press, 2015.

Asad, Talal. "Thinking About Religion, Secularism, and Politics." Lecture delivered at the University of California at Berkeley, Berkeley, CA, October 2, 2008. YouTube Video. October 17, 2008. 57:02. https://www.youtube.com/watch?v=kfAGnxKfwOg.

Atlanta Botanical Garden. "Alice's Wonderland Reimagined." Online. https://atlantabg.org/plan-your-visit/atlanta-garden-calendar/imaginary-worlds.

Au, Willie, and Noreen Cannon. *Urgings of the Heart: A Spirituality of Integration.* Mahwah, NJ: Paulist, 1996.

Baker, Don. *Catholics and Anti-Catholicism.* Honolulu: University of Hawai'i Press, 2017.

Barad, Karen. *Meeting the Universe Halfway: Quantum Physics and the Entanglement of Matter and Meaning.* Durham, NC: Duke University Press, 2007.

Bauman, Zygmunt. *Wasted Lives: Modernity and Its Outcasts.* Cambridge: Polity, 2004.

Beaty, Daniel. *Knock Knock: My Dad's Dream for Me*. Boston: Little, Brown, and Co., 2013.

Beaudoin, Tom. "Why Does Practice Matter Theologically." In *Conundrums in Practical Theology*, edited by Bonnie J. Miller-McLemore and Joyce Mercer, 8–32. Leiden: Brill, 2016.

Beaudoin, Tom, and Katherine Turpin. "White Practical Theology." In *Opening the Field of Practical Theology: An Introduction*, edited by Kathleen A. Cahalan et al., 251–69. New York: Rowman and Littlefield, 2014.

Benjamin, Walter. *Illuminations: Essays and Reflections*. New York: Schocken, 1969.

Bhabha, Homi. *The Location of Culture*. New York: Routledge, 1994.

Birch, Kean. *A Research Agenda for Neoliberalism*. Cheltenham, UK: Edward Elgar, 2017.

Bivins, Charles. "Digital Colonialism and the Skycoin's Skywire Solution." *Medium*, December 21, 2018. Online. https://medium.com/@bivins1/digital-colonialism-and-the-skycoins-skywire-solution-4fe57e60f39d.

Blue, Rose. *Ron's Big Mission*. New York: Dutton Children's Books, 2009.

Bodhi, Bhikkhu, ed. *The Buddha's Teachings on Social and Communal Harmony: An Anthology of Discourses from the Pali Canon*. Somerville, MA: Wisdom, 2016.

Boelts, Maribeth. *A Bike Like Sergio's*. Somerville, MA: Candlewick, 2016.

Boisen, Anton T. *The Exploration of the Inner World: A Study of Mental Disorder and Religious Experience*. Chicago; New York: Willett, Clark, 1936.

Brickman, Celia. *Aboriginal Populations in the Mind: Race and Primitivity in Psychoanalysis*. New York: Columbia University Press, 2003.

Brown, Wendy. *In the Ruins of Neoliberalism: The Rise of Antidemocratic Politics in the West*. New York: Columbia University Press, 2019.

———. "Suffering Rights as Paradoxes." *Constellations* 7.2 (2000) 230–41.

———. *Undoing the Demos: Neoliberalism's Stealth Revolution*. Cambridge, MA: MIT Press, 2015.

Brubaker, Pamela K. *Globalization at What Price*. Cleveland: Pilgrim, 2007.

Buber, Martin. *I and Thou*. Translated by Walter Kaufmann. New York: Scribner's Sons, 1971.

Buswell, Robert, and Donald Lopez Jr., eds. *The Princeton Dictionary of Buddhism*. Princeton: Princeton University Press, 2014.

Capps, Don. "Resistance in the Local Church: A Psychoanalytic Perspective." *Pastoral Psychology* 64 (2015) 581–601.

Cazdyn, Eric. *The Already Dead: The New Time of Politics, Culture, and Illness*. Durham, NC: Duke University Press, 2012.

Chakrabarty, Dipesh. "Climate and Capital: On Conjoined Histories." *Critical Inquiry* 41.1 (2014) 1–23.

———. "The Climate of History: Four Theses." *Critical Inquiry* 35.2 (2009) 197–222.

———. *The Crises of Civilization: Exploring Global and Planetary Histories*. London: Oxford University Press, 2018.

———. *Provincializing Europe: Postcolonial Thought and Historical Difference*. Princeton, NJ: Princeton University Press, 2007.

Cigna and Ipsos. *Cigna US Loneliness Index*. New York: Cigna, 2018. Online. https://www.multivu.com/players/English/8294451-cigna-us-loneliness-survey/docs/IndexReport_1524069371598-173525450.pdf.

Clebsch, William A., and Charles R. Jaekle. *Pastoral Care in Historical Perspective.* New York: Rowman and Littlefield, 1964.

Clinebell, Howard. *Basic Types of Pastoral Care and Counseling.* New York: Abingdon, 1984.

Coleman, Gabriella. *Hacker, Hoaxer, Whistleblower, Spy: The Many Faces of Anonymous.* London: Verso, 2015.

Coles, Robert. *The Story of Ruby Bridges.* New York: Scholastic, 1995.

Cone, James H. "Whose Earth Is It Anyway?" *Cross Currents* 50.1–2 (2000) 36–46.

Cooper, Floyd. *The Ring Bearer.* New York: Philomel, 2017.

Cooper-White, Pamela. *Shared Wisdom: Use of the Self in Pastoral Care and Counseling.* Minneapolis: Fortress, 2004.

Culbertson, Phillip. *Caring for God's People: Counseling and Christian Wholeness.* Minneapolis: Fortress, 2000.

Damaraju, Sarita, et al. "Meet the Class of 2021: Beliefs and Lifestyle." *The Harvard Crimson,* August 30–September 1, 2017. Online. https://features.thecrimson. com/2017/freshman-survey/lifestyle.

Danticat, Edwidge. *Brother, I'm Dying.* New York: Vintage. 2007.

———. *Create Dangerously: The Immigrant Artist at Work.* New York: Vintage, 2011.

———. *Mama's Nightingale: A Story of Immigration and Separation.* New York: Penguin, 2015.

Das, Veena. *Life and Words: Violence and the Descent into the Ordinary.* Berkeley: University of California Press, 2006.

Davies, William. "The Democratic Critique of Neo-Liberalism." *Renewal* 23.3 (2015) 86–92.

Davis, Jim. *Garfield.* Los Angeles: KABOOM!, 2004.

Didron, Adolphe N. *Christian Iconography: The History of Christian Art in the Middle Ages.* Translated by E. J. Millington. New York: Frederick Ungar, 1965.

Dreyer, Jaco, et al., eds. *Practicing Ubuntu: Practical Theological Perspectives on Injustice, Personhood, and Human Dignity.* Zürich: Lit Verlag, 2017.

Dykstra, Robert. *Finding Ourselves Lost: Ministry in the Age of Overwhelm.* Eugene, OR: Cascade, 2018.

———. *Images of Pastoral Care: Classic Readings.* St. Louis: Chalice, 2005.

Eitzen, D. Stanley, and Maxine B. Zinn, eds. *Globalization: The Transformation of Social Worlds.* 3rd ed. Belmont, CA: Wadsworth, 2012.

Ellison, Gregory C., II. *Cut Dead But Still Alive: Caring for African American Men.* Nashville: Abingdon, 2013.

———. *Fearless Dialogues: A New Movement for Justice.* Louisville: Westminster John Knox, 2017.

———. "From My Center to the Center of All Things: Hourglass Care (Take 1)." *Pastoral Psychology* 59.6 (2010) 747–67.

———. "Late Stylin' in an Ill-Fitting Suit: Donald Capps's Artistic Approach to the Hopeful Self and Its Implications for Unacknowledged African American Young Men." *Pastoral Psychology* 58.5–6 (2009) 477–89.

Emerson, Bo. "'Imaginary Worlds' Exhibit Returns to Atlanta Botanical Garden." *Atlanta Journal-Constitution,* May 1, 2018. Online. https://www.ajc.com/ entertainment/attractions/imaginary-worlds-exhibit-returns-to-atlanta-botanical-garden/43wzCHe3emSGwtuOoVPflO.

Eng, David L., and Shinhee Han. *Racial Melancholia, Racial Dissociation: On the Social and Psychic Lives of Asian Americans.* Durham: Duke University Press, 2019.

Entwistle, Vikki A., and Ian S. Watt. "Treating Patients as Persons: A Capabilities Approach to Support Delivery of Person-Centered Care." *American Journal of Bioethics* 13.8 (2013) 29–39.

Epstein, Greg. *Good Without God: What a Billion Nonreligious People Do Believe.* New York: Harper Collins, 2010.

Erikson, Erik H. *Identity: Youth and Crisis.* New York: Norton, 1968.

Evans, Mari. *A Dark and Splendid Mass.* New York: Harlem River, 1992.

Eyerman, Ron. "Cultural Trauma: Slavery and the Formation of African American Identity." In *Cultural Trauma and Collective Identity*, edited by Jeffrey C. Alexander et al., 60–111. Los Angeles: University of California Press, 2004.

Fanon, Frantz. *Black Skin, White Masks.* Translated by Charles Lam Markmann. New York: Grove, 1967.

———. *The Wretched of the Earth.* Translated by Richard Philcox. New York: Grove, 1963.

Ferguson, Niall. "American Democracy: The Perils of Imperialism?" In *America at Risk: Threats to a Liberal Self-Government in an Age of Uncertainty*, edited by Robert Faulkner and Susan Shell, 29–54. Ann Arbor: University of Michigan Press, 2009.

Fitzgerald, Timothy. *The Ideology of Religious Studies.* Oxford: Oxford University Press, 2000.

Fowler, James W. "The Emerging New Shape of Practical Theology." In *Practical Theology: International Perspectives*, edited by Friedrich Schweitzer and Johannes A. van der Ven, 75–92. Erfahrung und Theologie 34. Frankfurt: P. Lang, 1999.

Francis, Leah Gunning. *Ferguson and Faith: Sparking Leadership and Awakening Community.* St. Louis: Chalice, 2015.

Gallegos, Joseph S., et al. "The Need for Advancement in the Conceptualization of Cultural Competence." *Advances in Social Work* 9.1 (2008) 51–62.

Gates, Henry Louis. *The Trials of Phillis Wheatley: America's First Black Poet and Her Encounters with the Founding Fathers.* NY: Basic, 2010.

Gebara, Ivone. *Longing for Running Water: Ecofeminism and Liberation.* Minneapolis: Fortress, 1999.

Gehl, Robert W. *Weaving the Dark Web: Legitimacy on Freenet, Tor, and I2p.* Cambridge, MA: MIT Press, 2018.

Gill, Penny. *What in the World Is Going On?* Bloomington: Balboa, 2014.

Gill-Austern, Brita L. "Engaging Diversity and Difference: From Practices of Exclusion to Practices of Practical Solidarity." In *Injustice and the Care of Souls: Taking Oppression Seriously in Pastoral Care*, edited by Sheryl Kujawa-Holbrook et al., 29–44. Minneapolis: Fortress, 2009.

Gillon, Raanan. "Ethics Needs Principles—Four Can Encompass the Rest—and Respect for Autonomy Should be 'First Among Equals.'" *Journal of Medical Ethics* 29.5 (2003) 307–12.

Gilroy, Paul. "Suffering and Infrahumanity." In *Tanner Lectures on Human Values 34*, edited by Mark Matheson, 21–50. Salt Lake City: University of Utah Press, 2015. Online. https://tannerlectures.utah.edu/Gilroy%20manuscript%20PDF.pdf.

Graham, Larry K. *Care of Persons, Care of Worlds: A Psychosystems Approach to Pastoral Care and Counseling.* Nashville: Abingdon, 1992.

————. "Pastoral Theology and Catastrophic Disaster." *Journal of Pastoral Theology* 16 (2006) 1–17.

Greider, Kathleen J. "Religious Pluralism and Christian-Centrism." In *The Wiley-Blackwell Companion to Practical Theology*, edited by Bonnie J. Miller-McLemore, 452–61. Chichester, UK: Blackwell, 2012.

Gunnar, M. R., et al. "Salivary Cortisol Levels in Children Adopted from Romanian Orphanages." *Dev Psychopathol* 13.3 (2001) 611–28. Online. https://www.ncbi.nlm.nih.gov/pubmed/11523851.

Gunning, Isabelle R. "Arrogant Perception, World-Travelling, and Multicultural Feminism: The Case of Female Genital Surgeries." *Columbia Human Rights Review* 23 (1992) 189–248.

Gunning Francis, Leah. *Ferguson and Faith: Sparking Leadership and Awakening Community*. St. Louis: Chalice, 2015.

Halley, Janet. *Split Decisions: How and Why to Take a Break from Feminism*. Princeton: Princeton University Press, 2006.

Hamid, Shadi. "Resist the Lure of Theological Politics." *Atlantic*, December 22, 2018. Online. https://www.theatlantic.com/ideas/archive/2018/12/how-resist-making-politics-theological/578851.

Harris, Melanie. *Ecowomanism: African-American Women and Earth-Honoring Faiths*. Maryknoll, NY: Orbis, 2017.

Harris, Robie H. *It's Perfectly Normal: A Book About Changing Bodies, Growing Up, Sex and Sexual Health*. Cambridge, MA: Candlewick, 1994.

Harvey, David. *A Brief History of Neoliberalism*. New York: Oxford University Press, 2005.

Hayek, Friedrich A. *The Constitution of Liberty*. Chicago: University of Chicago Press, 1960.

————. *The Fatal Conceit: The Errors of Socialism*. London: Routledge, 1988.

————. *The Road to Serfdom*. Chicago: University of Chicago Press, 1944.

Hegel, Georg W. F. *The Phenomenology of Spirit*. Translated by Terry Pinkard. 1807. Cambridge: Cambridge University Press, 2018.

————. *Philosophy of Subjective Spirit*. New York, NY: Springer, 1978.

Helsel, Phil B. "Loving the World: Place Attachment and Environment." *Journal of Pastoral Theology* 28.1 (2018) 22–33.

Herman, Judith. *Trauma and Recovery: The Aftermath of Violence*. New York: Basic, 1992.

Hidaka, Brandon H. "Depression as a Disease of Modernity: Explanations for Increasing Prevalence." *Journal of Affective Disorders* 140 (2012) 205–14.

Hiltner, Seward. *Preface to Pastoral Theology*. Nashville: Abington, 1958.

Hoffman, Mary. *Amazing Grace*. New York: Dial Books for Young Readers, 1991.

Hong, Christine. "Teaching Practical Theology De-Colonially." Paper presented at The Future of Practical Theology: Emerging Scholars and Themes, American Academy of Religion, Denver, CO, November 2018.

Hook, Joshua N., et al. "Cultural Humility: Measuring Openness to Culturally Diverse Clients." *Journal of Counseling Psychology* 60.3 (2013) 1–14. Online. https://doi:10.1037/a0032595.

hooks, bell. *Teaching Critical Thinking*. NY: Routledge, 2010.

Humanists International. "What is Humanism?" *Humanists International*. Online. https://humanists.international/what-is-humanism.

Hwang, Kyung Moon. *A History of Korea: An Episodic Narrative*. New York: Palgrave Macmillan, 2017.

Jacoby, Russell. *Picture Imperfect: Utopian Thought for an Anti-Utopian Age*. New York: Columbia University Press, 2005.

Jezewski, Mary Ann. "Evolution of a Grounded Theory: Conflict Resolution Through Culture Brokering." *Advanced Nursing Science* 17.3 (1995) 14–30.

Johann, Robert. *The Meaning of Love: An Essay Towards a Metaphysics of Intersubjectivity*. Glen Rock, NJ: Paulist, 1966.

Johnson, Cedric C. *Race, Religion, and Resilience in the Neoliberal Age*. New York: Palgrave, 2015.

Jones, Robert P., et al. "The 2012 American Values Survey: How Catholics and The Religiously Unaffiliated Will Shape the 2012 Election and Beyond." Washington, DC: Public Religion Research Institute, 2012. Online. http://publicreligion.org/site/wp-content/uploads/2012/10/AVS-2012-Pre-election-Report-for-Web.pdf.

———. "A Generation in Transition: Religion, Values, and Politics among College-Age Millennials." Washington, DC: Public Religion Research Institute, 2012. Online. http://publicreligion.org/site/wp-content/uploads/2012/04/Millennials-Survey-Report.pdf.

Jordison, Sam. "How Could *The Overstory* Be Considered a Book of the Year?" *Guardian*, December 18, 2018. Online. https://www.theguardian.com/books/2018/dec/18/how-could-the-overstory-be-considered-a-book-of-the-year-richard-powers.

Katz, Josh. "Drug Deaths in America Are Rising Faster Than Ever." *New York Times*, June 5, 2017. Online. https://www.nytimes.com/interactive/2017/06/05/upshot/opioid-epidemic-drug-overdose-deaths-are-rising-faster-than-ever.html.

Keller, Catherine. *Cloud of the Impossible: Negative Theology and Planetary Entanglement*. New York: Columbia University Press, 2015.

———. *From a Broken Web: Separation, Sexism, and Self*. Michigan: Beacon, 1988.

Kim, Eun Jung. *Curative Violence: Rehabilitating Disability, Gender, and Sexuality in Modern Korea*. Durham, NC: Duke University Press, 2017.

Kimball, Penn. "Magna Cum Nonsense." *New York Times*. March 16, 1952. SM68.

Kimmerer, Robin Wall. *Braiding Sweetgrass: Indigenous Wisdom, Scientific Knowledge, and the Teachings of Plants*. Minneapolis: Milkweed, 2013.

Klein, Lori. "Doing What's Right: Providing Culturally Competent Reunification Services." *Berkeley Journal of Gender, Law & Justice* 12.1 (1997) 20–44.

Klein, Naomi. *This Changes Everything: Capitalism Vs. The Climate*. New York: Simon & Schuster, 2014.

Kwak, Jung, and William E. Haley. "Current Research Findings on End-of-Life Decision Making Among Racially or Ethnically Diverse Groups." *Gerontologist* 45 (2005) 634–41.

Lakoff, George, and Mark Johnson. *Metaphors We Live By*. Chicago: University of Chicago Press, 1980.

LaMothe, Ryan. "This Changes Everything: The Sixth Extinction and its Implications for Pastoral Theology." *Journal of Pastoral Theology* 26.3 (2017) 178–94.

Lartey, Emmanuel Y. *In Living Color: An Intercultural Approach to Pastoral Care and Counseling*. 2nd ed. London: Jessica Kingsley, 2003.

———. *Pastoral Counseling in Inter-Cultural Perspective*. London: Peter Lang, 1987.

———. *Postcolonializing God: An African Practical Theology*. London: SCM, 2013.

LeCain, Timothy. "Heralding a New Humanism: The Radical Implications of Chakrabarty's 'Four Theses.'" *RCC Perspectives: Transformations in Environment and Society* 2 (2016) 15–20.

Leech, Garry. *Capitalism: A Structural Genocide*. London: Zed, 2012.

Lester, Andrew. *Hope in Pastoral Care and Counseling*. Louisville: Westminster John Knox, 1995.

Lloyd, Maggie. "Religion at MIT." *The Tech* 132.25 (2012) 11–20. Online. http://tech.mit.edu/V132/N25/religion/breakdown.

Locke, John. *A Letter Concerning Toleration*. 1689. Edited by James H. Tully. Indianapolis: Hackett, 1983.

———. *Second Treatise of Government*. 1690. Edited by C. B. Macpherson. Indianapolis: Hackett, 1980.

Lorde, Audre. *Sister Outsider: Essays and Speeches by Audre Lorde*. New York: Ten Speed, 2007.

Louw, Daniel J. "Dreaming the Land in Hope: Towards a Practical Theological Ecclesiology of Cura Terrae." In *Dreaming the Land: Theologies of Resistance and Hope*, edited by Hans-Georg Ziebertz and Friedrich Schweitzer, 10–29. Berlin: Lit Verlag, 2007.

Love, Jessica. *Julián Is a Mermaid*. Somerville, MA: Candlewick, 2018.

Lynn, Barry C. *Cornered: The New Monopoly Capitalism and the Economics of Destruction*. Hoboken, NJ: Wiley & Sons, 2010.

Madhava, Achary. *Sarva-Darsana-Samgraha*. Translated by E. B. Cowell and A. E. Gough. London: Trubner and Co., 1882.

Magesa, Laurenti. *What Is Not Sacred? African Spirituality*. Maryknoll, NY: Orbis, 2013.

Maina, Ivy W., et al. "A Decade of Studying Implicit Racial/Ethnic Bias in Health Care Providers Using the Implicit Association Test." *Social Science Medicine* 199 (2017) 219–29.

Maldonado-Torres, Nelson. "On the Coloniality of Being." *Cultural Studies* 21.2–3 (2007) 240–70.

Manigault-Bryant, LeRhonda S. "An Open Letter to White Liberal Feminists." *African American Intellectual History Society*, November 19, 2016. Online. https://www.aaihs.org/an-open-letter-to-white-liberal-feminists.

———. *Talking to the Dead: Religion, Music, and Lived Member Among Gullah/Geechee Women*. Durham: Duke University Press, 2014.

Marcel, Gabriel. *Homo Viator: Introduction to a Metaphysic of Hope*. Translated by Emma Craufurd. Gloucester, MA: Peter Smith, 1951.

Marques, José M., et al. "The 'Black Sheep Effect': Extremity of Judgments Towards Ingroup Members as a Function of Group Identification." *European Journal of Social Psychology* 18 (1988) 1–16.

Martin, Randy. *Financialization of Daily Life*. Philadelphia: Temple University Press, 2002.

Marx, Karl. "Economic and Philosophic Manuscripts of 1844." In *The Marx-Engels Reader*, edited by Robert C. Tucker, 66–125. New York: Norton, 1978.

———. "The Grundrisse." In *The Marx-Engels Reader*, edited by Robert C. Tucker, 221–93. New York: Norton, 1978.

Matsumura Shinji, et al. "Acculturation of Attitudes Toward End-of-Life Care: A Cross-Cultural Survey of Japanese Americans and Japanese." *Journal of General Internal Medicine* 17.7 (2002) 531–39.

Mbiti, John S. *African Religions and Philosophy*. Portsmouth, NH: Heinemann, 1969.

McChesney, Robert W. *Digital Disconnect: How Capitalism Is Turning the Internet Against Democracy*. New York: New Press, 2013.

Merton, Thomas. *Contemplative Prayer*. New York: Doubleday, 1971.

Metz, Johann Baptist. *Faith in History and Society: Toward a Practical Fundamental Theology*. Translated by J. Matthew Ashley. New York: Crossroad, 1977.

Miéville, China. "Silence in Debris: Towards an Apophatic Marxism." *Salvage* 6 (2018) 115–44.

Mignolo, Walter D. *The Darker Side of Western Modernity: Global Futures, Decolonial Options*. Durham: Duke University Press, 2011.

———. "Epistemic Disobedience, Independent Thought and De-Colonial Freedom." *Theory, Culture & Society* 26.7–8 (2009) 1–23.

Mikkelson, David. "Fred Rogers—'Look for the Helpers.'" *Snopes*, April 15, 2013. Online. https://www.snopes.com/fact-check/look-for-the-helpers.

Miller, Alice. *The Drama of the Gifted Child: The Search for the True Self*. New York: Basic, 1997.

Miller-McLemore, Bonnie J. *Christian Theology in Practice: Discovering a Discipline*. Grand Rapids: Eerdmans, 2012.

———. "The Hubris and Folly of Defining a Discipline: Reflections on the Evolution of *The Wiley-Blackwell Companion to Practical Theology*." *Toronto Journal of Theology* 29.1 (2013) 143–74.

———. "The Human Web: Reflections on the State of Pastoral Theology." *The Christian Century* 110.11 (1993) 366–69.

———. "The Living Human Web: A Twenty-Five Year Retrospective." *Pastoral Psychology* 67.3 (2018) 305–21.

———. "A Tale of Two Cities: The Evolution of the International Academy of Practical Theology." *HTS Teologiese Studies/Theological Studies* 73.4 (2017) 1–11. Online. http://www.hts.org.za/index.php/HTS/article/view/4718.

———. "The Theory-Practice Binary and the Politics of Practical Knowledge." In *Conundrums in Practical Theology*, edited by Bonnie J. Miller-McLemore and Joyce Mercer, 190–218. Leiden: Brill, 2016.

———. "Trees and the 'Unthought Known': The Wisdom of the Nonhuman (or Do Humans 'Have Shit for Brains'?")." Unpublished article.

———, ed. *The Wiley Blackwell Reader in Practical Theology*. Hoboken, NJ: Wiley & Sons, 2019.

Mills, Charles. *The Racial Contract*. Ithaca: Cornell University Press, 1997.

Moellendorf, Darrel. "Racism and Rationality in Hegel's Philosophy of Subjective Spirit." *History of Political Thought* 13.2 (1992) 243–55.

Moody, Anne. *Coming of Age in Mississippi*. New York: Random, 1968.

Moon, Hellena. "Fictions of Liberation: A Paradoxical 'Palimpsest of Colonial Identity' of *Chŏng (Jeong)*." *Journal of Pastoral Theology*, 28.3 (2018) 160–74.

———. "The 'Living Human Web' Revisited: An Asian American Pastoral Care and Counseling Perspective." *Sacred Spaces: The e-Journal of the American Association of Pastoral Counselors* 3 (2010) 14–43. Online. https://secureshopper.bisglobal.net/_templates/74/hmoon_pastoral_care.pdf.

———. *Mask of Clement Violence Amid Pastoral Intimacies: A Feminist Liberation Critique of the Violence Against Wo/men Discourse*. Eugene, OR: Pickwick (forthcoming).

Mora, Richard, and Mary Christianakis. "Feeding the School-to-Prison Pipeline: The Convergence of Neoliberalism, Conservatism, and Penal Populism." *Journal of Educational Controversy* 7.1 (2013) 1–10. Online. https://cedar.wwu.edu/jec/vol7/iss1/5.

Morales, Yuyi. *Dreamers*. New York: Neal Porter, 2018.

Morrison, Toni. "Twelve of Toni Morrison's Most Memorable Quotes." *New York Times*, August 6, 2019. Online. https://www.nytimes.com/2019/08/06/books/toni-morrison-quotes.html.

Murray, Gilbert. *Five Stages of Greek Religion*. New York: Doubleday, 1955.

Nader, Kathleen, et al. *Honoring Differences: Cultural Issues in the Treatment of Trauma and Loss*. New York: Brunner-Mazel, 1999.

National Center for Cultural Competence (NCCC), et al. *Bridging the Cultural Divide in Health Care Settings: The Essential Role of Cultural Broker Programs*. Washington, DC: Georgetown University, 2004. Online. https://nccc.georgetown.edu/culturalbroker/Cultural_Broker_EN.pdf.

Nhất Hạnh, Thích. *The Heart of the Buddha's Teaching: Transforming Suffering into Peace, Joy, and Liberation*. New York: Harmony, 1998.

———. "The Island of the Self." Transcription of a talk given in Plum Village, France, July 28, 1998. Online. http://www.purifymind.com/IslandSelf.htm.

———. *Tri kỷ của Bụt* (*Soulmate of the Buddha*). Hanoi: Nhà Xuất Bản Phương, 2014. Unpublished translation by Thích Chân Pháp Lưu.

Norton, M. M. H. *Letters to a Young Poet: Rainer Maria Rilke*. New York: Norton, 1954.

Nouwen, Henri J. M. *Here and Now: Living in the Spirit*. New York: Crossroad, 1994.

———. *Out of Solitude*. Notre Dame, IN: Ave Marie, 1984.

Nyengele, M. Fulgence. "Cultivating Ubuntu: An African Postcolonial Pastoral Theological Engagement with Positive Psychology." *Journal of Pastoral Theology* 24.2 (2014) 4.1–4.35.

Ofri, Danielle. *What Doctors Feel: How Emotions Affect the Practice of Medicine*. Boston: Beacon, 2013.

Oliver, Kelly. *The Colonization of Psychic Space: A Psychoanalytic Social Theory of Oppression*. Minneapolis: University of Minnesota Press, 2004.

Opala, Joseph A. *The Gullah: Rice, Slavery, and the Sierra Leone-American Connection*. Freetown, Sierra Leone: US Information Service, 2009.

Ortega, Robert M., and Katherine Coulborn Faller. "Training Child Welfare Workers From an Intersectional Cultural Humility Perspective: A Paradigm Shift." *Child Welfare* 90.5 (2011) 27–49.

Palmer, Parker J. *The Courage to Teach*. San Francisco: Jossey-Bass, 2017.

———. *Healing the Heart of Democracy: The Courage to Create a Politics Worthy of the Human Spirit*. San Francisco: Jossey-Bass, 2014.

Parker, Marjorie Blain. *Jasper's Day*. Toronto: Kids Can, 2002.

Parks, Sharon Daloz. *Big Questions, Worthy Dreams: Mentoring Young Adults in Their Search for Meaning, Purpose, and Faith*. San Francisco: Jossey-Bass, 2000.

Parnell, Peter, and Justin Richardson. *And Tango Makes Three*. New York: Little Simon, 2005.

Pateman, Carole. *The Sexual Contract*. Stanford: Stanford University Press, 1988.

Pateman, Carole, and Charles W. Mills. *Contract and Domination*. Malden, MA: Polity, 2007.

Pauly, Bernadette, et al. "Framing the Issues: Moral Distress in Health Care." *HealthCare Ethics Committee Forum: An Interprofessional Journal on Healthcare Institutions' Ethical and Legal Issues* 24.1 (2012) 1–11.

Pearsall, Judy, and Bill Trumble, eds. *The Oxford English Reference Dictionary*. 2nd ed. Oxford: Oxford University Press, 1996.

Piketty, Thomas. *Capital in the Twenty-First Century*. Cambridge, MA: Belknap, 2014.

Polacco, Patricia. *Thank You, Mr. Falker*. New York: Philomel, 1998.

Powers, Richard. *The Overstory*. New York: Norton, 2018.

Proulx, Annie. *Barkskins*. New York: Scribner, 2016.

Raven, Margot Theis. *Circle Unbroken*. New York: Square Fish, 2004.

Rilke, Rainer Maria. *Letters to a Young* Poet. Translated by M. D. Herter Norton. 1953. Reprint, New York: Norton, 1993.

Rivera, Lauren A. "Hiring as Cultural Matching: The Case of Elite Professional Service Firms." *American Sociological Review* 77.6 (2012) 999–1022.

Rodriguez, Diego. "Hiring: It's About Cultural Contribution, Not Cultural Fit." *Linkedin* (blog), September 10, 2015. Online. https://www.linkedin.com/pulse/how-i-hire-its-all-cultural-contribution-fit-diego-rodriguez.

Rogers-Vaughn, Bruce. "Blessed Are Those Who Mourn: Depression as Political Resistance." *Pastoral Psychology* 63.4 (2014) 503–22.

———. *Caring for Souls in a Neoliberal Age*. New York: Palgrave Macmillan, 2016.

———. "Recovering Grief in the Age of Grief Recovery." *The Journal of Pastoral Theology* 13.1 (2003) 36–45.

Rowley, Genny C. "Intersystemic Care: How Religious Environmental Praxis Expands the Pastoral Theological Norm of Relational Justice." *Journal of Pastoral Theology* 25.2 (2015) 107–21.

———. "Practicing Hope: Congregational Environmentalism as Intersystemic Care." PhD diss., Brite Divinity School, 2013.

Ruether, Rosemary Radford. *Gaia and God: An Ecofeminist Theology of Earth Healing*. New York: HarperCollins, 1992.

Ruskoff, Douglas. *Team Human*. New York: Norton, 2019.

Safi, Omid. "How to Reach Out to Someone Who Is Struggling." *On Being* (blog), October 11, 2017. Online. https://onbeing.org/blog/omid-safi-how-to-reach-out-to-someone-who-is-struggling.

Saha, Somnath, et al. "Patient Centeredness, Cultural Competence, and Healthcare Quality." *Journal of the National Medical Association* 100.11 (2008) 1275–85.

Said, Edward. *Culture and Imperialism*. New York: Vintage, 1994.

Sartre, Jean-Paul. "Preface." In *The Wretched of the Earth*, by Franz Fanon, 7–34. New York: Grove, 1963.

Sassen, Saskia. *Expulsions: Brutality and Complexity in the Global Economy*. Cambridge, MA: Belknap Press of Harvard University Press, 2014.

Schermerhorn, Seth. *Walking to Magdalena: Personhood and Place in Tohono O'odham Songs, Sticks, and Stories*. Lincoln: University of Nebraska Press, 2019.

Schüssler Fiorenza, Elisabeth. *Congress of Wo/men: Religion, Gender, and Kyriarchal Power*. Cambridge, MA: Feminist Studies in Religion, 2016.

———. *Jesus and the Politics of Interpretation*. New York: Continuum, 2000.

Scott, Joan W. *Sex and Secularism*. Princeton: Princeton University Press, 2017.

Sendak, Maurice. *Where the Wild Things Are*. New York: Harper & Row, 1963.

Sharma, Rashmi K., et al. "Traditional Expectations Versus US Realities: First-and Second-Generation Asian Indian Perspectives on End-of-Life Care." *Journal of General Internal Medicine* 27 (2012) 311–17.

Sharp, Melinda McGarrah. *Creating Resistance: Pastoral Care in a Postcolonial World.* Leiden: Brill, 2019.

———. *Misunderstanding Stories: Toward a Postcolonial Pastoral Theology.* Eugene, OR: Pickwick, 2013.

———. "Prelude to Decolonizing Immersion Pedagogy: Four Movements." *Sacred Spaces* 10 (2018) 105–41. Online. https://cdn.ymaws.com/www.aapc.org/resource/resmgr/files/sacredspaces/vol._10.sacredspaces.2018.fi.pdf.

Shore-Goss, Robert E. "Gay and Lesbian Theologies." In *Liberation Theologies in the United States: An Introduction,* edited by Stacey M. Floyd-Thomas and Anthony B. Pinn, 181–208. New York: New York University Press, 2010.

Silverman, Laura. "Sendak's Legacy: Helping Kids 'Survive Childhood.'" *NPR,* May 8, 2012. Online. https://www.npr.org/2012/05/08/152250644/sendaks-legacy-helping-kids-survive-childhood.

Simard, Suzanne W., et al. "Net Transfer of Carbon between Tree Species with Shared Ectomycorrhizal Fungi." *Nature* 40 (1997) 579–82.

Skloot, Rebecca. *The Immortal Life of Henrietta Lacks,* New York: Crown, 2010.

Smith, Clint (@ClintSmithIII). 2015. "Nor did Jefferson believe that black people possessed the ability to be creative or be artists. He refused to call Phyllis Wheatley a poet." Twitter, September 11, 2015, 8:44 a.m. https://twitter.com/ClintSmithIII/status/642362996673642497.

Soss, Joe, et al. *Disciplining the Poor: Neoliberal Paternalism and the Persistent Power of Race.* Chicago: University of Chicago Press, 2011.

Spencer, Marguerite L. "Environmental Racism and Black Theology." *University of St. Thomas Law Journal* 5.1 (2008) 288–311.

Spencer-Oatey, Helen, ed. "What is Culture? A Compilation of Quotations." *GlobalPAD Core Concepts,* 2012. Online. https://warwick.ac.uk/fac/soc/al/globalpad/openhouse/interculturalskills/global_pad_-what_is_culture.pdf.

Spivak, Gayatri. *Outside in the Teaching Machine.* New York: Routledge, 1993.

Stamwitz, Alicia von. "If Only We Would Listen: Parker J. Palmer on What We Could Learn About Politics, Faith, and Each Other." *The Sun* 443 (2012). Online. https://thesunmagazine.org/issues/443/if-only-we-would-listen.

Stirrat, Gordon M., and Robin Gill. "Autonomy in Medical Ethics After O'Neill." *Journal of Medical Ethics* 31 (2005) 127–30.

Storr, Will. "The Metamorphosis of the Western Soul." *New York Times,* August 24, 2018. Online. https://www.nytimes.com/2018/08/24/opinion/the-metamorphosis-of-the-western-soul.html.

Stuermer, Amanda. "Meet the Muse: An Interview with Gloria Steinem." *World Muse,* December 19, 2015. Online. http://theworldmuse.org/meet-the-muse-an-interview-with-gloria-steinem.

Su, Christopher Thomas, et al. "Family Matters: Effects of Birth Order, Culture, and Family Dynamics on Surrogate Decision Making." *Journal of the American Geriatrics Society* 62.1 (2014) 175–82.

Sue, Derald, et al. "Racial Microaggressions in Everyday Life: Implications for Clinical Practice." *American Psychologist* 62.4 (2007) 271–86.

Tanis, Justin. *Trans-Gendered: Theology, Ministry, and Communities of Faith.* Center for Lesbian and Gay Studies in Religion and Ministry. Cleveland: Pilgrim, 2003.

Taylor, John V. *The Primal Vision: Christian Presence Amid African Religion.* London: SCM, 1963.

Taylor, Mark L. *The Executed God: The Way of the Cross in Lockdown America.* Minneapolis: Fortress, 2001.

Teo, Alan R., et al. "Does Mode of Contact with Different Types of Social Relationships Predict Depression in Older Adults?" *Journal of the American Geriatrics Society,* 63 (2015) 2014–22.

Tervalon, Melanie, and Jann Murray-García. "Cultural Humility Versus Cultural Competence: A Critical Distinction in Defining Physician Training Outcomes in Multicultural Education." *Journal of Health Care for the Poor and Underserved* 9.2 (1998) 117–25.

Thien, Madeleine. *Do Not Say We Have Nothing.* New York: Norton, 2016.

Thurman, Howard W. "How Good to Center Down!" In *Meditations of the Heart,* by Howard W. Thurman, 28. New York: Harper, 1953.

———. *Jesus and the Disinherited.* Boston: Beacon, 1996.

Tillich, Paul. *Dynamics of Faith.* New York: HarperCollins, 2001.

"Tohono O'odham Baskets." *Bahti Indian Arts.* Online. http://mark-bahti-btof. squarespace.com/tohono-oodham-baskets.

Torpy, Jason. "Humanist Chaplains in the Dutch Military." *Military Association of Atheists and Freethinkers* (blog), March 29, 2013. Online. http://militaryatheists. org/news/2013/03/humanist-chaplains-in-the-dutch-military.

Tsai, Jeanne L. "Ideal Affect: Cultural Causes and Behavioral Consequences." *Perspectives on Psychological Science* 2.3 (2007) 242–59.

Tucci, Veronica, and Nidal Moukaddam. "We Are the Hollow Men: The Worldwide Epidemic of Mental Illness, Psychiatric and Behavioral Emergencies, and Its Impact on Patients and Providers." *Journal of Emergencies, Trauma, and Shock* 10.1 (2017) 4–6.

Turkle, Sherry. "Connected, But Alone?" *TED Talks,* February 2012. Video, 19:33. Online. https://www.ted.com/talks/sherry_turkle_connected_but_alone.

Twain, Mark. *The Adventures of Tom Sawyer.* New York: Bantam, 1875.

Twenge, Jean M., et al. "Increases in Depressive Symptoms, Suicide-Related Outcomes, and Suicide Rates Among US Adolescents After 2010 and Links to Increased New Media Screen Time." *Clinical Psychological Science* 6.1 (2017) 3–17. Online. https://journals.sagepub.com/doi/10.1177/2167702617723376.

Unamuno, Miguel de. *Tragic Sense of Life.* Translated by J. E. Crawford Flitch. New York: Dover, 1954.

United Nations General Assembly. *Universal Declaration of Human Rights.* December 10, 1948. Online. https://www.humanrights.com/what-are-human-rights/ universal-declaration-of-human-rights/preamble.html.

Walker, Carl. *Depression and Globalization: The Politics of Mental Health in the Twenty-First Century.* New York: Springer, 2008.

Wentworth, Marjory. "One River, One Boat." *Marjory Wentworth,* May 20, 2015. Online. http://www.marjorywentworth.net/newmarj/one-river-one-boat.

Wheatley, Phillis. *The Poems of Phillis Wheatley: With Letters and a Biographical Note.* Mineola, NY: Dover, 2010.

Wintz, Sue, and George Handzo. *Patient's Spiritual and Cultural Values for Health Care Professionals.* New York: HealthCare Chaplaincy Network, 2014. Online. http://www.healthcarechaplaincy.org/docs/publications/landing_page/cultural_sensitivity_handbook_from_healthCare_chaplaincy_network_8_15_2014.pdf.

Wolski Conn, Joann. "Spirituality and Personal Maturity." In *Clinical Handbook of Pastoral Counseling*, edited by Robert J. Wicks et al., 37–57. Mahwah, NJ: Paulist, 1993.

Yoon, Sunkyung, et al. "Are Attitudes Towards Emotions Associated with Depression? A Conceptual and Meta-Analytic Review." *Journal of Affective Disorders* 232 (2018) 329–40.

Young, Robert J. C. *Postcolonialism: A Very Short Introduction.* New York: Oxford University Press, 2003.

Zapeda, Ofelia. *Ocean Power: Poems from the Desert.* Tucson: University of Arizona Press, 1995.

Zevallos, Zuleyka. "What Is Otherness?" *Other Sociologist* (blog), October 14, 2011. Online. http://othersociologist.com/otherness-resources.

Made in the USA
Coppell, TX
27 August 2021